STUDIES IN WELSH HISTORY

Editors

RALPH A. GRIFFITHS   CHRIS WILLIAMS
ERYN M. WHITE

24

'INTELLIGENT TOWN'

AN URBAN HISTORY OF SWANSEA, 1780–1855

'INTELLIGENT TOWN'

AN URBAN HISTORY OF SWANSEA, 1780–1855

by

LOUISE MISKELL

*Published on behalf of the
History and Law Committee
of the Board of Celtic Studies*

CARDIFF
UNIVERSITY OF WALES PRESS
2006

© Louise Miskell, 2006
Reprinted 2018

British Library Cataloguing-in-Publication Data
A catalogue record for this book is available from the British Library.

ISBN-13 978-0-7083-2510-0

All rights reserved. No part of this book may be reproduced, stored in a retrieval system, or transmitted, in any form or by any means, electronic, mechanical, photocopying, recording or otherwise, without clearance from the University of Wales Press, 10 Columbus Walk, Brigantine Place, Cardiff, CF10 4UP.
www.wales.ac.uk/press

The right of Louise Miskell to be identified as author of this work has been asserted by her in accordance with sections 77 and 78 of the Copyright, Designs and Patents Act 1988.

Printed by CPI Group (UK) Ltd, Croydon CR0 4YY

EDITORS' FOREWORD

Since the foundation of the series in 1977, the study of Wales's history has attracted growing attention among historians internationally and continues to enjoy a vigorous popularity. Not only are approaches, both traditional and new, to the study of history in general being successfully applied in a Welsh context, but Wales's historical experience is increasingly appreciated by writers on British, European and world history. These advances have been especially marked in the university institutions in Wales itself.

In order to make more widely available the conclusions of original research, much of it of limited accessibility in postgraduate dissertations and theses, in 1977 the History and Law Committee of the Board of Celtic Studies inaugurated this series of monographs, *Studies in Welsh History*. It was anticipated that many of the volumes would originate in research conducted in the University of Wales or under the auspices of the Board of Celtic Studies, and so it has proved. But the series does not exclude significant contributions made by researchers in other universities and elsewhere. Its primary aim is to serve historical scholarship and to encourage the study of Welsh history.

CONTENTS

EDITORS' FOREWORD	v
PREFACE	ix
LIST OF ILLUSTRATIONS	xi
LIST OF TABLES AND FIGURES	xii
ABBREVIATIONS	xiii
Introduction	1
I 'Prejudicial to our ancient rights and privileges': Urban governance, c.1780–1800	18
II 'Many advantages not to be found in any other part of Wales': Improvement and identity, c.1800–1820	41
III 'A degree of commercial and manufacturing importance': Industrialization and regional status	70
IV 'The content and comfort of the workmen': The Swansea populace and social relations	98
V 'Cutting each other's throats by our unhappy divisions': Local government in the post-reform era	132
VI 'There is a spirit of intelligence abroad': Urban elites and urban culture	158
Conclusion	182
BIOGRAPHICAL APPENDIX	194
BIBLIOGRAPHY	205
INDEX	221

PREFACE

The writing of this book was made possible by an innovative collaboration between the University of Wales Swansea, and the National Museums and Galleries of Wales. Beginning in September 2000, these two institutions jointly funded a research post in the department of history at Swansea. It was an initiative inspired by Swansea's choice as the location for a new national museum charting Wales's industrial and maritime past. As the person appointed to this new post, I was presented with an opportunity to conduct the research on which this book is based. It would not have been written without the foresight and commitment of the two chief collaborators, Dr David Jenkins, curator of the national museum's industrial and maritime collections, and Professor Ralph Griffiths of the history department at Swansea.

My own route towards the writing of an urban history of Swansea originated much earlier. As an undergraduate at Aberystwyth in 1989, I was fortunate enough to come under the tutelage of a succession of superb historians, including Professor Rees Davies, Professor Geraint H. Jenkins, Dr John Davies and later, as a postgraduate, Dr Paul O'Leary. Along with their colleagues in the department of history and Welsh history, they provided me with encouragement and rigorous academic scrutiny whenever it was needed. In 1997 I became a research assistant at the University of Dundee where I began work on a research project that was specifically urban in focus. Professor Chris Whatley, Dr Bob Harris and Professor Charles McKean all provided invaluable guidance as I began to familiarize myself with the Scottish urban landscape and, inevitably, to draw comparisons with the history of Welsh towns. I owe my former colleagues in Dundee a tremendous debt of thanks. Their influences are clear for all to see in this book.

Since joining the department of history at Swansea in September 2000 and embarking on the research for this book, I have benefited from advice and support from numerous different quarters. My departmental colleagues, especially Professor David Howell, have been a constant source of encouragement. Staff at the university library and archives, in particular the university archivist, Elisabeth Bennett, and the history subject librarians, Dr Ian Glen and Bernadette Matthias, have been unfailingly cooperative. Staff at the West Glamorgan Archives Service, especially Kim Collis and Andrew Dulley, were extremely helpful during the months spent wading through volumes of corporation minutes. Elsewhere in Swansea, members of staff at the Glynn Vivian Art Gallery, particularly Jenni Spencer-Davies and Ellie Dawkins, and at Swansea Museum, Bernice Cardy and Bernard Morris, have given generously of their time and expertise in helping me to locate suitable illustrative material. Other Swansea experts who have kindly shared their knowledge with me include Gerald Gabb, Dr Owen Roberts and Dr Robert Anthony.

My frequent research visits to other institutions, principally the National Library of Wales and the National Archives at Kew, were made easier by the efficiency and friendliness of the staff who dealt with my queries, and I am especially grateful to Jenny Mountain at the Bank of England Archives for her interest in, and assistance with, my research. During the writing of the book, the series editors have kept an attentive eye on my progress, and I am also indebted to the generosity of Neil Evans who undertook to read and comment on an earlier draft of the text. The finished product would have been much the poorer without his observations.

My final thanks are reserved for the people who make up my personal 'support networks'. They have, some of them unknowingly, helped me through the inevitable ups and downs of a lengthy research project. They are my family in Port Talbot, Mike and our neighbours in Aberdare, and my running friends in Swansea. I am grateful to them all.

Louise Miskell

ILLUSTRATIONS

1. Moses Harris, *A Welsh Corporation Meeting*, 1787 (Swansea Museum). Thomas Powell attacks Charles Collins as the Quaker, William Padley (centre, wearing his hat), looks on.
2. Paul Padley, *Panorama of Swansea in the 1790s* (Swansea Museum). The scale of the Cambrian Pottery can be gauged from the four large kilns visible on the left.
3. Paul Padley, *Panorama of Swansea in the 1790s* (Swansea Museum). Jernegan's Countess of Huntingdon's chapel is clearly visible in the new area of development on the Burrows.
4. G. O. Delamotte, *Constable John Luce* (Swansea Museum). Appointed by the paving commission in 1821 to impound stray animals found on Swansea's streets.
5. G. O. Delamotte, untitled sketch (WGAS). This untitled sketch shows the poor condition of some of Swansea's streets by the second decade of the nineteenth century. The street shown here, the Strand, was described by the paving commissioners in their survey of 1819 as being 'in bad repair throughout'.
6. George Yates, extract from map of Glamorgan, 1799 (WGAS). This extract shows Swansea's well developed urban core and spacious harbour, with good canal and road links to the surrounding district.
7. G. O. Delamotte, *Caswell Bay* (undated) (WGAS). This sketch of c.1820 shows a well-dressed group of excursionists gathered near a Gower cave to view the rock and plant life of the coastline near Swansea.
8. G. O. Delamotte, *Muffins or Crumpets!* (NLW) Cake-seller dressed in the traditional hat, shawl and apron attire worn by female traders in early nineteenth-century Swansea.

TABLES

1.1	Occupational profile of Swansea burgesses, 1760–89	21
1.2	Occupational profile of Swansea burgesses, 1789–92	30
3.1	Annual rateable value of property in selected Glamorgan towns, 1826	92
4.1	Population growth in four south Wales towns, 1801–41	103
5.1	Occupations of Swansea burgesses, 1760–92 and 1835	136
5.2	Swansea's first town council, 1836	138
6.1	Occupational status of RISW subscribers, 1839	164
6.2	Residential distribution of RISW subscribers, 1839	171

FIGURES

3.1	Occupations of Swansea householders, 1838	86
4.1	Comparison of occupations in Cardiff, Merthyr Tydfil and Swansea, 1841	124

ABBREVIATIONS

BAAS	British Association for the Advancement of Science
BoEA	Bank of England Archives
CUHB	*Cambridge Urban History of Britain*
GCH	*Glamorgan County History*
GGF	George Grant Francis collection
GRO	Glamorgan Record Office
NLW	National Library of Wales
PP	Parliamentary Papers
RISW	Royal Institution of South Wales
SCL	Swansea Central Library
TNA	The National Archives
UWSA	University of Wales Swansea Archives
WCR	William Cyril Rogers collection
WGAS	West Glamorgan Archive Service
WHR	*Welsh History Review*
YIM	Yorkshire Imperial Metals

INTRODUCTION

On 6 October 1802, Swansea, it was said, was 'never was so full'. Crowds gathered in the fields and hills surrounding the town, took up vantage points in houses and on board ships in the harbour. People from 'the most distant parts of the country' flocked to swell the ranks of the population, all with an excited sense of anticipation at what they were about to witness.[1] Preparations for the day had long been in the making. Handbills had been published and circulated and a subscription raised. A temporary wooden stage had been erected in the 'Ball Court' outside the George Inn, around which an estimated 8,000 people had gathered for an on-the-spot view of proceedings. The focus of their attention, and the cause of all the excitement in the town that day, was the activity on the stage where a Mr Francis Barrett was conducting a chemical reaction using iron filings and vitriol (sulphuric acid). His object was to generate sufficient gas to inflate a vast expanse of limp material attached to a basket or 'car'. Looking on was a local doctor, William Turton, waiting for the instruction to take his seat in the basket at the appropriate moment along with Barrett. For the first time, the residents of this part of south Wales had gathered to observe a manned balloon flight.

It was almost two decades since the Montgolfier brothers had successfully carried out the first balloon flight in Annonay, south of Lyons in the Rhone-Alpes region, in 1783. Since then, aeronautical feats of increasing daring had been undertaken, including the first manned flight from the dauphin's residence at Château La Muette in October 1783 and a successful crossing of the English Channel by Blanchard and Jeffries in 1785. The ballooning 'mania', although a little slower to take hold in Britain, had gathered pace in the mid-1780s with a number of successful ascents in London followed by provincial tours by some of the successful early aeronauts, including Vincent Lunardi, who achieved the first manned balloon ascent in Britain in September 1784. Spellbound crowds from Exeter to

---

[1] *The Times*, 12 October 1802.

Bath, and from Liverpool to Cork and Aberdeen, had been treated to the spectacle of these daring pioneers of air travel ascending in their flimsy carriages to heights at which atmospheric effects were previously unknown and covering extended distances in seemingly impossibly short times.[2] Ballooning exploits had ground to a halt by the end of the 1780s, however. A few well-publicized fatalities, including one at Newcastle upon Tyne in 1786, had understandably dampened enthusiasm, and war with France put a halt to the visits of pioneering French aeronauts to Britain for the remainder of the century. It was not until after the Peace of Amiens was signed in March 1802 and the subsequent visit to Britain of a new French balloonist, Monsieur Garnerin, that interest was rekindled.[3]

It was during this second flowering of balloon mania that the first manned ascent from Swansea was planned. Several successful demonstrations by Garnerin at Ranelagh Gardens, Lord's cricket ground and Vauxhall over the course of the summer had inspired a number of home-grown balloonists, including Francis Barrett, to try to emulate his success. The assembled thousands at Swansea, however, were to be left bitterly disappointed. Barrett could not get the balloon to inflate. He was not the first aeronaut to encounter difficulties with this stage of the endeavour. The inflation process was often slow and tedious. At Moorfields in London in 1784, Vincent Lunardi had had to run the gauntlet of serious disorder among the estimated 150,000 people who grew increasingly agitated as the balloon in which he was to make his historic flight took its time to inflate.[4] Some of the French pioneers, to avoid this sort of problem, had taken the prudent step of keeping out of the public gaze until the balloon was ready for launch, but not Barrett. He had commenced the inflation process at eight in the morning, but by three in the afternoon it was still not complete and, not surprisingly, the crowds surrounding the stage were beginning to lose patience. Stories of the similar failure of a Barrett balloon in Greenwich a few months earlier were bandied about and the mood quickly turned from expectation to cynicism. Barrett tried to deflect the

---

[2] For further details of the early history of ballooning, see L. T. C. Rolt, *The Aeronauts. A History of Ballooning, 1783–1903* (Gloucester, 1985).
[3] J. Penny, 'Up, up and away. An account of ballooning in and around Bristol and Bath, 1784–1999', *Historical Association Local History Pamphlets (Bristol Branch)* (Bristol, 1999), pp. 7–8.
[4] Rolt, *The Aeronauts*, pp. 50–1.

criticism, blaming the delay on the local chemist for failing to supply sufficient quantities of vitriol, but as he mounted the stage to offer some words of apology, disaster struck. The temporary podium collapsed, taking Barrett and his balloon down with it. The planned ascent, needless to say, was abandoned in a scene of chaos and disarray as Barrett retrieved what was left of his balloon after pleading with the disgruntled crowds not to destroy it.

Despite the almost farcical outcome, the attempted balloon launch at Swansea and the interest it excited provide a vantage point from which to begin an examination of the modern town and its place in British urban society. Barrett was a showman and something of an entrepreneur. His attempted balloon ascent was a money-making venture which, first and foremost, required a large, paying audience. Locating the right venue was vital to its success and the choice of Swansea was therefore significant. It presented virgin territory for ballooning at a time when the craze was very much in its second flowering and practitioners were casting about for parts of the country where manned flights were still unprecedented. Although ascents had become an increasingly common feature of fêtes, galas and celebrations in the leisure gardens of the metropolis, south Wales presented a relatively populous part of the country where the phenomenon was still novel. Successful ascents had been carried out in Bristol and Bath and throughout the south of England in the mid-1780s, but in south Wales the majority of the population had 'never witnessed anything of the kind'.[5] Barrett had found an untapped audience. With over 6,000 inhabitants, Swansea was Wales's second most populous town.[6] It was also relatively easily accessible. Barrett and his family made the crossing by sea from Devon, whilst his balloon was conveyed by road.[7]

There were other respects in which Swansea was an ideal venue. Two key characteristics, in particular, made it a very promising location for a balloon ascent. These were its twin advantages as a recognized tourist centre as well as a town with serious industrial and scientific credentials. Although its resident population numbered only 6,000, the prospect of seeing a 'fire balloon' was enough to bring visitors flocking to Swansea in numbers estimated at around 20,000. Local people were used to coping with these sorts

[5] *The Times*, 19 October 1802.
[6] J. Williams, *Digest of Welsh Historical Statistics*, Volume 1 (Cardiff, 1985), p. 63.
[7] *The Times*, 22 October 1802.

of influxes. For residents like linen draper, Mr Griffiths, with whom Barrett and his family were staying,[8] the opening up of their homes to seasonal visitors in need of lodgings was a regular feature of the summer months and an opportunity to earn some extra money. The town had become something of a centre for leisure and entertainment by the latter years of the eighteenth century. A thriving bathing resort in summer, pleasure seekers, travellers and sea bathers were customarily accommodated and entertained in the inns and guesthouses along its shores. Barrett even speculated at one point whether, in such a bustling resort town, 'it would not be more profitable to cut up my balloon, and set up a manufactory of bathing caps, umbrellas and hat-covers'.[9] Nevertheless, he stuck to his original plan in the knowledge that 'the sight of a proper aerostatic machine, with its apparatus, must be an entire novelty to some hundreds of the inhabitants'. He certainly seemed to have judged the interest levels accurately.

He may also have been aware that a balloon ascent at Swansea was likely to interest the serious-minded scientist as well as the casual tourist. As a growing centre for copper smelting since the 1720s, Swansea had become home to a number of skilled chemists, engineers and industrialists for whom scientific experimentation was part of the everyday process of trying to improve economic productivity. Industrialists like the Vivians looked to their native Cornwall and further afield to northern Europe, where they kept an agent, to recruit men skilled in their knowledge of copper ore and how to smelt and refine it.[10] But there was also a wider scientific fraternity in the town, made up of local gentry collectors, educated medical men and lawyers who were making their presence felt in the expanding urban centre. The would-be balloonist, Dr William Turton, was a part of this burgeoning Swansea intelligentsia. Turton was no ordinary doctor. A pioneer in the use of vaccination to combat smallpox, he was also well known as an eminent conchologist and a fellow of the Linnean Society.[11] For men like Turton ballooning was more about scientific experimentation than public

---

[8] Ibid.
[9] Ibid.
[10] R. Toomey, *Vivian and Sons, 1809–1924. A Study of the Firm in the Copper and Related Industries* (London, 1985), p. 146.
[11] T. G. Davies, *Deeds not Words. A History of the Swansea General and Eye Hospital, 1817–1948* (Cardiff, 1988), p. 7.

spectacle. Many of the early balloonists were skilled scientists first and foremost and the involvement of doctors was not uncommon.[12] No great scientist himself, Barrett's failed ascent at Swansea was blamed in the press on his insufficient knowledge of chemistry.[13] He certainly looked amateurish compared with pioneers like John Jeffries, who carried scientific instruments with him on his historic cross-channel flight with Blanchard in 1785, and the Birmingham engineers and scientists, Boulton and Watt, who were using balloons for scientific experimentation even earlier.[14] By the second half of the nineteenth century, long after the novelty value of ballooning had diminished, it was being ever more firmly embraced by the scientific establishment, as evidenced by the formation of the Royal Aeronautical Society in 1866.[15]

Accounts of the attempted manned balloon flight thus offer some insights into Swansea's character as an urban centre at the beginning of the nineteenth century. Its role as a centre for tourism and leisure as well as science and industry gave it some distinction among Welsh towns in this period, but its wide range of functions has also made it difficult to categorize by any conventional models of urban 'type'. Harold Carter, in his classification of Welsh towns by their 'origins', grouped Swansea together with other 'castle-towns affected by industrial growth'. It could as easily have been included in either of his chapters on 'industrial towns' and 'resorts and ports', and does figure in his analysis of late eighteenth-century planned settlements.[16] It was a centre for the mining and shipping of coal for decades before coal became 'king' of the Welsh economy. It attained international renown as a centre for copper smelting without experiencing an industrial 'revolution' in the conventional sense of a take-off in output levels brought about by technological innovation or organizational restructuring. It had a flourishing pottery turning out practical earthenware for domestic use as well as more decorative pieces for affluent buyers at home and abroad. It had a tourist trade, built on the late eighteenth-century fashion for sea bathing among the social elites, and its inhabitants had a

---

[12] Caleb Hillier Parry, MD, FRS, for example, made a name for himself with a successful balloon ascent at Bath in 1794. See Penny, 'Up, up and away', p. 2.
[13] *The Times*, 19 October 1802.
[14] Rolt, *The Aeronauts*, p. 185.
[15] Ibid., p. 198.
[16] H. Carter, *The Towns of Wales. A Study in Urban Geography* (Cardiff, 1965).

reputation for culture, refinement and intelligence rarely attributed to other commercial and industrial centres.

Perhaps inevitably historians have had difficulty in categorizing such a multi-faceted place. Variously labelled 'Copperopolis' and the 'Brighton of Wales',[17] few accounts have succeeded in portraying Swansea's diversity, or in coming to terms with its apparent contradictions, most memorably summed up by Dylan Thomas who described it as an 'ugly, lovely town'. For some the solution has been to view Swansea as a divided place in the early part of the nineteenth century, and to see its different economic functions as competing influences on the town's development.[18] Certainly to present-day eyes, the environmental impact of copper smelting appears incompatible with the attractions of a bathing resort,[19] but in the early decades of the nineteenth century things were far less clear cut. Such seemingly conflicting functions could quite happily coexist. This was evident not only in Swansea but also in the Hampshire town of Southampton, where leisure and commercial life existed side by side. The similarities between these two towns in the early decades of the nineteenth century are worth exploring in brief.

Both towns developed as fashionable resorts in the second half of the eighteenth century, although in Southampton's case this role was supported not only by the availability of sea bathing but also by the local spa waters which purportedly had health-giving properties.[20] Rates of population growth were also similar. The residents of Southampton numbered 7,629 in 1801, rising to 9,260 a decade later and 12,913 in 1821.[21] Swansea's population grew at a comparable pace, from 6,099 in 1801 to 8,196 in 1811 and 10,255 in 1821.[22] Southampton did not have the industrial base which Swansea had acquired with the growth of copper smelting in the vicinity of the town from the early decades of the eighteenth century, but it did have a thriving port with coastal and foreign

---

[17] S. R. Hughes, *Copperopolis. Landscapes of the Early Industrial Period in Swansea* (Aberystwyth, 2000); D. Boorman, *The Brighton of Wales. Swansea as a Fashionable Seaside Resort, c.1780–1830* (Swansea, 1986).

[18] R. Rees, *King Copper: South Wales and the Copper Trade, 1854–1895* (Cardiff, 2000), p. 19.

[19] R. Rees, 'The great copper trials', *History Today*, 43, no. 12 (1993), 38–44.

[20] E. M. Sandell, 'Georgian Southampton: a watering place and spa', in J. B. Morgan and P. Peberdy (eds.), *Collected Essays on Southampton* (Southampton, 1958), pp. 79–87.

[21] A. Temple Patterson, *A History of Southampton, 1700–1914*, Volume 1: *An Oligarchy in Decline, 1700–1835* (Southampton, 1966), p. 36.

[22] Williams, *Digest*, Volume 1, p. 63.

trade. From the 1820s, with the growth of passenger-carrying steam packets, it developed an increasingly important role as the 'gateway to the Continent'. Like Swansea, however, it appeared by no means inevitable in the 1820s and 1830s that these commercial functions would supersede or displace the role of the resort. The best of both worlds seemed a perfectly plausible option.

Swansea, then, was not unique in British terms, but within Wales its experience of urbanization does appear unusual. This is partly because much of the existing historiography of nineteenth-century urban Wales has been dominated by research on towns linked to the coal and iron belt. In consequence, Welsh urban life in this period has come to be seen as essentially an industrial experience. Chris Evans's excellent study of early industrial Merthyr Tydfil, and E. D. Lewis's survey of the growth of the Rhondda from 1800, for example, both deal primarily with the effects of economic conditions and workplace relations on urban life.[23] Towns where coal and iron were not the primary catalysts of urban growth, or where these were combined with a range of other functions, have been less prominent in the historical literature. Towns like Carmarthen, for example, a thriving market centre and county town with a population of over 5,500 in 1801, making it one of Wales's largest urban centres, has attracted surprisingly little attention.[24] The urbanization of Newport, a town of over 7,000 people in 1831 and a serious rival to the ports of Swansea and Cardiff, has received little recent notice.[25] Similarly, the sizeable north Wales urban centres of Caernarfon, Wrexham and Bangor, all of which were more populous than Cardiff for at least the first two decades of the nineteenth century, have figured little in recent historical research.[26]

Swansea, it must be said, has fared rather better than these towns. Philip Jenkins points out that for the Tudor period it is 'one

---

[23] C. Evans, 'The Labyrinth of Flames'. Work and Social Conflict in Early Industrial Merthyr Tydfil (Cardiff, 1993); E. D. Lewis, The Rhondda Valleys. A Study in Industrial Development from 1800 to the Present Day (London, 1959); B. Thomas, 'The growth of industrial towns', in A. J. Roderick (ed.), Wales Through the Ages, Volume 2 (Llandybïe, 1960); D. Gwyn, 'The industrial town in Gwynedd', Landscape History, 23 (2001), 71–89.

[24] E. G. Bowen, 'Carmarthen: an urban study', Archaeologia Cambrensis, 17 (1968), 1–17.

[25] Information on the growth of Newport is contained in D. Williams, John Frost. A Study in Chartism (Cardiff, 1939); C. Williams, '"Decorous and creditable": the Irish in Newport', in P. O'Leary (ed.), Irish Migrants in Modern Wales (Liverpool, 2004), pp. 54–82.

[26] O. V. Jones, 'Bangor; the growth of a city during the first half of the nineteenth century', Transactions of the Caernarvonshire Historical Society, 46 (1985), 23–43; A. H. Dodd (ed.), A History of Wrexham, Denbighshire (Wrexham, 1957).

of the best covered of the Welsh boroughs'.[27] In fact, as the subject of two scholarly essay collections and a detailed pamphlet series, there has been a significant pooling of historical effort towards charting Swansea's development since its origins, possibly as a Viking settlement, up to the late twentieth century.[28] What has been lacking hitherto, however, is a single-authored history of the town to set the story of Swansea's modern phase of urbanization in a wider Welsh and British context. Without this, Swansea has been easily overshadowed by more thoroughly researched towns that expanded faster and further. The industrial hub of Merthyr Tydfil, in particular, has attracted greater attention thanks to its role, from the late eighteenth century, as the capital of the iron belt and its reputation as a centre of social unrest.[29] Cardiff's transformation from modest borough to Welsh capital, and the role of the Bute family in the process, has proved equally compelling.[30]

Swansea's experience of urban growth cannot be likened to either of these models of rapid industrial expansion or gentry-led civic development. Its growth was gradual and incremental. A recognized centre for copper smelting from the 1720s and for sea bathing from the 1780s, it was well ahead of other Welsh industrial towns in developing its urban infrastructure. In recent years, however, the tendency has been for historical research on urban and industrial Wales to focus predominantly on the late nineteenth and early twentieth centuries and this has meant that Swansea's earlier prominence has been overlooked. Martin Daunton's study of Cardiff's reign as Wales's *Coal Metropolis* commences in 1870 and extends as far as the outbreak of the First World War.[31] Exactly the same period was chosen by Andy Croll for his examination of popular culture and public space in Merthyr Tydfil.[32] Chris

---

[27] P. Jenkins, 'Wales', in P. Clark (ed.), *CUHB*, Volume 2: *1540–1840* (Cambridge, 2000), p. 134.

[28] G. Williams (ed.), *Swansea. An Illustrated History* (Swansea, 1990); R. A. Griffiths (ed.), *The City of Swansea. Challenges and Change* (Stroud, 1990); *Social and Economic Survey of Swansea and District, Pamphlets 1–6* (Cardiff, 1940).

[29] See, for example, G. A. Williams, *The Merthyr Rising* (London, 1978); H. Carter and S. Wheatley, *Merthyr in 1851. A Study of the Spatial Structure of a Welsh Industrial Town* (Cardiff, 1982).

[30] See, for example, J. Davies, *Cardiff and the Marquesses of Bute* (Cardiff, 1981); J. Davies, *Cardiff. A Pocket Guide* (Cardiff, 2002).

[31] M. J. Daunton, *Coal Metropolis. Cardiff, 1870–1914* (Leicester, 1977).

[32] A. Croll, *Civilizing the Urban. Popular Culture and Public Space in Merthyr, c.1870–1914* (Cardiff, 2000).

Williams's work on the vast and varied urban societies of the Rhondda has an even later chronological focus.[33] The late nineteenth century has also provided the backdrop for some valuable studies of municipalization and the urban experience in Wales. Owen Roberts's thesis on public health in Victorian Swansea and John Wyn Pritchard's examination of water supply in Welsh towns take a lead from the research of John Hassan on the politics of water in England.[34] This tendency in recent studies to concentrate on the late nineteenth century period is not only apparent in the field of urban history. Historians of Welsh politics, too, have mainly focused their efforts on charting the emergence of a Welsh political 'nation' in the period after 1850.[35]

As far as urban history in Wales is concerned, there are some sound demographic explanations for the preponderance of studies on the second half of the nineteenth century. It was in this period that the growth and increasing urban concentration of the Welsh population were most pronounced. Between 1851 and 1914 the proportion of Wales's inhabitants resident in Glamorgan and Monmouthshire rose from roughly one-third to two-thirds. Even more dramatic was the rate of population growth in the coalfield. The Rhondda valley (Ystradyfodwg parish) was home to just 951 people in 1851, but 55,000 thirty years later.[36] Only by the late nineteenth century do the population figures for Wales's main urban centres appear in any way comparable to those of large towns elsewhere in Britain. The *General Report* published after the 1901 census of England and Wales listed seventy-five 'urban districts' with populations of over 50,000; five of these were located in Wales. Cardiff, seventeenth on the list, with a population of over 164,000, was now on a par with northern industrial towns like Bolton and Sunderland. Twenty-fourth was Rhondda with a total of 113,735

---

[33] C. Williams, *Capitalism, Community and Conflict. The South Wales Coalfield, 1898–1947* (Cardiff, 1998); idem, *Democratic Rhondda. Politics and Society, 1885–1951* (Cardiff, 1996).

[34] O. G. Roberts, 'Sanitary reform, civic politics and ideas of health in Wales, 1870–1900' (unpublished Ph.D. thesis, University of Wales Aberystwyth, 2003); J. W. Pritchard, 'Water supply in Welsh towns, 1840–1900. Control, conflict and development', *WHR*, 21, no. 1 (2002), 24–47; J. Hassan, *A History of Water in Modern England and Wales* (Manchester, 1998).

[35] This observation is made in M. Cragoe, *Culture, Politics and National Identity in Wales, 1832–1886* (Oxford, 2004), p. 3.

[36] Lewis, *Rhondda Valleys*, pp. 229–30. Note that the large increase in population by 1881 can be partly accounted for by the inclusion of parts of Llantrisant and Llanwynno within the parish of Ystradyfodwg in 1879.

in its collection of settlements. Swansea was fortieth with 94,500, sandwiched between Wolverhampton and Huddersfield, and Merthyr Tydfil and Newport weighed in at fifty-fourth and fifty-fifth with 69,000 and 67,000 respectively, placing them comfortably ahead of towns like Wigan, Barrow-in-Furness, Grimsby and Warrington.[37]

While these figures go a long way towards explaining the chronological focus on the late nineteenth and early twentieth centuries, the consequence has been to create the impression that nothing much happened in Welsh towns in earlier decades. It was in the late eighteenth and early nineteenth centuries, however, that English and Scottish urban leaders were busily engaged in setting up commissions for street cleaning, policing and lighting and, in some cases, embarking on large-scale 'new town' projects to refashion their central streets. The cultural life of towns also developed in these years with the foundation of literary and scientific societies, mechanics' institutes and charitable institutions for the promotion of health and knowledge amongst urban dwellers. These were also the decades when local government leaders in the towns changed from being unelected and unaccountable, to having a measure of public scrutiny imposed upon them for the first time. We know comparatively little about any of these developments in a Welsh context.[38] Partly this is because some Welsh towns were indeed slow to implement the kind of street improvements and sanitary reforms taking place elsewhere. Chris Evans points out that 'The new standards of urban sophistication – schemes for street lighting and repaving, new town halls and market buildings ... did not arrive at Merthyr until the second half of the nineteenth century.'[39] Merthyr, of course, was far from typical, but because research on other parts of urban Wales in this period has been so scanty, there has been little to counter the idea that Welsh towns may have lacked the 'improvement' ethos that was reshaping town life in other parts of Britain. As a result, Wales appears to have been out of step with the developments shaping urban life elsewhere. Indeed, this notion that

[37] *Census of England and Wales, 1901. General Report with Appendices* (London, 1904), pp. 27–8.
[38] Notable exceptions to this include D. C. James, 'The genesis of sanitary reform in Cardiff, 1774–1850', *WHR*, 11, no. 1 (1982), 50–66; G. Roderick, 'Educating the worker: the Mechanics' Institute movement in south Wales', *Transactions of the Honourable Society of Cymmrodorion* (1991), 161–74.
[39] Evans, *Labyrinth of Flames*, pp.145–6.

Welsh towns may have lagged behind urban developments more generally, or reflected a rather paler version of them, has gained recent currency in British urban history.[40]

To some extent, by focusing mainly on the period from the late nineteenth century onwards, historians of Wales have reinforced this idea and, in the process, detached themselves from key debates in recent British urban history. The 1980s and 1990s, in particular, saw the publication of a number of new urban histories, including excellent studies of Glasgow and Manchester which opened up new avenues of interpretation of cities previously seen as one-dimensional industrial metropolises.[41] Interest in the emergence of an urban middle class also featured prominently in a number of works. The textile towns of the north of England provided the backdrop for some of the best research on Britain's middle classes, such as Bob Morris's study of early nineteenth-century Leeds and Theodore Koditschek's book on Bradford.[42] As well as charting the rise of the middle classes in general, urban historians have been eager to identify the real 'movers and shakers' in towns and cities who formed a distinctive 'urban elite'. The activities of elites have increasingly come to be seen as influential in shaping urban development and urban life.[43] Our knowledge of the cultural life of towns, too, has benefited from recent research by historians such as Simon Gunn.[44]

These explorations, central to recent research in British urban history, have largely passed Wales by. Its historians have not readily engaged with the middle classes, urban elites and urban culture as have their counterparts in England and Scotland. There are, of course, some important exceptions. David Howell's research on eighteenth-century Pembrokeshire towns has revealed their roles as

---

[40] P. Clark and R. A. Houston, 'Culture and leisure', in Clark (ed.), *CUHB*, Volume 2, pp. 577–8.

[41] T. M. Devine and G. Jackson (eds), *Glasgow*, Volume 1: *Beginnings to 1830* (Manchester, 1995); W. H. Fraser and I. Maver (eds), *Glasgow*, Volume 2: *1830–1912* (Manchester, 1996); M. Hewitt, *The Emergence of Stability in the Industrial City. Manchester, 1832–1867* (Aldershot, 1996).

[42] R. J. Morris, *Class, Sect and Party. The Making of the British Middle Class, Leeds, 1820–1850* (Manchester, 1990); T. Koditschek, *Class Formation and Urban-Industrial Society: Bradford, 1750–1850* (Cambridge, 1990).

[43] R. Trainor, *Black Country Elites. The Exercise of Authority in an Industrial Area, 1830–1900* (Oxford, 1993); J. Smith, 'Urban elites c.1830–1930 and urban history', *Urban History*, 27, no. 2 (2000), 255–75.

[44] S. Gunn, *The Public Culture of the Victorian Middle Class. Ritual and Authority in the English Industrial City, 1840–1914* (Manchester, 2000).

centres of polite culture and social life for the county gentry.[45] Martin Daunton's study of Cardiff includes a detailed analysis of the local government leaders and social elites who presided over the town's reign as Wales's 'coal metropolis'.[46] The same town is the focus of Neil Evans's studies of the philanthropic activities and developing civic consciousness of Welsh urban elites, demonstrating that it is possible to examine the middle classes in a Welsh context.[47] This research has shown that, at least in Cardiff, there was an identifiable urban middle class engaged in many of the same kinds of activities as absorbed their counterparts elsewhere in Britain. There have been few attempts, however, to extend the inquiry to other Welsh towns. John Wyn Pritchard's discussion of the characteristics of town councillors in the town of Denbigh in the post-reform period is one of the few Welsh studies to engage directly with E. P. Hennock's valuable work on the status and motivations of those in public life.[48] And Julie Light has made the first serious attempt to chart the characteristics and activities of the Welsh urban middle classes in a multi-town context.[49]

Other historians of Wales have chosen to follow different agenda.[50] Growing interest in the study of labour history, especially from the 1970s, has meant that for many modern social historians the workplace rather than the town provided a more compelling focus of attention. Equally, interest in the issue of Welsh identity and the survival of distinctive linguistic and cultural traditions in Wales may have deterred some from examining the spread of urban influences, especially where these were seen as imported.

---

[45] D. W. Howell, 'Pembrokeshire gentry in the eighteenth century', in T. R. Barnes and N. Yates (eds), *Carmarthenshire Studies. Essays presented to Major Francis Jones* (Carmarthenshire, 1974), pp. 158–85; idem, 'Society, 1660–1793', in B. Howells (ed.), *Pembrokeshire County History*, Volume 3: *Early Modern Pembrokeshire* (Haverfordwest, 1987), pp. 293–6.

[46] Daunton, *Coal Metropolis*, pp. 147–77.

[47] N. Evans, 'Urbanisation, elite attitudes and philanthropy: Cardiff, 1850–1914', *International Review of Social History*, 27 (1982), 290–323; N. Evans, 'The Welsh Victorian city. The middle class and civic and national consciousness in Cardiff, 1850–1914', *WHR*, 12, no. 3 (1985), 350–87.

[48] J. W. Pritchard, '"Fit and proper persons": Councillors of Denbigh, their status and position, 1835–1894', *WHR*, 17, no. 2 (1994), 186–204; E. P. Hennock, *Fit and Proper Persons. Ideal and Reality in Nineteenth Century Urban Government* (London, 1973).

[49] J. Light, '"Of inestimable value to the town and district"? A study of the urban middle classes in south Wales with particular reference to Pontypool, Bridgend and Penarth, c.1850–1890' (unpublished Ph.D. thesis, University of Wales Swansea, 2003).

[50] N. Evans, 'Writing the social history of modern Wales: approaches, achievements and problems', *Social History*, 17, 3 (1992), 479–92.

INTRODUCTION

The Anglo-Norman conquests of the 1070–1280 period in particular, and the effects of immigration and castle building on town development, have done much to promote the idea of urbanization as a fundamentally English influence in Wales.[51] In the early modern period, the association between urban growth and Anglicization seemed to be reinforced by the significance of non-Welsh towns such as Liverpool, London, Shrewsbury, Chester and Bristol, as urban centres serving parts of Wales.[52] Such associations may have made for an ambivalent relationship between modern Welsh and urban history.

One of the aims of this volume is to address some of these historiographical issues. Its broader endeavour is to offer a case-study in the late eighteenth and early nineteenth centuries which goes some way to revise the perception that this was a latent period in the urbanization of Wales. Swansea's experience in these years suggests otherwise. The town achieved a number of significant 'firsts' which indicated healthy levels of urban development. It earned a reputation as a centre for print culture in Wales by virtue of the fact that it was home to the first weekly newspapers to be published in both the English and Welsh languages, from 1804 and 1814 respectively. Chosen by the Bank of England as the location of its first Welsh branch in 1826, its importance as a commercial and financial centre was also widely acknowledged in this period. Credited with planning, constructing and stocking the first purpose-built museum in Wales, it distinguished itself as a centre for urban culture and learning with a reputation that extended beyond Wales. These and other developments in the early years of the nineteenth century helped to propel Swansea to a position as Wales's capital town in all but name.

Partly because of Swansea's success in developing a range of urban institutions and facilities, the sources available to the historian of the late eighteenth-century and early nineteenth-century town are plentiful. As well as the columns of a weekly newspaper from 1804, full sets of minutes survive for all of Swansea's main institutions of local government, namely the corporation, the harbour trust from 1791 and the paving commission from 1808. The many charitable, cultural and commercial institutions of the day generated their own

---

[51] For a discussion of this, see R. A. Griffiths, 'Wales and the Marches', in D. M. Palliser (ed.), *CUHB*, Volume 1: *600–1540* (Cambridge, 2000), pp. 681–714.

[52] P. Jenkins, 'Wales', in Clark (ed.), *CUHB*, Volume 2, p. 133.

written records, including the infirmary from 1819, the Bank of England branch from 1826, and the scientific society from 1835. The town's role as a bathing resort meant that it was featured in a number of contemporary travel guides such as those published by the Worcestershire printer, George Nicholson,[53] and publishers of early nineteenth-century trade directories thought Swansea worthy of note both in dedicated town guides and as part of wider, regional surveys. It was also a town large enough to merit inclusion in some of the many royal commissions and parliamentary select committee investigations into aspects of urban life in the nineteenth century. It was one of the fifty places visited by the commissioners investigating the state of 'large towns and populous districts' in 1844, and it received the attention of the select committees investigating the state of local government in corporate towns and advising on the redrawing of municipal boundaries in 1834.[54]

Added to this substantial body of official documentation and published description are a number of very good visual depictions of the town and its people in the early nineteenth century. Two artists in particular, Paul Padley, a talented local man, and George Orleans Delamotte, who spent time in the late 1810s and early 1820s in Swansea and its vicinity, produced fine drawings and watercolours of local scenes. From these it is possible to discern the state of streets and buildings and, in some cases, the dress and general appearance of local inhabitants. Other contemporaries chose to make their personal observations on town life in written form, including a number of prominent local townsmen who were active in Swansea's public life. Lewis Weston Dillwyn, whose activities spanned town, county and national politics as well as local industry and cultural life, was a keen diarist; George Grant Francis, one-time mayor of Swansea and commentator on all of the major urban issues of the day, was an antiquarian who not only preserved his own correspondence but also the documentary history of the town. Their accounts, although partial, tantalizingly incomplete and idiosyncratic, like any other personal reflections, nevertheless provide the historian with detailed contemporary views of the town from within.

[53] G. Nicholson, *The Cambrian Traveller's Guide and Pocket Companion* (Stourport, 1808, 2nd enlarged edition, 1813).
[54] B. Ll. James, *Parliamentary Papers, 1801–1914, as Sources of the History of Wales: A Guide and Bibliography* (Library Association, 1973).

Such sources provide a rich diet for the urban historian but they offer, at best, a limited window on town life. Written almost exclusively by middle-class participants in municipal, cultural and commercial affairs, they leave little scope for examining the lives and experiences of those who did not move in such influential circles. The poor, for example, appear only fleetingly in this account of Swansea, on occasions when their actions left a lasting impression on the wealthy. The sick woman who interrupted breakfast at the Phillips household to plead for assistance is a case in point. Her actions prompted Richard Phillips to start a subscription for a dispensary in Swansea.[55] Similarly moving was the 'afflicting scene', witnessed by Lewis Weston Dillwyn, of the widow of a collier killed in an accident, who knelt in despair in the aisle at Llangyfelach church with her head resting on her dead husband's for the duration of his funeral service.[56] While these incidents provide poignant reminders of the world away from municipal politics and cultural life, they do little more than sketch the faintest outline of what urban life was like for this section of the population.

Such problems are by no means unique to the study of Welsh towns, but further difficulties apply specifically to urban history in Wales. In particular, there is a danger that accounts based to a large extent on the English-language minutes, reports and correspondence of the institutions and personalities of public life will seriously under-represent the impact of Welsh linguistic and cultural influences on urbanization. The problem is compounded by the lack of any reliable statistics on language patterns before the census of 1891. Without such figures we can hope for no more than an impressionistic grasp of the linguistic balance in towns like Swansea. With migrants from rural Welsh counties primarily taking up residence in the industrial villages on the outskirts of the town, there is perhaps a case for viewing the Welsh language as peripheral to Swansea's urbanization. Yet not all historians have been willing to accept the existence of such a stark linguistic divide. Ieuan Gwynedd Jones has countered that 'a Welsh stamp was given to the culture of the entire borough, not merely to those parts of it where the Welsh were in a majority'.[57] Occasional fragments of evidence appear to bear him out. Why else would the Swansea surgeon

---

[55] M. Phillips, *Memoir of the Life of Richard Phillips* (London, 1841), pp. 39–40.
[56] NLW, Lewis Weston Dillwyn 1, 19 September 1819.
[57] I. G. Jones, 'The city and its villages', in Griffiths (ed.), *City of Swansea*, p. 87.

advertising for an apprentice in August 1818 have stipulated that 'a knowledge of the Welsh language [is] indispensable',[58] or the printers of the fictional *Dialogue between John Bull and Bonaparte* have decided to produce 500 copies of the pamphlet in Welsh as well as 500 in English for distribution in Swansea in 1803?[59]

The present study offers an account of Swansea's urban 'coming of age' in the half-dozen or so decades after 1780. The people who were central to the processes of urban cultural and economic development necessarily provide the key to understanding this late eighteenth-century and early nineteenth-century flowering. Their names and activities will become familiar during the following chapters, and further information on some of the most influential among them is provided in a biographical appendix. This is intended not as a comprehensive listing of Swansea's 'urban elite', but as a selection of those who enjoyed some degree of local fame owing to their participation in commercial, cultural or political life. As well as identifying these 'celebrities', consideration is also given to the impact of their activities on the population at large. In this way an attempt is made to extend the analysis to encompass, if not the town's poor, then at least its working population. Chapter IV, in particular, examines the extent to which ordinary men and women shared in the benefits of Swansea's apparent elevation in status and prosperity by the 1840s. Linguistic issues are inevitably confronted in the course of this analysis, and addressed again in chapter VI as the degree to which Welsh cultural influences pervaded the literary and scientific institutions of Swansea is assessed. There are other themes which receive relatively little attention. Swansea's religious history, which has been explored in depth by Glanmor Williams,[60] is not afforded a dedicated chapter, although its influence, particularly in cultivating educational and literary life in the town, is examined. Similarly, the experience of women in the early nineteenth-century urban environment, a subject which undoubtedly merits a full-length study of its own, is not addressed in detail.

Gaps such as these are perhaps inevitable in a study which has been undertaken with a broader agenda in mind: that of viewing Swansea's development of flagship commercial and cultural institutions within the larger framework of British urbanization. In recent

[58] *The Cambrian*, 1 August 1818.
[59] D. and M. Walker, 'An Anglo-Welsh town', in Griffiths (ed.), *City of Swansea*, p. 14.
[60] G. Williams, 'Religion and belief', in Griffiths (ed.), *City of Swansea*, pp. 17–33.

years historians have sought to probe the reasons why Wales seemed to be peripheral in some of the key debates in modern British history. L. J. Williams posed the question, *Was Wales Industrialised?* in an attempt to gauge whether the experience of technological innovation, increased output levels and workplace reorganization were sufficient to allow it to be located as part of the British industrial revolution.[61] R. J. W. Evans has asked, 'Was there a Welsh Enlightenment?', pointing out that Wales is almost entirely absent from standard accounts of enlightenment culture in Britain and Europe.[62] This study of late eighteenth-century and early nineteenth-century Swansea has been written with a similar endeavour in mind, and in an attempt to engage more closely with the debates current in British urban history.

---

[61] L. J. Williams, *Was Wales Industrialised? Essays in Modern Welsh History* (Llandysul, 1995).
[62] R. J. W. Evans, 'Was there a Welsh Enlightenment?' in R. R. Davies and G. H. Jenkins (eds), *From Medieval to Modern Wales. Historical Essays in Honour of Kenneth O. Morgan and Ralph A. Griffiths* (Cardiff, 2004), pp. 142–59.

I
'PREJUDICIAL TO OUR ANCIENT RIGHTS AND PRIVILEGES': URBAN GOVERNANCE, c.1780–1800

By the end of the eighteenth century, contemporary commentators and modern historians alike agree that Swansea had attained a position of prominence in Wales's urban hierarchy. It lay at the heart of the most productive part of the south Wales coalfield as well as at the centre of the UK's most important non-ferrous metal smelting region. Its diverse economic base encompassed a range of smaller trades and manufactures from brewing to pottery. In addition, it had a thriving sea-bathing industry during the summer season as locals and visitors alike took advantage of its 'singularly beautiful' bay and 'commodious' shore.[1] As early as 1729, locals were aware that their town was 'a considerable sea port and for trade, business and number of inhabitants is inferior to few towns in Wales'.[2] For much of the early modern period it had shared prominence with Carmarthen, Haverfordwest, Caernarfon, Brecon and Wrexham as Wales's most important urban centres,[3] but by 1801 its population had reached a new high of 6,099. This put clear demographic distance between Swansea and the rest, and propelled it into a new position as Wales's second most populous town, behind Merthyr Tydfil, which was already home to 7,705 people by 1801 thanks to the growth of the iron industry.[4] Unlike Merthyr, Swansea had also developed an urban infrastructure to match its increasing size. With a market place, town hall, ballroom, circulating libraries and pockets of fine housing for its more affluent citizens, by 1800 it was, according to one historian, 'clearly the nearest Wales had to a capital'.[5] Other commentators predicted that the influence of the

---

[1] *The Swansea Guide: containing such information as was deemed useful to the traveller through the counties of Glamorgan and Monmouthshire* (Swansea, 1802), p. 7.
[2] University of Wales Swansea Archives (UWSA), Morris 1, 'A history of the copper concern, 1717–1730'. Historical notes and memoranda by Robert Morris junior, relating to Robert Morris senior's copper-smelting works in Swansea (1774), p. 43.
[3] P. Jenkins, 'Wales', in P. Clark (ed.), *CUHB*, Volume 2: *1540–1840*, p. 141.
[4] J. Williams, *Digest of Welsh Historical Statistics*, Volume 1 (Cardiff, 1985), p. 63.
[5] P. Jenkins, 'Tory industrialism and town politics: Swansea in the eighteenth century', *Historical Journal*, 28, no. 1 (1985), 104.

town would soon extend far beyond the principality. Visiting Swansea in 1804, Benjamin Malkin declared that 'the copper works and collieries have increased in so great a degree, that it is not at all improbable it may at some distant period rival Bristol or Liverpool'.[6]

A number of important studies of the medieval and early modern town have shown that Swansea's emergence as an urban centre was long in the making.[7] In the period before the Acts of Union its status was derived from its position as capital of the lordship of Gower and as a garrison town and port. Thereafter, commercial growth and, in particular, the thriving trade of the harbour sustained its economic buoyancy and regional influence. The population of the town grew unspectacularly but steadily. From a figure of around 1,000 in the last quarter of the sixteenth century, it was still under 2,000 by 1750.[8] Throughout this period, the main feature of urban governance was its growing exclusivity. The office of portreeve, the head of the corporation, was dominated by a few leading local families. The interests of the principal landowner of the area in the eighteenth century, the duke of Beaufort, also loomed large over the governance of the town. His authority was exercised through the person of his steward, who effectively controlled the appointment of burgesses and the selection of the twelve aldermen; they acted as a kind of executive council, holding office for life. To a large extent, this pattern of town governance remained unaltered until the municipal reforms of the 1830s but, in this chapter, it will be argued that the 1780–1800 period witnessed the beginnings of a significant change in the role and activities of Swansea corporation, and that this change was fundamental to the advancement of the town's urban status by 1800.

The significance of the decades after 1780 for Swansea's flowering urban status has not escaped the notice of historians of local

---

[6] B. H. Malkin, *The Scenery, Antiquities and Biography of South Wales* (London, 1807), p. 586.

[7] W. S. K. Thomas, *The History of Swansea: From Rover Settlement to the Restoration* (Llandysul, 1990); W. H. Jones, *History of Swansea and of the Lordship of Gower*, Volume 1: *From the Earliest Times to the Fourteenth Century* (Carmarthen, 1920); E. Evans and C. J. Spurgeon, *Swansea Castle and the Medieval Town* (Swansea, 1983).

[8] W. S. K. Thomas, 'Municipal government in Swansea, 1485–1640', in S. Williams (ed.), *Glamorgan Historian*, Volume 1 (Cowbridge, 1963), pp. 27–8; A. H. John, 'Introduction. Glamorgan, 1700–1750', in G. Williams and A. H. John (eds), *GCH*, Volume 5: *Industrial Glamorgan* (Cardiff, 1980), p. 5.

government in the town. Rosemary Sweet, for example, identified a brief period of factionalism in the late 1780s which gave way to an 'age of improvement', characterized by a more actively interventionist phase of corporation activity.[9] In a British context, there was nothing unusual about this. From the mid-eighteenth century onwards many towns experienced conflict and debate prior to the passing of local improvement acts.[10] Within Wales, the picture was varied. Cardiff did not experience any real factionalism in local government until 1818, when an anti-Bute contingent emerged in the corporation, one principally made up of families resentful of the new men brought in by the second marquess.[11] In Swansea the impact of eighteenth-century industrial growth brought matters to a head rather earlier. The factionalism of the 1780s coincided with a crucial phase of economic and commercial expansion, during which the corporation's traditionally narrow range of municipal activity was exposed as deficient for the needs of the growing town. In some quarters the corporation came to be seen in these years as obstructing rather than facilitating growth. The short period of factionalism which took place in this climate of industrial expansion prompted a change of direction in local government and, from the early 1790s, the corporation appears to have been more responsive to the changing needs of a growing population and an expanding commercial and industrial sector. It was increasingly inclined to work with, rather than guard against, local initiatives for improvement and, as a result, the town became better equipped to take on a more prominent role in the urban life of the region.

Throughout the eighteenth century, membership of Swansea's corporation was restricted. This was typical of local government arrangements in many towns throughout Britain in this period.[12] Participation in public life was confined to a small circle of families. This was particularly true of the upper echelons of local government, where access to principal posts was limited to a few key

---

[9] R. Sweet, 'Stability and continuity: Swansea politics and reform, 1780–1820', *WHR*, 18, no. 1 (1996), 14–39.

[10] J. Innes and N. Rogers, 'Politics and government', in Clark (ed.), *CUHB*, Volume 2, pp. 536–43.

[11] L. Hargest, 'Cardiff's "spasm of rebellion" in 1818', *Morgannwg*, XXI (1977), 69–88; J. Davies, 'Aristocratic town makers and the coal metropolis: the marquesses of Bute and Cardiff, 1776–1947', in D. Cannadine (ed.), *Patricians, Power and Politics in Nineteenth-Century Towns* (Leicester, 1982), p. 34.

[12] See, for example, P. Cadogan, *Early Radical Newcastle* (Consett, 1975), p. 10.

Table 1.1 Occupational profile of Swansea burgesses, 1760–89

Occupational category	No. of burgesses
Construction	5
Craft	8
Gentleman	15
Merchant	2
Professional	3
Retail/Processing	2
Transport	7
Clerk	1
Unknown	12

Source: J. R. Alban, *Calendar of Swansea's Freemen's Records from 1760* (Swansea, 1982).

individuals. The position of portreeve, in particular, was held by a very select few men. From 1782 to 1805, for example, Rowland Pritchard and Thomas Maddocks, the latter a banker and prosperous shipwright,[13] each held the post of portreeve three times. Other families, such as the Powells and Jeffreys, regularly took their turn.[14] The forging of useful connections with the established order in the town helped these men rise to the top in Swansea's local government circles. Rowland Pritchard, for example, was married to Sarah Bassett, sister of the Reverend Miles Bassett, who was vicar of Swansea for almost fifty-seven years.[15] Various members of the Powell family, meanwhile, held the post of steward of the duke of Beaufort in the eighteenth and early nineteenth centuries, thus providing them with direct influence on corporation activity.[16]

As well as enjoying privileged access to the top posts in Swansea's local government, these men were also able to use their influence to preserve the narrow power base in the town. In particular, tight control was exercised over burgess admissions, both in terms of number and the character of the recipients. This was significant

[13] UWSA, Misc. 3, 'File of notes by H. M. Stevens on banking in Swansea', December 1791.
[14] J. R. Alban, *Portreeves and Mayors of Swansea* (Swansea, 1982), pp. 8–11.
[15] West Glamorgan Archives Service (WGAS), D/D W. C. Rogers collection, biographical notes, vol. 129.
[16] Ibid., vol. 122.

because candidates for corporation membership could only come from the burgess body. Between 1760 and 1789, only fifty-five men were granted burgess membership in Swansea.[17] An analysis of the occupational groups from which they were drawn is presented in Table 1.1. Although the large number of 'unknown' occupations makes a precise analysis difficult, it appears from the figures that very few came from the ranks of important and high status middle-class occupations such as those of merchants, professionals and industrialists. A large proportion of them, some 27 per cent, were described simply as 'gentleman' in the freemen's roll. This group spanned the upper ranks of local society and included a number of titled landowners, notably the duke of Beaufort, Sir Thomas Stepney and Sir Watkin Lewes, as well as lesser Swansea property owners such as Iltid Thomas, Rowland Pritchard and Gabriel Jeffrey. The remainder of the new burgesses consisted primarily of craftsmen, including shipwrights, cabinetmakers, shoemakers and coopers, and those engaged in transport, particularly mariners such as Hugh Mason, John Rosser and William Fleming. There is a sense here that Swansea's leaders were anxious not to advance the interests of that section of the new commercial and industrial elite of the town which might have posed a threat to their own established order.

The range of activities and responsibilities undertaken by the corporation on behalf of the town was also very narrow. Aside from promoting facilities for the sea bathers who frequented the town in the summer months,[18] it played little active role in the development or improvement of the urban environment. Instead its principal objective was to protect its own rights and interests, and those of the duke of Beaufort. First and foremost, like every other similar institution of town government in the period, it was a body concerned with property management.[19] Two common attorneys were charged with the task of collecting the rents owing to the corporation, and much of the business conducted at its meetings revolved around the granting or renewing of leases on buildings or tracts of land. Some of these were for industrial or commercial

[17] J. R. Alban, *Calendar of Swansea's Freemen's Records from 1760* (Swansea, 1982), p. 3.
[18] D. Boorman, *The Brighton of Wales. Swansea as a Fashionable Seaside Resort, c.1780–c.1830* (Swansea, 1986), p. 14.
[19] F. H. Spencer, *Municipal Origins. An Account of Private Bill Legislation relating to Local Government, 1740–1835* (London, 1911), p. 3.

purposes, such as the 99-year lease at £5 per annum granted to Mr Phillips of Kendal in May 1792, to build a 'public brewery' in the town.[20] Others permitted the use of land for recreational purposes. In 1786 Charles Collins was granted permission on behalf of 'several gentlemen' of the town who 'hath applied for leave to level a part of the open burrows for playing cricket'.[21] This is one of the earliest recorded references to cricket playing in south Wales,[22] and it is likely that the corporation's willingness to support the playing of the game on the foreshore helped Swansea to become an early centre for the sport.

By the end of the eighteenth century the property functions of the corporation were becoming increasingly onerous. At a meeting in 1797 it was agreed that, 'As the receiving of the rents and doing the business of the Corporation is become too burdensome for the ordinary mode of doing it by the common attorneys – it is proposed that a receiver be appointed to assist them in it.'[23] Besides property management, its other responsibilities included the running of a street market in the town, which was established in 1774,[24] but beyond this its operations were limited. Its only other main area of activity was the performance of ceremonial functions, including the observance of customs traditionally carried out on public occasions and feast days. King George III's return to health after his first serious bout of mental illness, for instance, was marked throughout the country with public celebrations in April 1789. In Swansea it was announced that 'The Corporation intend to go to church in the usual form ... being the day appointed for a public thanksgiving in commemoration of his majesty's happy recovery, and that cakes and wine be given in the Hall as usual on public days.'[25] Likewise, on 20 May of that year the corporation resolved that 'Tomorrow being Ascension Day it is ordered that the boundaries of the Corporation lands and franchise be walked in the usual mode.'[26] The walking of the boundaries and the serving of cake and wine to

[20] WGAS, B/S Corp, B7, Hall Day Minute Book, 1783–1821, 10 May 1792.
[21] Ibid., 19 July 1786.
[22] A. Hignell, *A 'Favourit' Game. Cricket in South Wales before 1914* (Cardiff, 1992), pp. 1–14.
[23] WGAS, B/S Corp, B7, 16 January 1797.
[24] T. Ridd, 'The development of municipal government in Swansea in the nineteenth century' (unpublished MA thesis, University of Wales, 1955), p. 28.
[25] WGAS, B/S Corp, B8, Hall Day Minute Book, 1789–1791, 17 April 1789.
[26] Ibid., 20 May 1789.

mark public celebrations were the sorts of uncontested activities by which the corporation demonstrated its authority to the townspeople at large. These sorts of activities were typical of the public rituals followed by similar bodies in other British towns in this period and constituted the public face of what was otherwise a very private and closed system of local government.[27]

For much of the eighteenth century, this traditionally narrow range of corporation functions proved adequate for the needs of the town. Where particular problems needed to be addressed, the corporation showed itself to be willing to cooperate with other interest groups in the town to effect appropriate remedies. In 1729, for instance, a joint petition was sent from the portreeve, aldermen and principal inhabitants of Swansea to the postmaster general to request that the number of weekly postal deliveries be increased from two to three.[28] There were also cases where potential conflicts of interest between the burgesses and the duke of Beaufort were settled amicably. In 1762, for example, the proposed enclosure of two large areas of the duke's lands in Swansea, Townhill and the Burrows, was successfully negotiated by the duke's steward to the mutual benefit of both parties.[29]

If anything, local politics in Swansea were considerably more quiescent in this period than was the case elsewhere. Before 1791 there were no separate administrative bodies in existence in the town of the kind that could become a focus for anti-corporation sentiments. In addition, many of the early industrialists, such as Dr John Lane, who moved to the area in the 1720s to set up smelting works, displayed Tory leanings. As Philip Jenkins has shown, the gradual intensification of industry in the Swansea region between about 1720 and 1770 was not characterized by a developing gulf between incoming industrial entrepreneurs and the incumbent landed gentry.[30] Instead, the early industrialists had every reason to try to foster good relations with the region's landowners, to whom they looked for favourable leases of land and mineral rights. Robert Morris, a partner in Swansea's Landore copper works from the

[27] Spencer, *Municipal Origins*, p. 141.
[28] UWSA, Morris 1, 'History of the copper concern', p. 43.
[29] B. Morris (ed.), *Gabriel Powell's Survey of the Lordship of Gower and Kilvey in 1764* (Swansea, 2000), pp. 26–7; N. A. Robins, *The Enclosure of Townhill. An Illustrated Guide* (Swansea, 1990), pp. 8–12.
[30] Jenkins, 'Tory industrialism', 103–23.

1720s, for example, went to considerable lengths to develop good relations with the duke of Beaufort after experiencing problems with coal supplies from collieries belonging to another local landowner, Thomas Popkin. By February 1728, when he was planning to build new mills, he specified to his engineer that they should be on Beaufort's rather than Popkin's lands. In the same year, he also began to forge contacts with Gabriel Powell, later the duke's steward, presenting him with gifts of oysters and butter, and urging his partner, Robert Lockwood, to 'rivet a lasting friendship with him as he may on many occasions be very serviceable to your interests.'[31]

The landowners, for their part, were acutely aware of the benefits to be derived from such links with the leading industrialists. The duke of Beaufort's estate was said to have improved in value by £50 per annum in the first year after the granting of a colliery lease to the Mackworths of Neath.[32] Not surprisingly, many of Glamorgan's other leading landowners, such as Thomas Mansel Talbot, were keen to derive similar financial benefits, and became active in trying to find coal on their estates and in looking to establish smelting works.[33] Disputes and rivalries were thus more likely to erupt between local gentry families, in competition with each other for the riches of industrial development, than between the gentry and the industrialists. Gabriel Powell was able to report with some enthusiasm to the duke of Beaufort in 1754 that Mr Morris had opened a new colliery on the duke's lands, 'so he is now out of Popkin's and Price's power'.[34] Like Popkin, the Price family of Penllergaer was another thorn in the side of the Beaufort interest. As well as being rival landowners, competing with Beaufort for industrialists' investments, the Prices also opposed the wishes of the duke's steward in a number of key debates on improvement in eighteenth-century Swansea. In 1768, the first real initiative to improve the town's harbour was led by Gruffydd Price, who chaired a public meeting to propose measures for improving the navigation of the port. Despite receiving the broad backing of the meeting, Price was opposed by Gabriel Powell who blocked the proposals, saying that the corporation would never approve the measure.[35] For much of

[31] UWSA, Morris 1, 'History of the copper concern', p. 105.
[32] Ibid., p. 153.
[33] Jenkins, 'Tory industrialism', 118.
[34] Quoted in Morris (ed.), *Gabriel Powell's Survey*, p. 17.
[35] W. H. Jones, *History of the Port of Swansea* (Carmarthen, 1922), p. 54.

the eighteenth century, then, it was disputes of this kind, between rival gentry and landowning interests, which provided the most potent sources of contention among Swansea's ruling elite. The early industrialists were not regarded as a separate interest group who were powerful enough to pose a challenge to their dominance of local affairs in the town and neighbourhood.

These relatively quiescent relations between gentry and industrialists in eighteenth-century Swansea, however, have been overshadowed to a large extent by a well-documented and interesting period of factionalism which began in the late 1780s. This has formed the basis for a number of unfavourable assessments of Swansea corporation's record in local government and, in particular, of Gabriel Powell's activities as the duke of Beaufort's steward in the 1770s and 1780s. During these years, anti-Powell feeling in the corporation gathered momentum. A number of key opponents emerged, including Charles Collins, burgess and surgeon in the town, William Padley, Quaker, merchant and boatyard owner, and Robert Morris, whose father of the same name had curried favour with the young Gabriel Powell in the name of good business. These men moved in different circles and developed social networks outside the Powell–Beaufort orbit and, in some cases, outside Swansea. Robert Morris was called to the Bar in 1767 and, while in London, developed connections with leading radicals, befriending, amongst others, John Wilkes and frequenting political clubs including the Society for the Supporters of the Bill of Rights.[36] The leading members of the Collins family made influential connections of a different kind, in particular with the Talbots of Margam and Penrice. The pocket diaries of the Reverend John Collins, himself a Swansea burgess and later alderman, are full of references to dinner engagements at Penrice Castle and visits of the Talbot children to his Gower home. When in Swansea he invariably dined with his brother Charles or with the Eaton family and mingled with the leading trading and commercial figures in the town in the Swansea Mercantile Society.[37] Visits to the Padleys were also frequent, illustrating that denominational divisions were no barrier

---

[36] W. Jones, 'Robert Morris, the Swansea friend of John Wilkes', in R. Denning (ed.), *Glamorgan Historian*, Volume 11 (Barry, 1975), pp. 127–8.

[37] WGAS, Royal Institution of South Wales (RISW), Collins Box 10. Collins records dining with the members of the Swansea Mercantile Society on 1 September 1783 at the Fountain, and his subscription payments are recorded in his accounts.

to political and social alliances between the Quaker family and the Anglican vicar and his brother.

It is clear that these three were among the most vocal critics of some of Gabriel Powell's more high-handed tactics in late eighteenth-century corporation meetings, but their collective reputation as Swansea's radical opposition is founded largely on accounts of a single meeting held on 2 November 1787. At this meeting, Collins and Padley made a number of proposals that were given short shrift by Powell. The first was to admit two new burgesses in response to letters of application from the sons of current burgesses resident outside the town. This Powell refused on the grounds that 'they must apply in person and being not resident should not be admitted'. The second was their suggestion that the records of the corporation should be kept in the town hall in a secure chest, rather than 'in the single possession of Gabriel Powell'. This proposal Powell refused to put to the vote. Instead he raised hackles still further by reading to the meeting a statement opposing the resolution, agreed at a general meeting in the town, to apply for an Act of Parliament to improve the harbour. The statement denounced the plan as one which was 'very prejudicial to this town and borough and may tend to the manifest destruction of many of our most valuable rights and privileges', and pledged the corporation to oppose the passage of the Act through Parliament.[38] What followed was an almost farcical set-to between the rival groups and their supporters, captured in a well-known cartoon image by Moses Harris.[39] An account of the events was later drawn up by Robert Morris on behalf of Charles Collins, who alleged that he had been physically attacked by the Reverend Thomas Powell, son of Gabriel Powell. Written from an uncompromisingly anti-Powell perspective, with a possible legal action in mind, Morris described Collins as 'the prosecutor' and Powell as 'the defendant':

> The defendant came up behind him as he was sitting ... and gave him a blow across his breast which threw him and the bench backwards and while he was on the ground the prosecutor saw the defendant's foot lifted up with an apparent effort to stamp on his breast, when at that moment some of the burgesses interfered and saved the prosecutor from the defendant's violence.[40]

[38] WGAS, B/S Corp, B7, 2 November 1787.
[39] The cartoon, entitled 'A Welsh Corporation Meeting', is reproduced in Jones, *History of the Port of Swansea*, pp. 60–1, and in this volume.
[40] WGAS, RISW, Collins Box 13, 'History of what passed in the Corporation, 2 November 1787', n.d., but accompanying letter dated 28 July 1789.

Morris's account of these events has done much to colour historical interpretations of late eighteenth-century town government in Swansea. Powell has been demonized by some commentators for using his position as steward to dominate the corporation and block a number of important improvement measures.[41] His opposition to the petition for an act to improve the harbour was not the first time he had used his influence as steward to be obstructive. In February 1787 a petition to Parliament for a local Act to pave the deteriorating streets was opposed by the corporation under Powell's direction and declared to be 'prejudicial to our ancient customs, rights and privileges'.[42] In some respects, Powell's suspicions of the motives behind these initiatives were justified. Philip Jenkins has shown that the paving issue was used by Robert Morris and his fellow radical, Watkin Lewes, as a platform from which to challenge the duke of Beaufort's authority.[43] In June 1788, Robert Morris was urging Swansea's inhabitants not to pay for paving because the corporation had borrowed money from Sir Herbert Mackworth's bank for the task.[44] In other towns, where separate administrative bodies had been set up to look after matters such as paving, watching or the relief of the poor, these often became the main instruments of opposition to local government. In Coventry, for example, the mayor and aldermen were not represented on the body set up to administer relief of the poor in 1801 and, consequently, it became a focus for the expression of anti-corporation views.[45]

The conservative reaction of Powell and his supporters towards external initiatives in town government was thus, to a large extent, typical of its time. A number of British towns in this era had similar figures at the helm of local government who were concerned to preserve corporation privileges and rights and to resist vesting powers in separate administrative bodies.[46] Attempts to set up

[41] T. Ridd, 'Gabriel Powell: the uncrowned kind of Swansea', in S. Williams (ed.), *Glamorgan Historian*, 5 (Cowbridge, 1968), pp. 152–8.
[42] WGAS, B/S Corp, B7, 5 February 1787; Ridd, thesis, pp. 15–16.
[43] P. Jenkins, 'Jacobites and freemasons in eighteenth-century Wales', *WHR*, 9, no. 3 (1979), 404.
[44] WGAS, RISW, George Grant Francis collection (GGF), B6, Broadsheets relating to Swansea and Glamorgan, 26 June 1788, p. 12.
[45] S. and B. Webb, *English Local Government from the Revolution to the Municipal Corporations Act*, Part 2 (London, 1924), pp. 435–7.
[46] See, for example, E. Gauldie, *One Artful and Ambitious Individual: Alexander Riddoch (1745–1822) (Provost of Dundee, 1787–1819)* (Dundee, 1989).

independent commissions to look after harbour improvement or paving, watching and lighting in late eighteenth-century and early nineteenth-century British towns were thus almost guaranteed to cause conflict between inhabitants and corporations whose main concern was to protect their own powers and customary rights.[47] In this context there was nothing unusual in Swansea corporation's attempt to resist improvement initiatives in the late 1780s. It was no more than a continuation of the low level of corporation activity that had characterized local government in the town since the Middle Ages. What does require explanation is that it was during this short period, in particular, that this traditional approach to town government in Swansea came to be seen, at least in some quarters, as unpalatable.

There is little doubt that Powell, in his late seventies by this time, had in some senses outstayed his welcome in local government. The impression that it was he, personally, who was responsible for holding up change in local government is heightened by the fact that his death, in January 1789, was closely followed by a flurry of new burgess appointments. After the creation of just fifty-five burgesses in the preceding thirty years, there were eighteen new additions to the burgess body in 1789 alone, and thirty-four in total between 1789 and 1792.[48] This was not a decisive break with the past. Table 1.2 shows that the bulk of new additions to the ranks did little to upset the existing occupational profile of the burgess body, with joiners, ropemakers, shipwrights and bakers all included amongst the new intake. But there were also signs of a small but significant occupational shift. Alongside the representatives of the craft sectors and the continuing large intake of 'gentlemen', there was now a handful of new merchant, professional and industrial members, including the surgeon, Nathaniel Seccombe, the merchant, William Jones, and the coal owner and industrialist, John Morris.

The first significant signs of change in the old order thus seemed to have appeared at the very time when Gabriel Powell's reign as steward came to an end. The problem of how to interpret the events following his death, and the period of factionalism that preceded it, has produced two very different types of responses

[47] Spencer, *Municipal Origins*, p. 40.
[48] Alban, *Calendar*, pp. 20–1.

Table 1.2 Occupational profile of Swansea burgesses, 1789–92

Occupational category	No. of burgesses
Construction	2
Craft	9
Gentleman	7
Merchant	4
Professional	1
Retail/Processing	4
Transport	3
Clerk	1
Industrialist	1
Unknown	2

Source: J. R. Alban, *Calendar of Swansea's Freemen's Records from 1760* (Swansea, 1982).

from historians. The first approach has been to emphasize the personality of Gabriel Powell, and his growing intransigence, as the key factor that increased levels of friction in Swansea's local government in this period.[49] The second has been to minimize the significance of the period, viewing the conflicts of the late 1780s as a blip in an otherwise largely tranquil era of town government.[50] What neither of these explanations offers is a sufficient degree of attention to the wider context of industrial and commercial development in the town. The 1780s were marked by a distinct change of pace in the pattern of industrial and commercial growth in Swansea. It was this that began to make the corporation's inactive approach to town government appear inadequate and ineffective whereas previously it had been accepted, and it was also this that was reflected in the subtle shifts taking place in burgess membership from 1789 onwards.

During the 1780s, industrialization in Swansea intensified as a number of new copper-smelting concerns were established in the vicinity of the town. The Anglesey 'copper king', Thomas Williams, took over the Upper Bank Works in 1782, Lockwood and Morris built a new works at Landore in 1793, and a number of

---

[49] See, for example, Ridd, 'Gabriel Powell', pp. 152–8.
[50] Sweet, 'Stability and continuity', 15.

Birmingham metal manufacturers also saw the potential of Swansea as a smelting site and opened works, including the Rose Copper Works. By the end of the eighteenth century there were seven copper-smelting businesses in production in the lower Swansea valley, producing a combined output of 7,000 tons per annum, or 90 per cent of the total UK output.[51] Some of the larger smelters were also investing in Boulton and Watt steam engines in this period. Popkin and Mackworth had one installed at Landore in 1788 at a cost of £5,000.[52] In response to this increased industrial activity, the population of Swansea showed a marked growth in the second half of the eighteenth century, from under 2,000 in 1750 to over 6,000 in 1800.[53] Recent research has shown that in-migration was largely responsible for this growth, making Swansea a more diverse and cosmopolitan urban centre than other Welsh towns in this period.[54] At the same time, Swansea moved ahead of Cardiff in terms of population size and industrialization. A divergence in the patterns of development in the two towns had been evident before 1750, but the latter two decades of the eighteenth century saw a widening of the gulf. In these years, the Swansea region experienced an intensification of industry and a growth of population which gave it a new level of prominence among Welsh towns. Cardiff, although it also displayed a 'new vigour' in the same period, with the growing prosperity of its port, improvements to the streets and a growth of urban services, did not experience the same level of population increase and still ranked only twenty-fifth among Welsh towns in 1801.[55]

Closely linked to Swansea's increased industrial activity were some significant developments in the provision of transport facilities. The 'canal mania' of the 1790s saw inland industrialists working to secure improved transport waterways to the coast. The Neath Canal Act was passed in 1791 and a group of seventy-one, mainly industrialist, subscribers from the Merthyr Tydfil region

---

[51] An additional works was also located at Penclawdd. P. R. Reynolds, 'Industrial development', in G. Williams (ed.), *Swansea. An Illustrated History* (Swansea, 1990), p. 32.

[52] D. T. Williams, 'The economic development of Swansea and of the Swansea district to 1921', *Social and Economic Survey of Swansea and District*, 4 (Cardiff, 1940), p. 35.

[53] T. Boyns and C. Baber, 'The supply of labour, 1750–1914', in Williams and John (eds), *GCH*, Volume V, p. 316.

[54] C. R. Anthony, 'Seaport, society and smoke. Swansea as a place of resort and industry, c.1700–1840' (unpublished Ph.D. thesis, University of Leicester, 2002), ch. 4.

[55] J. Davies, *Cardiff. A Pocket Guide* (Cardiff, 2002), pp. 28–35.

funded the Glamorganshire Canal between Cardiff and Abercynon which opened in 1794. The need for more effective links between the Swansea region's coastal strip and the mineral-rich interior was also becoming evident, as higher levels of output from the smelters demanded ever greater quantities of coal and lime.[56] From 1783 to 1785, John Smith, the coal proprietor who married the daughter of Chauncey Townsend, built a three-mile stretch of canal from Llansamlet to Foxhole, which one historian has described as 'the classic Swansea siting for its copper smelters'.[57] Plans in 1793 to build a new canal up the vale of Tawe and into Breconshire were greeted warmly by the corporation. A meeting was called for consideration of the plans. It was agreed that 'such a canal will be of very great utility' and that the venture would 'tend very much to augment the trade and manufacture of all its neighbourhood'.[58] In 1798 a 15-mile-long stretch of waterway along the Tawe valley was opened.

Plans for canal building involved negotiations over route and, crucially, over the point of termination where goods would be loaded and unloaded. Town rivalries came to the fore over such issues and forced local leaders to think about the future role their town should play in the urban and industrial setting. In Swansea, the minds of the corporation were concentrated on this issue when it was proposed, by the industrialist Morris family, that the Tawe valley canal should be terminated north of the town at Plasmarl. It was calculated that such a plan would cost the corporation some £500 per annum in lost revenues and would do untold harm to the town and its inhabitants.[59] In order to protect its interests, and those of the town, the corporation threatened to withdraw its £1,000 subscription to the project unless it received a guarantee that the canal would terminate in Swansea itself.[60] This action illustrated the new resolve of the corporation in the latter decades of the eighteenth century. Developments in industry, transport and commerce fostered a heightened awareness of Swansea's position in relation to other urban settlements in south Wales and generated among

[56] C. Hadfield, *The Canals of South Wales and the Border* (Cardiff, 1967), pp. 45–61.
[57] S. R. Hughes, *Copperopolis. Landscapes of the Early Industrial Period in Swansea* (Aberystwyth, 2000), p. 112.
[58] WGAS, B/S Corp, B7, 18 March 1793.
[59] Ibid., 18 March 1794.
[60] Ibid., 21 August 1795.

corporation members a greater sense of the need to act in the interests of the town.

From the end of the 1780s, then, there were clear signs of an improvement ethos permeating the corporation. It was prepared to move beyond its traditional ceremonial and property management roles and take a wider interest in the development of the town. Powell's death in 1789 did much to clear the way for this increased level of activity. Liberated from his restrictive influence, the corporation concerned itself with the appearance of the town, ease of access to and around it, and its trade and commerce. A 'committee for improvements' was in existence by 1791, and from the beginning of that decade, there was a marked shift in corporation rhetoric, which saw the old emphasis – on acting to protect the customary rights and privileges of corporation members – give way to a new concern for the wider benefit of the town.[61]

Evidence of these new corporation concerns at work can be seen in a number of activities in the late 1780s and early 1790s. In their approach to property leases, for example, the corporation began to demonstrate a greater interest in regulating the appearance of the built environment. The following direction was included in a lease of houses in the High Street in 1789: 'for the encouragement of such persons who have or shall hereafter purchase any part of the said property, to bring out the front of their buildings in a parallel line with the adjoining houses which will be a great ornament to that part of the town.'[62] Meanwhile, the corporation's bathing house committee was directed to look to the improvement of roads and avenues along the shore. In April 1790 it reported that 'the Ropewalk and the avenues leading to it may be made a public way of great utility ... and that it would be a great inducement to the future erection of buildings on the Corporation lands'.[63] The corporation's concern to improve trade was evident in its efforts to revive the traditional Tuesday market in the town in addition to the weekly Saturday market, and in its dealings with local manufacturers such as John Coles and George Haynes who ran the Cambrian pottery. In extending their lease, the corporation informed Coles and Haynes that it was 'ready and willing to grant them as much

[61] Reference to the committee for improvements can be found in ibid., 29 August 1791.
[62] WGAS, B/S Corp, B8, 11 September 1789.
[63] Ibid., 16 April 1790.

more ground as may be found convenient for increasing the manufactory'.[64] Concern to enhance the value of corporation lands was no doubt part of the incentive underpinning these and similar measures, but a nod in the direction of the wider benefits the town might accrue from such initiatives is also clearly evident, adding a new dimension to local governance in this period.

The benefits derived by local trades and manufacturers from this corporation backing were great. In particular, the production of pottery in the town went from strength to strength in this period. As E. Morton Nance has observed, the development of the pottery industry in Swansea 'was intimately connected with ... the growth and expansion of the town as a port and business centre and as a summer resort'.[65] The Cambrian pottery, established in Swansea in 1764 by William Coles, initially produced mainly coarse pottery products manufactured from local clay, primarily for the local market. By the 1780s the range of products had already extended to include finer earthenware goods made from imported Devon and Dorset clay, but the most notable phase of expansion came from 1789 when George Haynes, from a Warwickshire Quaker family, went into partnership with Coles. Haynes reorganized the pottery using Wedgwood's Staffordshire manufactory as a model, and introduced a number of skilled Staffordshire workmen to the Cambrian. With the cooperation of the corporation over the granting of leases, he was able to expand the business and, by 1790, there were four kilns in operation and some £1,200 had been spent on new buildings.[66]

Under Haynes's management, the variety of products grew to include a range of cream ware, similar to Wedgwood's 'Queen's ware'. By the second half of the eighteenth century, these light-coloured table wares were in common use among Britain's urban middle classes and in resort towns like Swansea, where tea drinking was gaining in popularity, the market for fine ceramic services was buoyant.[67] By the early nineteenth century the range of goods available for sale at the pottery included 'a large assortment of Dinner,

[64] Ibid., 8 February 1790.
[65] E. Morton Nance, *The Pottery and Porcelain of Swansea and Nantgarw* (London, 1942), p. 14.
[66] H. L. Hallesy, *The Glamorgan Pottery Swansea, 1814–38* (Llandysul, 1995), p. 2.
[67] G. B. Roberts, 'Swansea and Wedgwood', in J. Gray (ed.), *Welsh Ceramics in Context*, Part 1 (Swansea, 2003), pp. 77–9.

Desert [*sic*], Supper, Tea and other services in a great variety of new patterns and shapes, and of improved quality. Also vases, mantelpiece ornaments, bisket [*sic*] ware for ladies to paint on ...'[68] Markets also expanded to include the West Country and by the second decade of the nineteenth century, a thriving export trade with the Baltic, Italy, Ireland, the USA and the West Indies was in place.

The success of the Cambrian pottery in this era illustrated the increasing wealth of the town and its growing range of British and foreign trading links in the late eighteenth century. Although the arrival of Haynes in 1789 was crucial to this phase of expansion, the more active role of the post-Powell corporation from this date in promoting the improvement and prosperity of the town was also an important facilitating factor.

There was also evidence of a change in the approach of the corporation towards the promotion of more extensive improvement measures. In particular, the issue of harbour improvement was high on the agenda once again in the early 1790s. Earlier corporation attempts, led principally by Gabriel Powell, to obstruct the passing of legislation for improving the harbour meant that it was left largely to local initiative to try to extend harbour provision in the town. By the latter years of the eighteenth century, this was becoming a matter of some urgency. The industrial growth of the district in the preceding decades and the construction of canals in the vicinity had significantly increased the use of the harbour. In 1768 some 690 vessels entered the port of Swansea. By 1790 this had risen to 1,697 and a year later to 1,803.[69] This rate of growth exposed deficiencies in the existing harbour provision and, by the late 1780s, local initiative was being mobilized to act where the corporation had previously sought to obstruct. In 1789 a group of local gentry and leading townsmen set up a subscription fund in order to raise money to pay a harbour surveyor to give advice on the improvements necessary at Swansea. On this occasion, the corporation was not willing to stand by while others took the initiative. It resolved to 'advance a sum of money equal to what each of the other noblemen and gentlemen do advance for the purpose'.[70] It also took an active role in attempting to engage a suitably qualified person to undertake the survey work.

[68] Quoted in Nance, *Pottery and Porcelain*, p. 83.
[69] Williams, 'Economic development of Swansea', p. 39.
[70] WGAS, B/S Corp, B8, 26 October 1789.

After refusals from the harbour surveyor at Liverpool, it was resolved that the portreeve should

> write to know if the person ... engaged to view the port of Bristol for the purpose of making improvements therein, will come down to this place to inspect the harbour, communicate their judgement on the capability of improving the same, and to know for what sum they will proceed.[71]

Ultimately, when the issue of an Act of Parliament was again raised at a general meeting in the town, the corporation decided to throw in its lot with the 'burgesses of the borough of Swansea and of several proprietors of lands, copper works and ... several other persons concerned with the trade and navigation of the said port', in order to petition Parliament for a bill.[72] The result of this united action was the passing, in 1791, of An Act for Repairing, Enlarging and Preserving the Harbour of Swansea in the County of Glamorgan.

By responding to public pressure for a harbour act at this stage, the corporation, in all probability, avoided a future storm. In other towns where public demands for harbour legislation fell on deaf ears, the issue became a focus of anti-corporation resentment and opposition. In Dundee, for example, where the harbour was crucial to the town's growth as a centre for linen manufacture, resentment built up at what was seen as the council's neglect of the harbour for decades and, in 1814, a determined group of opponents wrested control of the harbour away from the council and established their own independent harbour commission.[73] By acting earlier, Swansea's local government leaders prevented any similar opposition from gathering momentum and, at the same time, secured for themselves a leading stake in the future management of the harbour improvements. In the new harbour trust set up under the 1791 act, corporation representation was dominant. The portreeve, aldermen and twelve annually elected burgesses became members. Theirs were not the only voices represented on the new body, however: in addition, twelve representatives of the district's collieries and manufactories were appointed to the trust. This brought into the public

---

[71] Ibid., 8 February 1790.
[72] Ibid., 7 December 1790.
[73] L. Miskell and W. Kenefick, '"A flourishing seaport": Dundee harbour and the making of the industrial town, c.1815–1850', *Scottish Economic and Social History*, 20, no. 2 (2000), 176–98.

life of the town for the first time a number of key figures from business and industry. George Haynes, banker and pottery manufacturer, John Smith, colliery proprietor and son-in-law of Chauncey Townsend, Richard Phillips, barrister, whose father was agent for the White Rock copper works, and Calvert Richard Jones, a prominent townsman and promoter of local commerce, were among the trustees appointed to represent the interests of Swansea's commercial and industrial groups.[74]

This new cooperative approach over the harbour did not, however, mark a new attitude to the range of corporation roles and responsibilities in town governance. Other areas of need received little attention from the corporation. Of particular concern was the maintenance of law and order, another issue brought increasingly into focus by the industrial and demographic growth of the second half of the eighteenth century. Poor harvests and inefficient distribution of foodstuffs caused particular concern in towns which had undergone recent population growth and, not surprisingly, Swansea experienced repeated outbreaks of corn rioting in the second half of the eighteenth century. Several incidents in the 1750s and 1760s, and increasing signs of lower class unrest thereafter, made the town's law enforcement provisions seem inadequate. Threats to authority were again felt in 1784 after an incident of rioting in March and an attack that resulted in the destruction of the public whipping post in June.[75] Swansea also figured prominently in the disturbances of the 1790s which broke out as a result of steadily rising corn prices. The corporation twice voted funds to buy up supplies of grain from England for sale to the poor of the town in a bid to head off disorder,[76] but their efforts were in vain. In 1793 copper workers from Llangyfelach marched into the town, raiding farms along the way, and took their complaints direct to the town hall where magistrates were sufficiently alarmed to send for a detachment of troops.[77] Trouble was again signalled in the winter of 1795 by an 'alarming and most atrocious paper having been put up on the door of the Town Hall holding out an insult to the magistracy of these districts and threatening pillage and destruction to the town'.[78]

[74] Jones, *History of the Port of Swansea*, p. 67.
[75] WGAS, B/S Corp, B7, 15 March 1784, 9 June 1784.
[76] Ibid., 13 February 1793, 27 January 1795.
[77] D. J. V. Jones, *Before Rebecca. Popular Protests in Wales, 1793–1835* (London, 1973), p. 20.
[78] WGAS, B/S Corp, B7, 12 November 1795.

Local merchants and businessmen inevitably felt vulnerable. Their response was to form an Association for the Prosecution of Felons in 1792, to 'pay the expenses of advertising, taking and prosecuting any person or persons who shall rob, feloniously defraud or otherwise injure person or property of any or either of the subscribers'.[79] This was less of an improvement initiative than a defensive response to heightened fears of lower-class unrest among a number of local businessmen. The committee included the draper, printer and banker John Voss, who was one of those threatened by food rioters in 1766.[80] Neither was it designed to address the longer-term problem of how to police the town effectively. It was not until 1803 that a more ambitious plan to address the question of regular policing for the town was put to the corporation by Charles Collins, setting out a structure of districts with constables, inspectors and magistrates with clearly defined duties.[81]

Another issue which local inhabitants in Swansea considered important enough for action was that of transport, more specifically the state of the roads in and around the principal towns of Glamorgan. In response to this problem, the South Wales Association for the Improvement of Roads was formed at a meeting chaired by the industrialist John Morris at Swansea's Mackworth Arms hotel in November 1789. The subscribers to the new group included Thomas Mansel Talbot of Margam, John Vaughan of Golden Grove and J. Weeks of Bristol, as well as a strong Swansea-based contingent led by the Morrises. They all agreed that the mail route from Bristol to Milford Haven and on to Ireland was 'of the greatest importance to the parts of South Wales through which it passes', and viewed 'the improvement of that line of road an object greatly to be desired'.[82] Similar privately organized initiatives were undertaken in this period in other south Wales towns. In Newport, for example, a 'thoughtful and influential group of gentlemen' took it upon themselves to apply to Parliament for an increase in the county rate in order to raise money to build a new stone bridge over the Usk.[83] The broad composition and perspective of the group formed at Swansea,

[79] WGAS, RISW, GGF, B6, Broadsheets relating to Swansea and Glamorgan, p. 39, 'Rules of the Association for the Prosecution of Felons', 13 February 1792.
[80] Jenkins, 'Tory industrialism', p. 122.
[81] WGAS, RISW, Collins Box 13, 'Plan for establishing some regular police in the town of Swansea' (1803).
[82] Ibid., GGF, B6, p. 37, 2 November 1789.
[83] B. P. Jones, *From Elizabeth I to Victoria. The Government of Newport (Monmouthshire), 1550–1850* (Newport, 1957), pp. 102–3.

however, were indicative of the town's growing awareness of its widening sphere of influence as a trading and commercial centre, both within south Wales and beyond.

By the end of the eighteenth century, then, there were signs that Swansea was adapting to the demands of commercial and demographic growth by a combination of local initiative and corporation good will. The range of corporation involvement in improvement measures was widening, just enough to justify Rosemary Sweet's use of the phrase 'age of improvement', though it was still largely in areas most likely to bring benefit to corporation property and interests. The corporation certainly had not been premature in pressing such matters as street paving. A host of other, and smaller, Welsh towns, including Cardiff, Brecon, Carmarthen and Abergavenny, all obtained improvement Acts with paving powers sooner.[84] But in Swansea the timing proved to be exactly right. Although Powell's intransigence had held up paving and harbour improvements, it did so just long enough to allow the momentum of commercial and demographic growth in the town to build to a level that was sufficient to prompt a new level of corporation activity after Powell's death. The effects of industrial and population growth in the latter decades of the eighteenth century thus probably played a more significant part than did the victory of any particular local government faction in prompting the corporation to broaden the scope of its activities.

There was a significant gear-shift in corporation activity in the last decade of the eighteenth century. A position of intense scepticism was replaced by one of cooperation, and it was a change which, arguably, had a greater transforming impact on local government in the town than the implementation of the 1835 Municipal Corporations Act.[85] This new spirit of cooperation manifested itself in a number of different ways. It was evident in the participation of representatives of commerce and industry in the affairs of the town for the first time, alongside members of the corporation in the newly established harbour trust. It underpinned the expressions of intent to benefit the town which became a common feature of corporation resolutions. It was also reflected in the greater range of activities in which the corporation became

[84] Anthony, 'Seaport, society and smoke', p. 215.
[85] For a discussion of the impact of this piece of legislation on local government in Swansea, see below, chapter V.

involved in the last decades of the eighteenth century. Without this gear-shift, Swansea would not have been propelled into the new position of urban prominence which it occupied by the turn of the century and on which it was able to build in the next two decades.

A Welsh Corporation Meeting, 1787 (Swansea Museum). Thomas Powell attacks Charles Collins as the Quaker, William Padley (centre, wearing his hat), looks on.

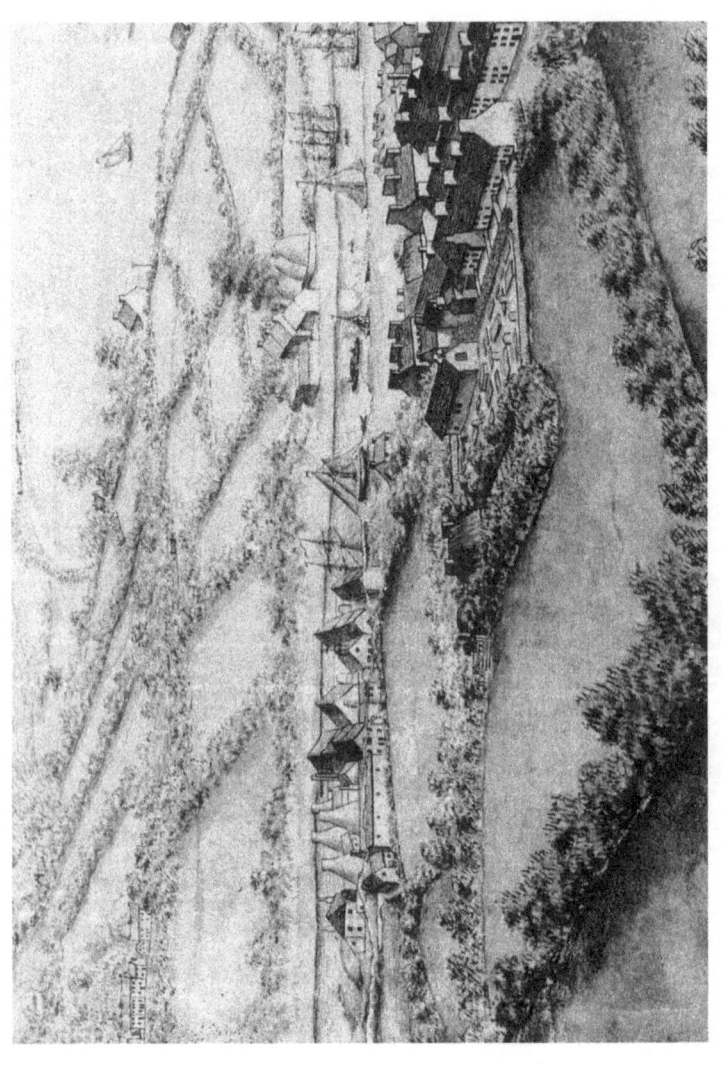

Panorama of Swansea in the 1790s (Swansea Museum). The scale of the Cambrian Pottery can be gauged from the four large kilns visible on the left.

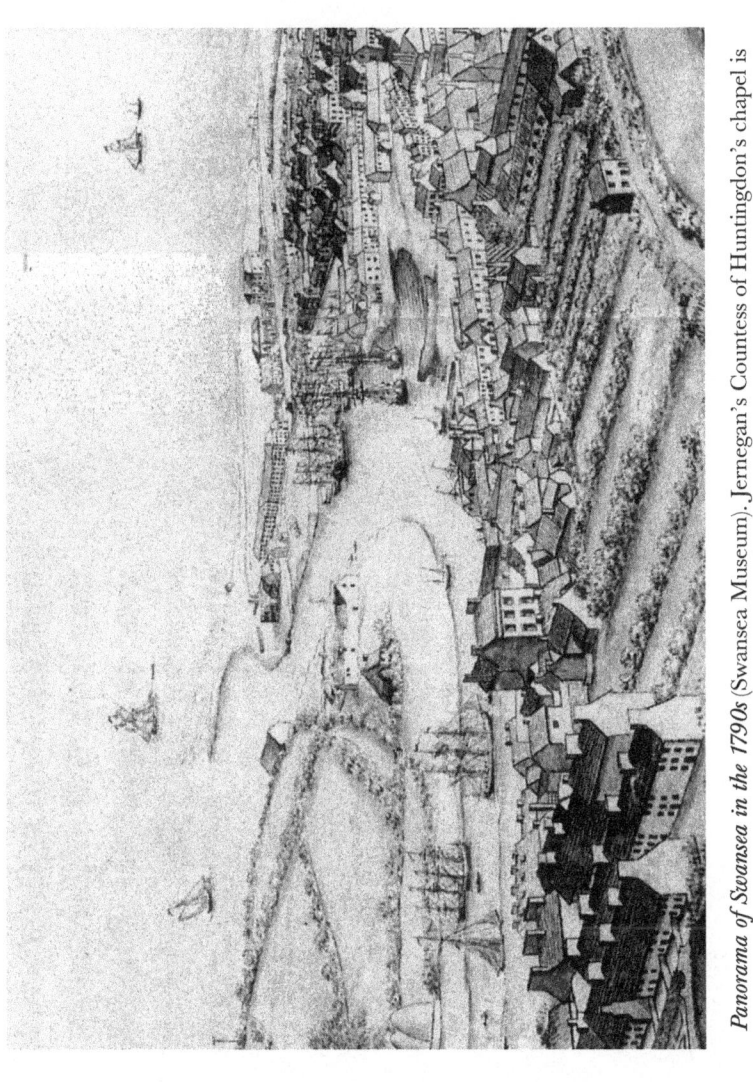

Panorama of Swansea in the 1790s (Swansea Museum). Jernegan's Countess of Huntingdon's chapel is clearly visible in the new area of development on the Burrows.

Constable John Luce (Swansea Museum). Appointed by the paving commission in 1821 to impound stray animals found on Swansea's streets.

This untitled sketch (WGAS) shows the poor condition of some of Swansea's streets by the second decade of the nineteenth century. The street shown here, the Strand, was described by the paving commissioners in their survey of 1819 as being 'in bad repair throughout'.

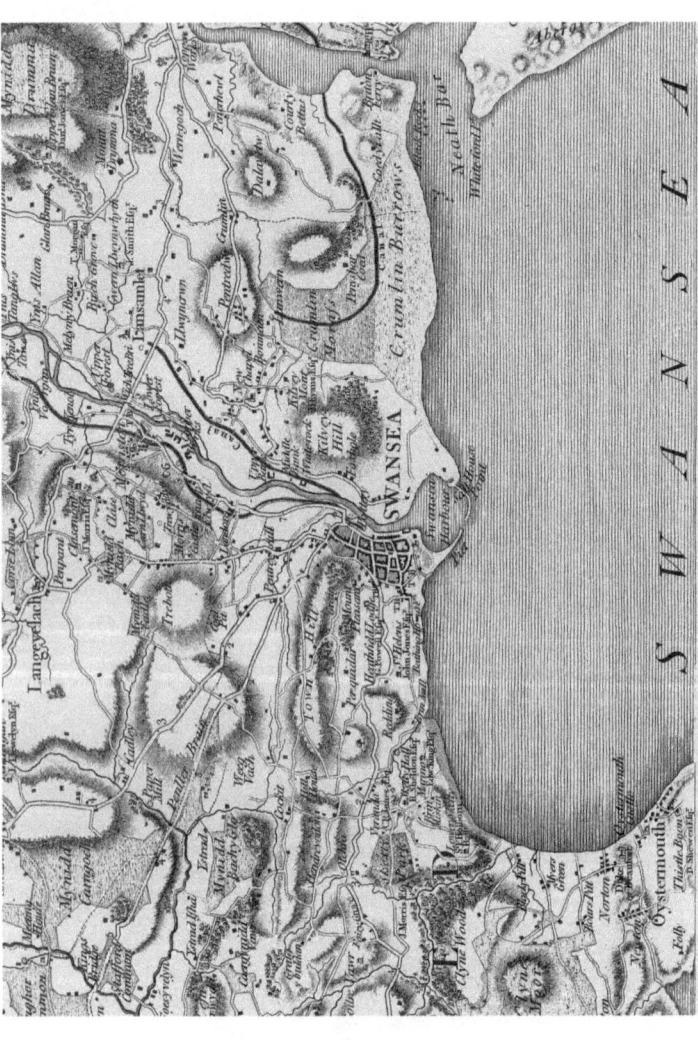

Extract from map of Glamorgan, 1799 (WGAS). This extract shows Swansea's well developed urban core and spacious harbour, with good canal and road links to the surrounding district.

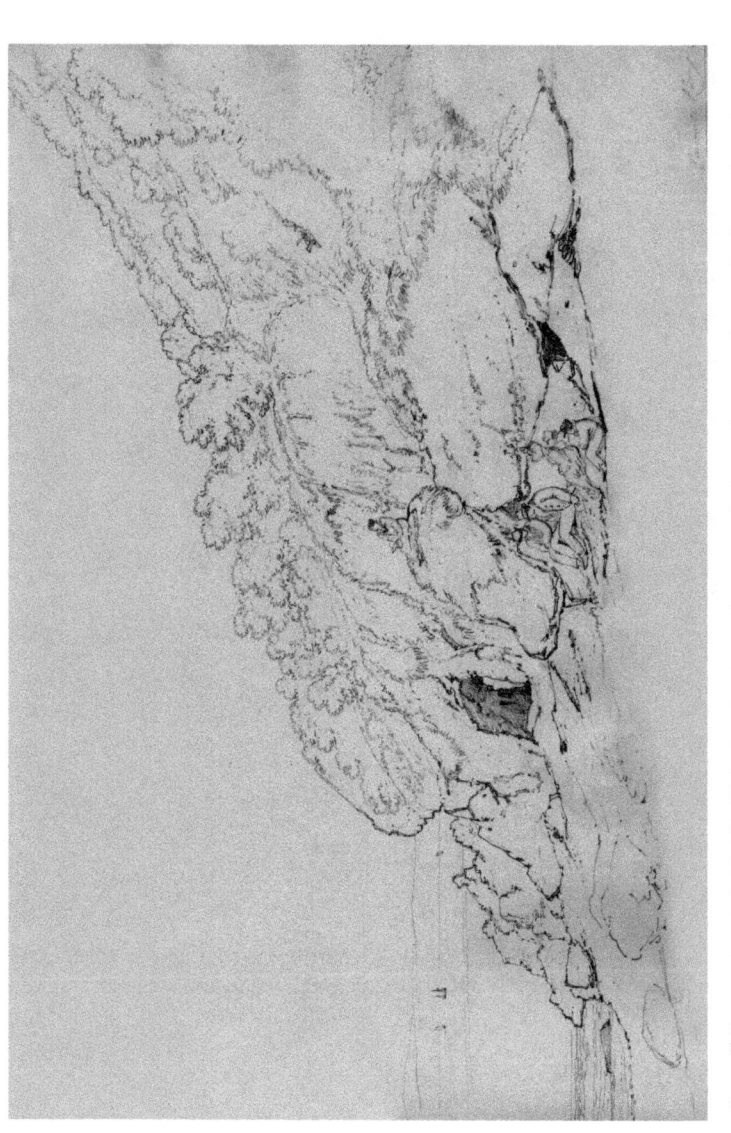

Caswell Bay (undated) (WGAS). This sketch c.1820 shows a well-dressed group of excursionists gathered near a Gower cave to view the rock and plant life of the coastline near Swansea.

Muffins or Crumpets! (NLW) Cake-seller dressed in the traditional hat, shawl and apron attire worn by female traders in early nineteenth-century Swansea.

II
'MANY ADVANTAGES NOT TO BE FOUND IN ANY OTHER PART OF WALES': IMPROVEMENT AND IDENTITY, c.1800–1820

The impetus for 'improvement', which Swansea corporation had shown signs of embracing in the last decade of the eighteenth century, became a more prominent feature of town life in the first two decades of the nineteenth. The idea of acting 'for the benefit of the town' became a much more conscious part of corporation activity in this period as a host of initiatives were undertaken to improve the thoroughfares, recreational spaces and public amenities of Swansea. The *New Swansea Guide*, published in 1823, assessed the developments which had taken place in the town in the first two decades of the nineteenth century and concluded that 'Within the last twenty years the town has astonishingly increased in wealth and population; an elegant theatre has been opened, public rooms erected, various new streets have been formed and its general appearance greatly improved.'[1]

This heightened contemporary awareness of improvement in early nineteenth-century Swansea was, of course, far from being exceptional. Asa Briggs's concept of an 'age of improvement', taking in the 'formative changes in the structure of the English economy, the shape of English society and the framework of government', mapped out a much broader improvement ethos in political and commercial as well as social life in the period.[2] From this concept, urban historians have distilled a number of key developments in the late eighteenth and early nineteenth centuries which collectively improved the condition of the towns. One of these was the provision of basic facilities, such as drainage, sewerage, street lighting and refuse collection. A second was concern with the appearance and accessibility of towns, with street widening and paving schemes and the attempt to regulate the appearance of new buildings. The third was the idea that towns should be able to offer a range of

---

[1] *The New Swansea Guide, 1823* (Swansea, 1823), p. 22.
[2] A. Briggs, *The Age of Improvement, 1783–1867* (Harlow, 1979), pp. 1–2.

urban amenities, including reading rooms, town halls, assembly rooms and theatres. Studies of English and Scottish towns have shown that these improvements, as well as being a sign of 'increasing enthusiasm for urban life',[3] could also provide much-needed solutions to problems of safety and public health.[4] Stark ideological differences over the best way to implement and fund such improvements meant that they could also become the battlefields of local politics.[5] Much less research has been undertaken on similar developments in urban Wales with the result that Welsh towns have not traditionally been associated with the late eighteenth-century and early nineteenth-century fashion for building new theatres and assembly rooms and attending to street paving and lighting.[6] In Swansea, there was activity on all of these fronts in the first two decades of the nineteenth century.

In examining Swansea's experience of urban improvement in this period, the intention is not to present it as typical of wider trends in urban Wales. In many ways Swansea presents a rather unusual Welsh case-study. Improvements to its streets, buildings and facilities were prompted to some extent by the pressure of demographic and commercial growth but these were not the only, or necessarily the principal, factors at work. Population growth in the town, from just over 6,000 in 1801 to 10,255 in 1821, was fast but not frenetic.[7] With the exception of the potteries and a soap manufactory, the growth of industry took place largely outside the town, with the location of smelting works upriver.[8] Of greater significance in shaping the character and range of urban facilities being developed in the town was Swansea's role as an elite bathing resort. Many of the urban improvement initiatives undertaken in this period were conceived, if not exclusively for the benefit of summer

[3] C. Smith, 'Urban improvement in the Nottinghamshire market town, 1770–1840', *Midland History*, XXV (2000), 98–114.
[4] C. Gill, 'Birmingham under the street commissioners, 1769–1851', *University of Birmingham Historical Journal*, 1, no. 2 (1948), 255–87.
[5] L. Miskell, 'From conflict to co-operation: urban improvement and the case of Dundee, 1790–1850', *Urban History*, 29, no. 3 (2002), 350–71.
[6] Notable exceptions to this include P. Jenkins, *The Making of a Ruling Class: The Glamorgan Gentry, 1640–1790* (Cambridge, 1983); J. W. Pritchard, 'Water supply in Welsh towns, 1840–1900. Control, conflict and development', *WHR*, 21, no. 1 (2002), 24–47; D. W. Howell, 'Society, 1660–1793', in B. Howells (ed.), *Pembrokeshire County History*, Volume 3: *Early Modern Pembrokeshire* (Haverfordwest, 1987), pp. 293–6.
[7] J. Williams, *Digest of Welsh Historical Statistics*, Volume 1 (Cardiff, 1985), p. 63.
[8] See below, chapter III.

visitors to its shores, then at least with their needs in mind. The town's role as a resort gave it a clear head start over other urban centres in south Wales in equipping itself with an attractive range of urban facilities, particularly for polite recreational pursuits. Moreover, these developments helped to give the town an elevated status within the south Wales region which was apparent to contemporaries and evident in a number of key developments dating from these years. In particular, the campaign hold a sitting of the Court of Great Sessions in Swansea and the move to have a branch of the Bank of England in the town were both products of a new, confident urban identity which two decades of urban improvement had helped to cultivate.

At the beginning of the nineteenth century, however, it seemed that improvement issues would have to take a back seat, as urban leaders were faced with more pressing and immediate concerns over public order and security. Food shortages continued to be a problem, just as they had been in the late eighteenth century, and the threat of public disorder at times of particular distress remained very real. In April 1801 the portreeve was again required, as in the 1790s, to buy up corn for sale at a reasonable price to the town's poor. The initiative failed to avert an outbreak of food rioting in the same month which the marquess of Bute's clerk, John Bird, who was in the town for the day to receive taxes, observed from his base in the Mackworth Arms. He was somewhat dismissive of the incident, in which 'a number of poor women' broke into a warehouse containing barley, 'but did not attempt taking any of it away'. The Swansea authorities, he suggested, were more worried by a rumour 'that a large mob of miners, colliers etc. meant to assemble the next day'.[9] Certainly the corporation took a more serious view of the 'dreadful and daring' proceedings, which acted as a further reminder, if one were needed, that the town was ill-equipped to deal with large-scale disorder and vulnerable at times of unrest.[10]

It was perhaps as a result of this that a more pre-emptive approach was adopted when economic distress again threatened to give rise to social unrest in 1816. On this occasion, the corporation passed a resolution requiring the portreeve to set aside £50 from corporation funds, 'in case a subscription be entered into at the

[9] H. M. Thomas (ed.), *The Diaries of John Bird of Cardiff, Clerk to the first Marquess of Bute, 1790–1803* (Cardiff, 1987), pp. 131–2.
[10] WGAS, B/S Corp, B7, 20 April, 16 October 1801.

town meeting this day for considering the best mode of employing the labouring poor'.[11] In addition it was resolved that 'the portreeve be requested not to give the usual dinner on the 26th in order to enable him to make a more liberal subscription for the employment of the labouring poor'. These decisions, taken against a background of serious industrial unrest elsewhere in south Wales, were no doubt intended to head off similar disturbances at Swansea, but they also illustrated an increased level of responsiveness on the part of the corporation to popular needs.

As well as the fear of disorder on the domestic front, worries over national security were never far away. In the latter years of the 1790s, the threat of a French invasion was as keenly felt in Swansea as anywhere in Britain. In March 1797, a jittery Thomas Mansel Talbot at Penrice had notified the corporation that 'a vessel supposed to be an enemy was in Rossily Bay' and requested that 'the Swansea Royal Volunteers might be sent'.[12] Coming only a month after the landing of a French invasion force just along the coast in Fishguard, Talbot's reaction indicated that, despite the ease with which the Pembrokeshire invaders had been repelled, fear of the French was still very much alive.[13] With such grave prospects seemingly on the horizon, the urgency of dealing with local matters such as paving understandably lessened and the corporation turned its attention instead to issues such as the recruitment of volunteers for the defence of the county.[14] Within the space of just a few years, however, the passing of the French threat and a diminution in unrest over food prices brought a greater sense of stability to the town. This was strengthened in August 1802 with the visit of the hero of the French conflict, Admiral Lord Nelson. His arrival in Swansea was part of a wider tour of south Wales in the company of Sir William and Lady Hamilton. At Monmouth, Tenby and Milford Haven, he was greeted with great enthusiasm by cheering crowds, and a similar level of excitement was felt in Swansea. The corporation made him a burgess in honour of his 'great and meritorious services to the United Kingdom',[15] but it was the mass

---

[11] Ibid., 10 December 1816.
[12] Ibid., 2 March 1797.
[13] R. Quinault, 'The French invasion of Pembrokeshire. A bicentennial assessment', *WHR*, 19, no. 4 (1999), 618–42.
[14] WGAS, B/S Corp, B7, 27 February 1798.
[15] Ibid., 14 August 1802.

celebrations that dominated the day. One account tells of how 'there were a number of sailors on leave, who drew one of the open carriages through the streets much to everyone's delight'.[16] In return, Nelson made a patriotic speech which was later printed and widely circulated 'for the encouragement of national enthusiasm among the young people of Swansea'.[17]

Although the period of the Napoleonic wars in some senses disrupted the day-to-day rhythms of urban life, in resort towns in particular it was also a time of opportunity. The decline in continental travel during the years of conflict stimulated increasing demand for leisure and resort facilities at home. Towns like Swansea, with an attractive coastline suitable for sea bathing, were in a position to capitalize if they could offer the necessary facilities to attract seasonal visitors. Much of Swansea's urban development in the first two decades of the nineteenth century was consequently geared towards meeting these demands. Individual initiative often took the lead in pushing forward improvements, but corporation resolve and participation were also clearly evident.

Attempts were made in the first decade of the nineteenth century to improve the range of entertainment facilities available in Swansea for the use of visitors. It was the gentry of the district, in particular, who took the initiative. In 1804 a group of them launched a tontine subscription to fund the building of a new theatre and assembly rooms. Swansea's old town hall had formerly served as a venue for theatrical productions, until the establishment of a purpose-built theatre in Wind Street.[18] This had ceased operating in 1798, however, and, by the time of the tontine subscription, theatrical facilities in the town appeared to be in a sorry state. The lack of public rooms, meanwhile, was seen as a particularly severe handicap for a resort town. It was the stated intention of the tontine subscribers to redress this deficiency: 'The influx of fashionable strangers during the summer months having been of late years much diminished by the want of public rooms for their accommodation and amusement.'[19] The only accommodation suitable for use as a ballroom, for example, was located in the Mackworth Arms, Swansea's

[16] E. C. Freeman and E. Gill, *The Story of Lord Nelson and Sir William and Lady Hamilton's Tour in Wales and Monmouthshire, Sunday 25 July–Friday 20 August* (Newport, 1962), p. 28.
[17] C. Hibbert, *Nelson: A Personal History* (2nd edition, London, 1995), pp. 304–6.
[18] D. Gwent, *The Swansea Stage. A Biographical and Anecdotal Sketch of its History* (n.d.).
[19] WGAS, RISW, GGF, B6, 7, List of subscribers to the Assembly Rooms at Swansea.

principal inn.[20] To find such facilities available at an inn was not entirely surprising: many large urban public houses aimed to cater for the entertainment needs of their increasingly well-to-do clientele in this period.[21] In the case of the Mackworth Arms, this was just one of the many roles it fulfilled. As the point of arrival and departure for travellers to and from Swansea by coach, it was 'admirably adapted for the accommodation of visitants and travellers, in style'.[22] It served as an administrative base for officials in town on formal business, as was the case on the occasion of John Bird's visit to collect taxes in 1801. It played, in short, a central role in the urban life of Swansea at the beginning of the nineteenth century.

Multi-functional though the Mackworth Arms was, it did not satisfy everyone's tastes. One visitor to Swansea in 1821 proclaimed it to be 'very so so', despite its reputation as 'the best inn in the principality'.[23] In seeking to provide new, purpose-built venues, it is likely that the gentry of the district were investing in better entertainment facilities for themselves, as well as for Swansea's summer visitors. Nicholson's *Cambrian Traveller's Guide* of 1808 noted that Swansea had 'long been a winter residence of the neighbouring gentry',[24] and the regional scope of the early subscription lists show that support was forthcoming from an impressive array of gentry and wealthy residents throughout south Wales and the south-west of England. Thomas Mansel Talbot of Margam, Lord Vernon of Briton Ferry and William Rees of Aberpergwm were some of the local gentry subscribers.[25] They were joined by Thomas Wyndham of Dunraven Castle, Samuel Homfray of Merthyr, John Hume Spry of Bath and the Gloucester legal firm of Fendall and Co. The regional scope of the subscription list illustrates the geographical extent of Swansea's influence as a centre for fashionable leisure and entertainment.

The efforts of the subscribers met with mixed success. In the case of theatre provision, there was rapid progress. The revenues raised

---

[20] D. Boorman, *The Brighton of Wales: Swansea as a Fashionable Seaside Resort, c.1780–1830* (Swansea, 1986), p. 41.
[21] P. Clark, *The English Alehouse. A Social History, 1200–1830* (London, 1983), pp. 313–14.
[22] *Mathews's Swansea Directory* (Bristol, 1816), p. 6.
[23] T. Lloyd, 'The diary of a visitor to Swansea and Gower in 1821', *Gower*, 34 (1983), 10.
[24] G. Nicholson, *The Cambrian Traveller's Guide* (Stourport, 1808), p. 602.
[25] WGAS, SL WM1/6, Swansea Tontine Society Account Book.

proved sufficient to fund the construction of new premises in the town's Goat Street which opened to the public in June 1806. The assembly rooms project proved more complicated. In 1805 Thomas Wyndham, John Llewelyn and Thomas Mansel Talbot, trustees of the Swansea Tontine Society, leased a piece of ground on which new public rooms could be built, but the project ran into financial difficulties a decade into its construction, and the assistance of the corporation was required in order to see it through. At a corporation meeting in July 1813, members resolved to 'subscribe £1,200 towards finishing the public rooms',[26] and this sum was subsequently augmented before the project reached its successful completion in 1821. The 1834 report of the commissioners on the municipal corporations of England and Wales, which included an assessment of financial expenditure over the foregoing decades, recorded that, in all, a total of £3,300 had been expended on the assembly rooms by the corporation.[27] This level of support demonstrated the importance attached to the facility. The town's capacity to provide recreational accommodation, attractive to seasonal visitors and local gentry alike, was clearly perceived to be a long-term obligation of the town and one worthy of a substantial investment. After its completion in 1821, the *New Swansea Guide* predicted that it would equally serve 'the amusement and accommodation of the resident gentry' as well as 'the numerous and highly respectable visitors'.[28]

As well as facilities for indoor entertainment, the provision of attractive outdoor recreational space for resident urban elites and visitors was also a feature of urban development in Swansea in this period. From the early eighteenth century, parks and pleasure gardens had been considered a desirable urban amenity in towns for social meeting and display. Although few towns had anything to rival London's Vauxhall Gardens, many developed public walks with the same purpose of providing designated outdoor leisure space for the respectable townsfolk.[29] Similar initiatives in Swansea dated from 1785, when the duke of Beaufort created a public walk on the 'burrows', and it was on the same area of corporation-owned

---

[26] WGAS, B/S Corp, B7, 16 July 1813.
[27] WGAS, SL 2/3, Report of the Commissioners on Municipal Corporations in England and Wales: Swansea (1834), p. 395.
[28] *New Swansea Guide, 1823*, p. 50.
[29] M. Reed, 'The transformation of urban space, 1700–1840', in P. Clark (ed.), *CUHB*, Volume 2: *1540–1840* (Cambridge, 2000), pp. 638–9.

land between the town and the sea that further efforts were directed in the early part of the nineteenth century. In 1804 the corporation signalled its intention to control land use in the area when it resolved to grant leases for the building of houses only if they conformed to an approved plan.[30] A further project, masterminded by local industrialist Sir John Morris, was adopted in 1810.[31] Its aim was to provide walks and gardens on the burrows for use by the respectable inhabitants of the town and by fashionable visitors. The determination to preserve the area as a high quality recreational space for the elite was further underlined in 1816, when gates and walls were erected to keep out unwanted and undesirable members of the public.[32]

The provision of public walks was just one manifestation of the level of attention being paid to the appearance and quality of the urban environment in Swansea in these years. Easily the greatest influence on how the town looked in these decades was exercised by one man, William Jernegan. Acclaimed by one commentator as the principal architect in south Wales by 1800, he was believed to have trained with the English architect John Johnson.[33] Some of his best-known works were outlying villas for the lesser gentry of the district, such as the Palladian-style Stouthall in Reynoldston, Gower, completed in 1793 for John Lucas, whose family had occupied the site since the Tudor period.[34] But Jernegan was also responsible for building key residential housing in the town itself. Certainly he was the nearest that Swansea had to a 'town architect' in the late eighteenth and early nineteenth centuries, although he worked privately on land leased from the corporation. His distinctive Regency style shaped the new maritime quarter where a series of elegant new terraces – Gloucester Place, Somerset Place, Adelaide Place and Cambrian Place – provided affluent residents with sought-after town-centre dwellings with gardens for decades to come. The streets of the maritime quarter were laid out around two key buildings, the countess of Huntingdon's chapel (1789) and the Assembly Rooms (commenced in 1806). This was town planning on a micro-scale – a

---

[30] WGAS, B/S Corp, B7, 29 August 1804.
[31] Ibid., 8 March 1810.
[32] J. A. Owen, *Swansea's Earliest Open Spaces. A Study of Swansea's Parks and their Promoters in the Nineteenth Century* (Swansea, 1995), p. 14.
[33] T. Lloyd, 'The architects of Regency Swansea', *Gower*, 41 (1990), 58–62.
[34] R. Lucas, *Reynoldston* (Swansea, 1998), p. 21.

far cry from the grand town-council-sponsored development of Edinburgh's new town by James Craig, or the ambitious city-centre redevelopment undertaken in Newcastle by Richard Grainger in the 1830s,[35] but a significant contribution to Swansea's evolving urban environment nonetheless. It provided a prestige residential area, popular with surgeons, magistrates, merchants and industrialists before the development of Uplands as an area of high-quality middle-class housing,[36] and it probably prevented that early departure of wealthy residents to the suburbs which some other towns experienced in the first half of the nineteenth century as the growth of town-based manufacturing took its toll on urban living conditions.[37]

Concern for the appeal of the urban environment to seasonal visitors may also have played a part in the renewal of demands from the inhabitants for better paving in the town in 1808. Since the earlier abortive attempt to establish a paving commission in Swansea in 1787, which was blocked by Gabriel Powell to the consternation of Collins, Padley and other reforming burgesses, there had been a deterioration in the condition of Swansea's streets. Benjamin Malkin, who visited the town in 1804, noted that conventional street-cleaning methods, traditionally the responsibility of the court leet, were inadequate to cope with the increasing levels of traffic now using the growing town:

> It was, till of very late years, remarkable for its cleanliness and neatness. The streets were every where swept very clean early in the morning, and strewed with sand. This usage is, as much as possible, still continued; but the greatly increased bustle of commercial thoroughfare, the great influx of occasional visitors, and its occupations, dirty in many of their departments, do not admit of the former nicety.[38]

The intervening years had also witnessed the establishment of improvement commissions in provincial towns throughout England. By 1831, only four of the forty or so English towns with populations

---

[35] A. J. Youngson, *The Making of Classical Edinburgh, 1750–1840* (Edinburgh, 1966); L. Wilkes and G. Dodds, *Tyneside Classical. The Newcastle of Grainger, Dobson and Clayton* (London, 1964); I. Ayris, *A City of Palaces. Richard Grainger and the Making of Newcastle upon Tyne* (Newcastle, 1997).

[36] J. C. M. Rees, 'Evolving patterns of residence in a nineteenth-century city: Swansea, 1851–1871' (unpublished Ph.D. thesis, University of Wales, 1983), pp. 160–1.

[37] See, for example, M. Hewitt, *The Emergence of Stability in the Industrial City. Manchester, 1832–1867* (Aldershot, 1996), p. 54.

[38] B. H. Malkin, *The Scenery, Antiquities and Biography of South Wales* (London, 1807), p. 586.

exceeding 11,000 were without an Act to provide for their paving, watching, lighting and other improvement.[39] When a public meeting was held in Swansea in 1808 to address the question of petitioning for a similar Act to improve the streets, the corporation on this occasion indicated its support for the measure. At a meeting in November 1808, it was resolved unanimously that:

> A resolution having been entered into at a meeting of the inhabitants of Swansea 'that it will be highly advantageous to the town and borough of Swansea to obtain an Act for paving, repairing, cleansing, lighting and watching the streets and other public passages and places within the said town and borough, and for removing and preventing nuisances and obstructions therein' ... this corporation approve of the principal measure.[40]

The Act establishing Swansea's paving commission was passed in May 1809 and a body of fifty-four commissioners, on which the portreeve, recorder and steward were represented, was subsequently set up. It used its powers to attempt to control and regulate the growth of the town and to maintain a habitable and orderly environment in the face of demographic and industrial expansion. Amongst its early activities was the appointment of a constable, John Luce, 'to seize all beasts and swine found wandering in the town', and the organization of house numbering in conjunction with the taking of the census enumeration in 1811.[41] Although historians of Swansea have found little merit in its early work, and have criticized its operations as amateurish and ineffective,[42] its experience was comparable with that of other provincial improvement commissions. In Bradford, for example, where a commission was established in 1803, there were no immediate solutions to pressing problems such as lighting in the town.[43]

In Swansea, the commissioners were at least remarkably frank about their failings. In a thorough review of their work in 1819, overseen by a local barrister and paving commissioner, Henry Sockett, it was admitted that the state of the streets was 'very unsatisfactory':

---

[39] J. Innes and N. Rogers, 'Politics and government', in Clark (ed.), *CUHB*, Volume 2, pp. 536–7.
[40] WGAS, B/S Corp, B7, 29 November 1808.
[41] WGAS, B/S Corp, F1, Minute Book of the Paving Commissioners, 1809–43, 7 November 1810; 5 June 1811.
[42] T. Ridd, 'The development of municipal government in Swansea in the nineteenth century' (unpublished MA thesis, University of Wales, 1955), pp. 54–5.
[43] G. Firth, *A History of Bradford* (Chichester, 1997), p. 83.

In respect to paving, pitching, lighting and watching it is become absolutely indispensable to the comfort and interest of the inhabitant householders and the morals of the lower classes that some general and liberal plan for the attainment of the above objects should be laid down.

There was no thought here about prettifying the town for seasonal visitors or of making purely cosmetic improvements. The commissioners instead viewed street maintenance as an issue of safety and public order, and resolved to go about their task in 'a scientific and workmanlike manner'. They set about borrowing £1,500, carrying out a detailed survey of the streets, which revealed some to be 'in bad repair throughout' and others 'exceedingly dangerous', and investigating the cost of procuring gas lights.[44] Such improvements were vital if the town was to be regarded as modern, civilized and safe. The provision of gas lighting, in particular, was an important symbol of progress. John Henry Vivian, while away from town on business in 1820, received the news that 'They are at last going to light this town with gas'. The letter, from his wife Sarah, went on to calculate how many candles might be saved by the new gas light she had ordered for the staircase.[45] The importance placed upon such initiatives in Swansea was signified by the award to Henry Sockett, in 1830, of the freedom of the town for his 'many and valuable services afforded to the town and borough of Swansea'.[46]

Gradually, early nineteenth-century Swansea began to look more like the sort of place which visiting socialites would want to frequent. It also showed increasing signs of being able to cater for their cultural and literary interests. Library provision in the town was fast improving in the early nineteenth century. Like the growth of entertainment facilities, libraries were integral to the range of attractions which bathing resorts were expected to provide for their visitors. Contemporary guidebooks commented on the quality of library provision available in various resort towns. Swansea's two circulating libraries in existence in 1802, for example, were described in the 1803 *Guide to the Watering and Sea-bathing Places* as being better equipped to entertain than to inform.[47] By 1815, however, their number and the quality of available reading matter had greatly improved. Five libraries were in existence in the town by that date,

[44] WGAS, B/S Corp, F1, 3 November 1819.
[45] NLW, Vivian A, 127b, S. Jones, Swansea, to J. H. Vivian, Truro, 24 February 1820.
[46] WGAS, B/S Corp, B9, Hall Day Minute Book, 1821-35, 17 November 1830.
[47] See Boorman, *Brighton of Wales*, p. 57.

including the Glamorgan Library in Wind Street which was the town's first public library established by, amongst others, the pottery manufacturer George Haynes.[48] This was a 'proprietory subscription' library which, by 1808, had thirty proprietors including prominent local gentry such as Lewis Weston Dillwyn and Thomas Mansel Talbot. Its stock was carefully compiled to appeal to intellectual tastes. Novels were excluded and books on law and religion subject to ballot. The strengths of the collection lay in topography, history, natural history and literature.[49] As a result of this improved provision, the authors of subsequent guidebooks were more favourable in their assessments of reading facilities in the town. The *Cambrian Tourist* guide, published in 1821, commented that 'the libraries are good, well-supplied and civil'.[50]

There was also a thriving book trade in Swansea, with some seven bookbinders, booksellers, printers and stationers listed in the 1823 town guide.[51] There was a strong link between the printing trade in this period and the appearance of libraries and reading rooms in the town. For example, the sisters Elizabeth and Georgina Jenkins, who operated the Cambrian circulating library, came from a family of booksellers and printers, while other smaller reading rooms and circulating libraries were attached to stationers' premises.[52] Not surprisingly, this blossoming literary culture gave rise to local writers who emerged from Swansea with ambitions to serve the literary tastes of the county as a whole. In 1803, William Davies of Swansea, inspired by the rapid industrial and demographic developments in the town and its vicinity, proposed to write a new history of Glamorgan, charting the topographical, cultural and commercial development of the county.[53]

The town's growing Nonconformist religious community cultivated further literary talent in the early decades of the nineteenth century. *Seren Gomer*, the first weekly Welsh-language newspaper, was launched in Swansea in January 1814, placing the town in the vanguard of Welsh-language publishing. The brainchild of Baptist minister, Joseph Harris, it was not an immediate success and had to

[48] H. L. Hallesy, *The Glamorgan Pottery Swansea, 1814–38*, p. 80.
[49] E. Rees and G. Walters, 'Swansea libraries in the nineteenth century', *Journal of the Welsh Bibliographical Society*, 10 (1966–71), 44.
[50] *The Cambrian Tourist* (London, 1821), p. 84.
[51] *New Swansea Guide, 1823*.
[52] Rees and Walters, 'Swansea libraries', 45–6.
[53] WGAS, RISW, GGF, B6, 62.

be relaunched in 1818, but, within a year, it was selling 1,500–2,000 copies per issue.[54] *Seren Gomer* was the product of a highly literate Nonconformist presence in Swansea from the late eighteenth century. Harris was awarded a medal for his services to Welsh literature by the Gwyneddigion Society in London in 1815,[55] but there were also significant earlier initiatives. Solomon Harris, a Presbyterian minister noted for his 'great abilities and sound learning', had relocated a training college for ministers from Carmarthen to Swansea in 1784. The Baptist and Wesleyan Methodist denominations each had chapels in the town by the turn of the nineteenth century and, later, the growth of Unitarianism in Wales brought two successive ministers from Gloucester Unitarian Church to Swansea. The first, Richard Aubrey, who arrived in 1814, became well known for his learned pamphlets refuting critics of Unitarianism in which he displayed an impressive knowledge of Hebrew and Greek. After his death in 1836 he was succeeded by G. B. Brock, who enjoyed a similar scholarly reputation and succeeded in attracting 'some of the most intellectual men in the town' to his congregation.[56] Not all were impressed. Lewis Weston Dillwyn, an erstwhile Quaker, first visited the Unitarian chapel in Swansea in October 1820, but found that he 'did not like it at all'.[57] Plenty of others were inspired. T. B. Essery, later mayor of Swansea, was an enthusiastic member of Richard Aubrey's congregation, even naming his son after him.[58]

The development which most firmly cemented Swansea's reputation as a centre for the production and dissemination of the printed word, however, was the establishment of a weekly English-language newspaper, the *Cambrian*. First published on 28 January 1804 by Thomas Jenkins of Swansea, and backed by a group of shareholders which again included the ubiquitous George Haynes, the new paper proudly proclaimed itself to be 'the first and only newspaper printed in Wales'. Its establishment came at a time when the provincial press was growing rapidly in Britain. The number of

---

[54] H. Walters, 'The periodical press to 1914', in P. H. Jones and E. Rees (eds), *A Nation and its Books. A History of the Book in Wales* (Aberystwyth, 1998), p. 199.

[55] A. G. Jones, 'Harris, Joseph (1773–1825)', *Oxford Dictionary of National Biography* (Oxford, 2004).

[56] W. Tudor Jones, *The Rise and Progress of Religious Free Thought in Swansea* (Swansea, 1900), pp. 27–68.

[57] H. J. Randall and W. Rees (eds), 'Diary of Lewis Weston Dillwyn', *South Wales and Monmouth Record Society*, 5 (Newport, 1963), p. 47.

[58] WGAS, D/D WCR 145, biographical information on Richard Aubrey Essery.

weekly papers published in England grew from 70 in 1800 to over 200 four decades later.[59] From the outset, the *Cambrian* was promoted not as a local venture, merely serving the immediate town and neighbourhood, but as a 'provincial paper ... intended more particularly for the use, convenience and advantage of the principality of Wales'. It promised to 'remove the inconveniences under which the various interests of Wales have long laboured, from the want of a newspaper establishment within the principality' and to report all foreign and domestic news as well as the important legal, commercial and financial developments. Its local department promised news of Welsh shipping, fairs, markets and news of visitors to the various places of resort, but its principal function was broadly defined as 'benefiting the principality by freely disseminating all communications calculated to produce that effect'.[60] This conscious promotion of the *Cambrian* as a Wales-wide newspaper testified to the growing sense that Swansea, even in the first decade of the nineteenth century, was moving ahead of other Welsh towns in terms of wealth, commercial importance and urban influence. The proprietors confidently predicted that the circulation would extend not only throughout Wales but also to neighbouring English counties, where it would face competition from established newspapers such as the *Gloucester Journal* and the *Bath Chronicle*.

While the founding of the *Cambrian* in 1804 was a landmark in the history of English-medium print culture in Wales, it was also an important indicator of the aspirations of the town. As Clark and Houston have shown, newspapers and other print media had an important role to play in the life of resort towns and entertainment centres, carrying advertisements for concerts, assemblies, shows and other local events.[61] They were also an important asset to towns aspiring to achieve county or regional capital status. Principal county centres in the Midlands, like Worcester and Nottingham, were ahead of their neighbours in establishing successful and long-running weekly newspapers.[62] In predicting principality-wide success for their new paper, the founders of the *Cambrian* in Swansea were not necessarily expressing unrealistic expectations. Their vision of Swansea as

---

[59] H. Barker, *Newspapers, Politics and English Society, 1695–1855* (Harlow, 2000), p. 29.
[60] WGAS, RISW, GGF, B6, 67A.
[61] P. Clark and R. A. Houston, 'Culture and leisure, 1700–1840', in Clark (ed.), *CUHB*, Volume 2, pp. 595–6.
[62] A. Dyer, 'Midlands', in Clark (ed.), *CUHB*, Volume 2, p. 102.

an urban centre serving the wider region, even the whole of Wales, was increasingly reflected in the comments of visitors and observers of the town in the opening decades of the nineteenth century. Feltham's 1806 guide to bathing and watering places described Swansea as the 'principal port' of Glamorgan and the 'first town in the county'.[63] Cooke's *Topographical and Statistical Description of the Principality of Wales* identified in Swansea 'many advantages not to be found in any other part of Wales' and described its market as 'the best attended in the Principality'.[64] Slowly but surely, Swansea was acquiring the trappings of a regional capital. Initiatives that had their origins in Swansea's role as a sea-bathing centre were thus reaping much wider rewards for the town.

It was not just the local and visiting social elites who benefited from these developments. From the second decade of the nineteenth century there were increasing efforts to initiate improvements aimed at assisting some of Swansea's poorer residents. The provision of health care for the poor was one such area where, again, Swansea's reputation as a bathing resort appears to have been an important factor in accelerating the pace of developments compared with those in other Welsh towns. Swansea's increasing population in the first two decades of the century was served by a growing cohort of doctors and physicians, including Dr William Turton and John Charles Collins, who were early practitioners of vaccination,[65] and Dr Thomas Hobbes, who was one of the few medical men in the town known to have gained university qualifications and whose status was consequently high among his fellow practitioners and within the town generally.[66] For those without the means to pay for the services of a doctor, however, there was no established health care provision. An attempt to remedy this situation was first made in 1808, when a subscription was launched, at a meeting in the Mackworth Arms Hotel, to establish a dispensary in the town. The prime mover in this initiative was the Quaker, Richard Phillips, son of John Phillips, the Cornish-born agent at White Rock copper works.[67] Having moved to London after his father's death and

---

[63] J. Feltham, *Guide to the Watering and Sea-bathing Places* (London, 1806), pp. 387–8.
[64] G. A. Cooke, *Topographical and Statistical Description of the Principality of Wales, part 2: South Wales* (n.d. but c.1820), pp. 93–6.
[65] T. G. Davies, *Deeds not Words. A History of the Swansea General and Eye Hospital, 1817–1948* (Cardiff, 1988), p. 7.
[66] T. G. Davies, 'Lewis Weston Dillwyn and his doctors', *Morgannwg*, XXIII (1988), 77.
[67] D. Salmon, *Swansea Hospital: History, 1817–1917* (Swansea, 1917), pp. 4–5.

established himself in the legal profession there, with the help of a maternal uncle, Richard Phillips became involved in numerous charitable ventures, including the setting up of a hospital for contagious diseases in the capital and the founding, in 1809, of a dispensary in Brighton, where he and his family often spent time for health reasons.[68] On a visit to his family in Swansea in 1808, he was reportedly prompted to initiate a campaign for a dispensary in the town after seeing a poor woman apply to their house for assistance, and hearing his sister lament the lack of facilities for such people in the town.[69]

The timing of these medical developments in Swansea coincided with a period of significant growth in the size and distribution of the medical profession in Britain. Between 1801 and 1850, over 8,000 university-educated men embarked on medical careers, and in the same period hospital accommodation in England and Wales grew from a capacity of 3,000 to 8,000.[70] In Wales, Swansea did not achieve the distinction of being the first town to possess a dispensary. Carmarthen had established such an institution in 1807 and other towns, notably Bangor (1809), were not far behind.[71] Once mooted though, support for the Swansea equivalent was widespread. The original governing body consisted of a number of prominent townsmen and corporation members including Sir John Morris, Robert Eaton, John Grove and Calvert Richard Jones.[72]

Within a short time, demand for the services of the dispensary grew. The annual report for 1811 recorded an official figure of 421 patients treated by the institution in the preceding year, although the actual number believed to have made use of its services was put at nearer 700. In 1813 the committee was advertising for a new dispenser, preferably one with knowledge of the Welsh language, to help with the growing numbers seeking medical help, and just three years later, and less than ten years into the dispensary's short life, the committee began the process of turning their institution into an infirmary.[73] The other dispensaries established in Welsh towns in the first half of the nineteenth century were much slower to develop

---

[68] M. Phillips, *Memoir of the Life of Richard Phillips* (London, 1841), pp. 130–8.
[69] Ibid., p. 140.
[70] B. Haley, *The Healthy Body and Victorian Culture* (London, 1978), pp. 4–5.
[71] Davies, *Deeds not Words*, p. 13; O. V. Jones, *The Progress of Medicine: A History of the Caernarfon and Anglesey Infirmary, 1809–1948* (Llandysul, 1984), pp. 15–16.
[72] Salmon, *Swansea Hospital*, p. 5.
[73] Ibid., p. 6.

into infirmaries or joint dispensary/infirmary institutions. In Bangor, despite the early establishment of a dispensary in 1809, an infirmary was not mooted until over thirty years later.[74] In Newport there was a gap of twenty years between the setting up of a dispensary and the renaming of the institution as the Newport Dispensary and Infirmary, and a further eight years before its new infirmary building was opened.[75] In Cardiff, the dispensary, established in 1823, became the Glamorgan and Monmouthshire Infirmary and Dispensary in 1837.[76]

The pace of developments in Swansea meant that it was the first town in Wales to establish an infirmary.[77] There was a considerable overlap in personnel between the original governing body of the dispensary and those who subsequently became involved in the infirmary venture. One-third of the 1818 infirmary committee was composed of men who had been on the original governing body of the dispensary in 1808.[78] The new institution opened its doors in 1817; conscious that its services were unique in the principality, its expressed mission was broadly defined as 'the relief of the sick and lame poor from every part of the kingdom'.[79] It also sought royal patronage from the princess of Wales, pressing its claim to be 'the first charity of the kind in the Principality'; her death later in 1817 meant that this particular ambition was never realized.[80]

The reasons for Swansea's success in establishing itself as a leader among Welsh towns in the provision of medical care to the poor were manifold. The demand created by the population growth of the town in the first two decades of the nineteenth century was an important factor. Also significant was the emergence of a committed core of people who were willing to play an active part in developing medical services in the town. Quite apart from the medical men themselves, such as Hobbes and Collins, who were closely associated with both the dispensary and the infirmary initiatives, there was what one historian has described as a 'philanthropic

[74] Jones, *Progress of Medicine*, p. 54.
[75] T. Baker Jones, *History of the Royal Gwent Hospital, 1839–1948* (Newport, 1948), p. 22.
[76] A. S. Aldis, *Cardiff Royal Infirmary, 1883–1983* (Cardiff, 1984), p. 1.
[77] Swansea's lead in this sector has not always been recognized. For details, see N. Evans, '"The first charity in Wales": Cardiff Infirmary and south Wales society, 1837–1914', *WHR*, 9, no. 2 (1979), 319–46.
[78] Salmon, *Swansea Hospital*, pp. 6–8.
[79] Davies, *Deeds not Words*, p. 18.
[80] Salmon, *Swansea Hospital*, p. 8.

spirit' among the commercial classes in the town in this period.[81] Personified by the Quaker, Richard Phillips, this greater awareness of the needs of the poor was also evident among 'the new type of industrial employer'.[82] It was perhaps not surprising to find the agents of a number of the leading coal and copper works of the locality listed among the members of the infirmary's early committees. For local industrialists there was an obvious incentive to support a venture that was likely to result in a healthier and more productive labour force. Yet it is clear from the minutes of early meetings of the infirmary's directors that a degree of cajoling was sometimes required to secure the support of these employers. In April 1818, for instance, an infirmary subcommittee was appointed 'to wait upon the Birmingham Mining and Copper Company committee to solicit their becoming subscribers'.[83] These tactics evidently met with some success. In 1818 Samuel Bordell of the Birmingham mining company, along with Henry Bath, agent to John Morris, and Thomas Bigg of the Ynishowell works, were named as infirmary committee members.[84]

The support of members of the commercial and industrial elite was one important factor in the success of these early nineteenth-century medical initiatives. A further issue of significance in cementing Swansea's early lead in this sphere was the role of the town as a sea-bathing resort. By the end of the eighteenth century, medical opinion in Britain was extolling the health-giving properties of sea water over those of hot springs, and coastal resort towns such as Brighton, Weymouth and Swansea began to break into the health tourism market previously dominated by the spa towns and other centres known for their hot mineral springs, such as Bath, Clifton and Tunbridge. The establishment of the Swansea Infirmary made this link between sea water and health even more explicit. The town's original infirmary was housed in the eastern part of the old bathing house on Swansea's Burrows, and it officially launched itself as 'The Swansea Infirmary for warm and cold sea water bathing and for the relief of the poor and sick lame ...'.[85] It

---

[81] G. D. Fielder, 'Public health and hospital administration in Swansea and West Glamorgan since the end of the eighteenth century to 1914' (unpublished MA dissertation, University of Wales, 1962), p. 12.
[82] Ibid., p. 16.
[83] WGAS, D/D H/S 1, Minutes of Swansea Infirmary, 28 April 1818.
[84] Salmon, *Swansea Hospital*, p. 8.
[85] Quoted in Davies, *Deeds not Words*, p. 18.

was apparent, then, that well-to-do visitors were not the only people to benefit from Swansea's emergence as a sea-bathing destination in the late eighteenth century. The closely associated developments in health care which followed were chiefly aimed at those lower down the social scale.

The establishment of the infirmary was not the only scheme from which the humbler members of the Swansea populace were to benefit in these years. One of the leading lights responsible for setting these important medical developments in motion was also instrumental in the promotion of educational facilities in his native town in the first decade of the nineteenth century. Richard Phillips, the London-based Quaker lawyer who had started the subscription for the Swansea dispensary, also had a hand in the improvement of educational provision. Quaker involvement was the common denominator in many of the earliest educational establishments in industrial Wales and elsewhere in Britain in the early nineteenth century. This was in no small part due to the work of the Quaker educational pioneer, Joseph Lancaster, who established a model school along non-denominational lines in London at the beginning of the century, and then went on a provincial tour from 1806 to 1808 to encourage the adoption of his school system elsewhere. Some ninety-five 'Lancasterian' schools (later known as British Schools) were established between 1808 and 1810 as a result.

Swansea's interest in the Lancasterian model, however, came early. In 1806, after correspondence with Lancaster, the Swansea Society for the Education of the Children of the Poor was formed, with the aim of establishing a boys' and later a girls' school, exclusively for children whose parents could not afford to pay for their education. John Llewelyn of Penllergaer was its first president and it attracted support from prominent townsmen, including the Reverend Miles Bassett, vicar of Swansea, and the duke of Beaufort, who subscribed £10 to the cause. Members of well-known Quaker families in the district, including Lewis Weston Dillwyn, Thomas Bigg and Robert Eaton, were also enthusiastic supporters for an initiative inspired by one of their co-religionists.[86] All three became members of the committee while Richard Phillips, also a subscriber, acted as a useful contact between the society and the Lancaster base

---

[86] A. L. Trott, 'The British School movement in Wales, 1806–1846', in J. L. Williams and G. R. Hughes (eds), *The History of Education in Wales*, Volume 1 (Swansea, 1978), p. 86.

in London, where he became a member of the central finance committee in 1810.[87]

The Swansea Lancasterian school was the first of its kind in Wales and also one of the earliest to be established outside London. Lancaster himself held it up as a model for other towns during his provincial tours and also in a number of pamphlets advertising his educational principles. Another was set up near Cardiff, again by a Quaker industrialist family, the Harfords, of the Melingriffith tinplate works, in 1808.[88] By this time, provision at Swansea had expanded thanks to the further efforts of Richard Phillips. He started a subscription for another boys' school in much the same way as he had done with the dispensary, calling from house to house to solicit support. At the same time he collected monetary contributions to improve the quality of the accommodation in which the Lancasterian girls' school was housed.[89]

The fact that Swansea achieved some important milestones in improving the health and education of its poorer residents, as well as in the development of facilities to cater for visiting elites, suggests that the improvement ethos in the town in these years was not narrowly conceived to lure greater numbers of wealthy tourists to the town. Rather it was based on a determination to secure benefits for the public at large. The effects of medical and educational improvements may well have played their part in shaping the relatively quiescent social relationships that marked Swansea in the first half of the nineteenth century, of which more will be said in chapter IV. Notwithstanding these considerations, however, it was undoubtedly the case that the major beneficiaries from this phase of urban improvement among Swansea's permanent residents were the growing ranks of middle-class businessmen, professionals, traders and merchants. The 1822–3 *Pigot's Provincial Directory* listed nine surgeons and two physicians, nine firms of attorneys, fifteen agents in the employ of either coal or copper works and eight customs and excise officers.[90] As a resort town, it had significant numbers of innkeepers and owners of lodging houses, proprietors of bathing machines and organizers of entertainment and leisure attractions for visitors. Along with the numerous merchants, ship-

[87] Ibid., p. 84.
[88] L. W. Evans, *Education in Industrial Wales, 1700–1900* (Cardiff, 1971), p. 158.
[89] Phillips, *Memoir of Richard Phillips*, pp. 139–41.
[90] *Pigot's London Provincial Directory* (London, 1823).

brokers, insurers, bankers and manufacturers involved in either metal smelting or earthenware manufacture, these people constituted an increasingly prosperous and confident commercial middle class.

It was people from within these expanding middle-class occupational ranks who occupied Jernegan's new high-quality town housing in the maritime quarter. It was they, too, who helped to attract new businesses to the town, like that of John Francis, a coach maker from Somerset, who purchased premises in High Street in 1811.[91] Previously served only by the Brecon, Hereford and Bristol coach-makers who advertised in the town, the potential for a designated coach-building business in Swansea was recognized by Francis, and his instinct was proved right. By 1831 he was one of seven coach makers in the town, serving wealthy customers in Swansea and the surrounding district.[92] Other businesses flourished in response to the consumer demands of the town's growing middle class. In 1814 George Haynes established a new earthenware manufactory, the Glamorgan Pottery, to rival the successful Cambrian Pottery which he had earlier helped to develop in partnership with Lewis Weston Dillwyn. The new venture was to some extent born out of a growing rift between Haynes and Dillwyn after the expiry of their partnership in 1810, but it was also a response to the success of the trade and the growing demand in the town and region for competitively priced earthenware products for domestic use. In 1814 Haynes began turning out table services, tea wares and commemorative jugs in designs similar to those of his rivals at the Cambrian, for a mainly local market but with additional customers further afield in the south-west of England and in Ireland.[93] The fact that he was able to compete successfully with the longer-established Cambrian Pottery testified to the strong market for these products among the expanding urban population of the town in the first two decades of the nineteenth century.

Banking establishments, too, began to thrive. Haynes was able to finance the new pottery via his own bank, located in Swansea's Wind Street, which he established in partnership with Henry Polkington in about 1800. It was one of a number of early banking ventures in the town initiated by local industrialists and

[91] S. Thomas, 'J. Francis, coach-maker', *Minerva*, 2 (1994), 29–30.
[92] See G. A. Williams, *The Merthyr Rising* (London, 1978), p. 56.
[93] Hallesy, *Glamorgan Pottery*, pp. ix, 8, 30.

businessmen who needed to keep money in circulation and increase their access to finance.[94] Although the first banks to open in the county of Glamorgan were located in the iron town of Merthyr Tydfil in the early 1770s, Swansea's growing industrial and commercial wealth from the 1780s onwards soon produced its own flurry of banking activity. The coal proprietor, Herbert Mackworth, operated banks at Neath and Swansea from the early 1780s. In 1791 his Swansea bank was taken over by one of the town's prominent corporation figures, Alderman Thomas Maddocks and, in the same period, a second banking venture, the Swansea Bank, was formed by two local tradesmen, Walters and Voss. In the early nineteenth century, the growing financial needs of the town drew in a number of other enterprising financiers, including the Thomas Mansfield and Henry Child partnership which established the Swansea and Llanelly Union Bank in 1810, and the Quakers, Joseph Gibbins and Robert Eaton, who took over the Swansea, Neath and Glamorganshire Bank in 1811.[95] These new banking establishments were crucial in supporting the growth of commerce and industry and increasing the circulation of capital in the town and its industrial suburbs. By 1823 it was calculated that 'the smelting establishments on the Swansea river alone, with the collieries and shipping dependent on them, support a population of from 8,000–10,000 souls and cause a circulation in their vicinity of from £2,000-£3,000 weekly'.[96]

There was, too, a demand for high-quality educational provision in the town from the new middle class, which led to improvements in the grammar school sector. To its credit, the corporation had demonstrated a long-standing interest in the Free Grammar School, originally founded in the town by Bishop Hugh Gore in 1682. In January 1789 a corporation resolution was passed to raise the annual income of the master to twenty guineas, a level that was more likely to lead to 'the acceptance of a person properly qualified'.[97] The competence of the master was the single most important factor that determined the effectiveness of the grammar school, and the corporation continued to keep a close eye on the operation of the various

---

[94] R. O. Roberts, 'Banking and financial organization, 1770–1914', in G. Williams and A. H. John (eds), *GCH*, Volume V: *Industrial Glamorgan* (Cardiff, 1980), p. 366.
[95] UWSA, Misc. 3, 1791–1953. File of notes by H. M. Stevens on banking in Swansea.
[96] *New Swansea Guide, 1823*, pp. 32–3.
[97] WGAS, B/S Corp, B8, 30 January 1789.

holders of the post throughout the early decades of the nineteenth century. Where it was dissatisfied with the performance of any master, it was willing to act to remove him for the good of the school and educational provision in the town in general. Such a situation arose during the term of the Reverend John Oldisworth, who was appointed master in 1801. After a lengthy period in the post, it became apparent that he was not up to the job. Bishop Burgess of St David's, who carried out an inspection of the various grammar schools in the district, concluded that he was not the person 'under whose superintendence the school is likely to flourish'.[98] In July 1815 the corporation resolved to act on the grounds that 'it was most essential to the inhabitants of the town of Swansea that the Free School should be restored to that high state of respectability it formerly possessed'.[99] Oldisworth was subsequently removed from the post with the help of a payment of £100 from the corporation to secure his retirement. Their intervention clearly paid dividends. By the third decade of the nineteenth century Swansea, along with Bristol, was the destination of choice for the sons of commercial elites from other Welsh towns seeking a good grammar-school education.[100]

By the 1820s, on the back of over two decades of improvements to the appearance and facilities of the town, many of which were prompted by the desire of individuals and the corporation to attract seasonal visitors, Swansea had reached a position of urban maturity unrivalled in Wales. It had a range of entertainment and leisure facilities, a hospital and an assortment of schools to suit pupils of different social backgrounds. It possessed a weekly newspaper, a host of libraries, an array of banks and several new businesses catering to the consumer demands of its wealthy residents. No other Welsh town could boast the same range of urban amenities by this date. More significant than the pace of improvements in Swansea relative to other towns in Wales, however, was the status that the corporation and the local commercial elite attempted to derive from it. Put simply, they endeavoured, purposefully, to bring to the attention of outsiders Swansea's recent advances, and to

---

[98] C. Smith, 'A history of the Swansea Grammar School', in C. Smith (ed.) *Bishop Gore's Grammar School. Founded 14 September 1682. A History Published to Celebrate the Tercentenary of Foundation* (Swansea, 1982), p. 9.
[99] WGAS, B/S Corp, B7, 10 July 1815.
[100] G. A. Williams, 'The Merthyr election of 1835', *WHR*, 10, no. 3 (1981), 360.

press the case for locating greater administrative functions, in both the legal and financial sectors, in the town. The first illustration of this was a campaign to relocate one sitting of the Great Sessions from Cardiff to Swansea.

Cardiff's position as the legal and administrative centre for the county of Glamorgan dated back to the period after the Acts of Union when Wales was administratively reorganized along the lines of the English shires. Circuit judges would visit the town twice yearly to preside over the county sessions, hearing cases from across Glamorgan.[101] By the early nineteenth century, however, demographic and commercial growth in the western part of Glamorgan was making Cardiff's position as the location for both the spring and summer sittings increasingly anomalous.[102] As the principal trading, industrial and commercial centre in the western portion of the county, with a growing population in the town and its hinterland, Swansea could convincingly claim to be an alternative legal centre for the county. Consequently, from 1815, the corporation began to press for the relocation of one session of the court to Swansea. At a corporation meeting in that year it was resolved that the portreeve should

> present to the judges on this circuit a memorial from the corporation setting forth the great inconvenience and expense incurred by the suitors resident in the western part of this county in attending the Spring and Summer Great Sessions at Cardiff, and praying that they will in future be pleased to hold one of those Great Sessions at Swansea.[103]

This was not just wishful thinking. The corporation gave a clear indication of their determination to secure the move by undertaking to provide upgraded accommodation for visiting judges, barristers, attorneys and jurors, in a new and enlarged town hall to be constructed from its own funds. This intention was clearly spelled out at a meeting in October 1817, when it was resolved: 'That this Corporation will at their own expense, build and fit up such sufficient accommodation for holding the Great Sessions in the town of Swansea.'[104]

The motives of the corporation in making such a clear commitment to securing the removal of the Great Sessions were clearly

---

[101] W. Rees, *Cardiff: A History of the City* (Cardiff, 1962), p. 42.
[102] Ridd, 'Development of municipal government', p. 31.
[103] WGAS, B/S Corp, B7, 10 July 1815.
[104] Ibid., 25 October 1817.

expressed at the same meeting. The scheme was conceived as a means of relieving 'the extreme hardship which a great part of the population of the county of Glamorgan labour under' as a result of the existing arrangements at Cardiff. In making their pitch the Swansea lobby attempted to portray Cardiff as being on the periphery of the area it was meant to serve, pointing out that it

> is within two miles of the extremity of the county, which extends itself westward nearly sixty-five miles from the present seat of justice, and that the greatest part of the business of the Great Sessions arises from the population and commerce which the town of Swansea and its neighbourhood affords.[105]

Interestingly, Swansea's central location was an argument that was again employed against Cardiff in the 1880s during the debate over the location of the new University College of South Wales.[106] On that occasion it was unsuccessful, but in the early decades of the nineteenth century Swansea's credentials as an alternative centre of administrative and legal life proved more convincing. William Jernegan was duly commissioned to produce a set of plans for the new town hall accommodation, and thus were Swansea's ambitions to usurp Cardiff's county-town status set firmly in motion.

Not surprisingly, the proposed move met with some resistance in Cardiff. When the vicar of Swansea tentatively broached the subject in a sermon during a church service for the judges and officials assembled for the sessions, a number of the Cardiff contingent, including Lord Bute's agent, 'marched publicly out of church'.[107] It took another decade and a half of lobbying before the vision of Swansea as a legal centre became a reality; in the mean time, the new Cardiff–Swansea rivalry was evident in the political sphere, too.

Cardiff castle's control of the unwieldy parliamentary constituency made up of the Glamorgan boroughs gave the Swansea burgesses a distinct feeling of remoteness from the seat of political power in their county. In May 1796 they had to ask their portreeve to 'write to the bailiffs of Cardiff to know who is the candidate for the borough' whose nomination they were expected to endorse in the forthcoming election.[108] By the end of the second decade of the

---

[105] Ibid.
[106] N. Evans, 'The Welsh Victorian city: the middle class and civic and national consciousness in Cardiff, 1850–1914', *WHR*, 12, no. 3 (1985), 371.
[107] Randall and Rees (eds), 'Diary of Lewis Weston Dillwyn', 18 March 1818, p. 20.
[108] WGAS, B/S Corp, B7, 24 May 1796.

nineteenth century, after a sustained period of commercial, industrial and demographic growth in their part of the county, such an arrangement began to appear less palatable to Swansea's newly assertive urban leaders. By 1818, when the second marquess of Bute's uncle decided not to stand for re-election, they felt confident enough to consider contesting a seat which had gone unchallenged since 1734. Opponents of the Bute interest sensed an opportunity to mount a challenge from the western part of the county and, for a while, attention focused on Lewis Weston Dillwyn, who had recently come into possession of his wife's family estate at Penllergaer, as a likely challenger. He was 'strongly urged' by John Morris to stand, and received pledges of support from burgesses in a number of the contributory boroughs, as well as from some of Bute's opponents in Cardiff.[109] In the event, his position as high sheriff of the county prevented him from standing, but the very fact that a challenge had been mooted served notice that the Swansea burgesses no longer saw themselves as duty-bound to follow Cardiff's lead.

The Butes' would-be challenger in 1818 was also at the centre of another bold initiative in the 1820s, when a group of Swansea's leading inhabitants sought to advance the status of their town as a provincial banking centre. Like the rest of Britain's financial markets, the expanding banking sector in early nineteenth-century Swansea was dealt a severe blow by the financial collapse of 1825–6 which saw a number of the local banks fail and which undermined confidence in the currency circulation of the private banks. Lewis Weston Dillwyn recorded in his diary on 20 December 1825 that: 'The banks both of Gibbins and Eaton and of Haynes and Co. abruptly and unexpectedly suspended their payments this morning and threw the whole town and neighbourhood into a state of indescribable consternation and distress.'[110] Swansea's local gentry and businessmen, appreciating the threat that this posed to the commerce and prosperity of the town, were not slow to react. New legislation had been passed in the wake of the crisis, allowing the establishment of branch banks and, in response, the Bank of England had established a Branch Bank Committee to consider suitable locations for the opening of branch outlets. In May 1826 it

---

[109] Randall and Rees, 'Diary of Lewis Weston Dillwyn', May–June 1818, pp. 21–4.
[110] NLW, Dillwyn 2, 20 December 1825.

sent requests to Liverpool, Leeds, Manchester, Birmingham and Gloucester for information on how a branch bank might be received there. Swansea did not wait for a similar invitation. Instead a powerful Swansea delegation which included Dillwyn visited the Bank of England's committee in person to press the case for the establishment of a Bank of England branch in the town:

> The committee received a deputation consisting of his grace the Duke of Beaufort, Sir John Morris, Mr Vivian and several others who presented a memorial signed by above 60 of the principal landowners, manufacturers and others, pointing out the great benefit the bank would confer on the principality of Wales by establishing a branch bank at Swansea and earnestly requesting that the bank would do this without delay as they were in the utmost distress for want of it, the banks at Swansea having broken, and the deputation stated the great circulation and probable profit to the bank, as well as their earnest entreaties that they would establish without delay.[111]

The proactive way in which Morris, Vivian and Dillwyn went about this provides some revealing insights into their perceptions of Swansea and their ambitions for the town at this time. They viewed the acquisition of a Bank of England branch as a likely source of prestige as well as a practical asset. To be amongst the first places in the country to have a branch established would confirm the town's commercial importance as well as secure its future role as a financial centre. Dillwyn, Morris and Vivian were confident enough of Swansea's economic importance to see its potential as a regional financial hub. They presented Swansea to the committee as Wales's representative town and their arguments made an impact. Following the deputation, Dillwyn recorded that 'I remained afterwards in private consultation with some of the directors and have no doubt of our success'.[112] At a subsequent meeting to consider 'the best place for establishing a branch bank in south Wales', Swansea was chosen as 'the most eligible' from a shortlist comprising several candidates including Cardiff, Newport and Merthyr Tydfil.[113]

The Bank of England branch at Swansea opened its doors on 23 October 1826 as only the third branch in Britain.[114] Its impact on

---

[111] Bank of England Archives (BoEA), M5/744 Branch Committee Minute Book A, 5 June 1826.
[112] NLW, Dillwyn 2, 5 June 1826.
[113] BoEA, M5/112 Branch Committee Minute Book B, 1 August 1826.
[114] For an account of its business, see R. O. Roberts, 'Bank of England branch discounting, 1826–59', *Economica*, n.s. XXV, no. 99 (1958), 230–45.

the town was twofold. Firstly, it helped to restore financial confidence and had the effect of revitalizing the local banking sector. The stability it brought to the area encouraged other banking enterprises to be established, such as that of local businessmen Robert Eaton, William Stroud and Henry Knight which opened within a year.[115] Other studies have confirmed that local banks generally reaped advantages from being located close to a Bank of England branch.[116] Secondly, the new branch bank had an impact on Swansea's urban status. There is no doubt that to be one of the first three towns in Britain to have a branch of the Bank of England was a significant coup for the town. Indignant articles appeared in the provincial press in towns which felt they had been unjustly overlooked in the first wave of branch openings. The editors of the *Liverpool Chronicle* lamented that they were 'at a loss to conceive' why Liverpool had been passed over.[117] Swansea, meanwhile, was firmly established as 'the main financial centre of south Wales' for the following two decades.[118]

The awareness of its local government leaders of the growing urban status of Swansea, along with the presence in the town of a corpus of public-spirited individuals like Robert Eaton, Lewis Weston Dillwyn, Henry Sockett and George Haynes, marks this period out as one of significant improvement in Swansea. A combination of corporation goodwill and private initiative resulted in improvements on many different fronts. By the end of the first two decades of the nineteenth century, Swansea, still a town of only 10,000 inhabitants, had equipped itself with an up-to-date market, theatre, schools and hospital facilities. It had built new houses, roads, walkways and recreational areas and established a paving commission. It had extended its library provision and established a weekly newspaper and it was well on the way to completing assembly-room accommodation complete with reading room, billiard room, coffee room, ballroom, card room and supper room.

By no means all visitors to the town were impressed with this list of achievements. Despite the progress made, for some there

[115] UWSA, Misc. 3, File of notes by H. M. Stevens on banking in Swansea; *The Cambrian*, 29 September 1827.
[116] M. Collins, 'The Bank of England at Liverpool, 1827–44', *Business History*, 12, no. 2 (1972), 157–8.
[117] Quoted in *The Times*, 25 July 1826. Liverpool gained its own branch the following year.
[118] Roberts, 'Banking and financial organization', p. 373.

remained much to be done. The *Cambrian Tourist* in 1821 pronounced Swansea to be 'a mixture of good and bad, of old streets and new, wide and narrow, pride and poverty, much show and little wealth'.[119] Nevertheless, it is difficult to avoid the sense that, by 1820, the town had, through a variety of disparate efforts and approaches, succeeded in embracing many of the ideas and initiatives characteristic of this period of urban improvement in Britain. Also difficult to ignore was the growing sense of confidence accompanying these developments. Aware that it had been ahead of other Welsh towns in establishing many of its facilities and institutions, an assertive urban self-image was also discernible. Swansea began to see itself in a county, regional and Wales-wide context as a focal point for recreational, commercial and administrative activities. This new-found sense of importance was evident at a number of different levels: in the promotional rhetoric of the newspaper proprietors and infirmary directors and in the way in which corporation members set about repositioning the town in relation to Cardiff as a rival county centre. The impetus for much of this had come from Swansea's early nineteenth-century status as a bathing resort. Ultimately, however, it was the growth of the town over the next decades as an industrial centre, in an increasingly important metal-smelting and coal-mining region, that turned the brash sense of optimism of Swansea's early nineteenth-century urban leaders into a fully matured sense of urban and civic identity.

---

[119] *The Cambrian Tourist* (London, 1821), p. 83.

III

'A DEGREE OF COMMERCIAL AND MANUFACTURING IMPORTANCE': INDUSTRIALIZATION AND REGIONAL STATUS

As Swansea was developing its range of attractions for the entertainment of the gentry of the neighbourhood and its seasonal visitors, it was also building a considerable reputation as an industrial centre. The *Swansea Directory*, published by the Bristol firm of Joseph Mathews in 1816, listed 'eight large copper-houses, collieries of binding coal, culm, and stone-coal, a copper rolling-mill, a brass-work, a large tin-work, two iron furnaces, an iron foundry, two potteries and a large brewery', and described the town as 'increasing and opulent'.[1] At first glance, industrial growth on this scale appears incongruous in a genteel bathing resort. It is tempting to concur with the author of the most recent history of the copper trade in south Wales that early nineteenth-century Swansea was being pulled in different directions by the rival promoters of leisure and industry:

> For a few decades at the turn of the eighteenth and nineteenth centuries, Swansea was a town divided both in body and spirit. While its corporation was ordering bathing machines, building parades and improving bathing facilities in the Burrows near the mouth of the river, a mile or two inland, entrepreneurs from Cornwall, London, Bristol and Anglesey were building copper works.[2]

Certainly industry had a profoundly damaging effect on the local environment. It was in Swansea in 1813, significantly, that Richard Ayton wrote about the 'degeneracy' that 'results from the increase of manufactories'.[3] Even earlier, in 1808, the *Cambrian Traveller's Guide* warned prospective visitors to the town that 'the volumes of smoke from the different manufactories are a great deduction to the general attractions of the place'.[4] Feltham's *Guide to the Watering and Sea-bathing Places* in 1806 went even further, describing how 'the

---

[1] *Swansea Directory* (Bristol, 1816), pp. 8, 1.
[2] R. Rees, *King Copper: South Wales and the Copper Trade, 1584–1895* (Cardiff, 2000), p. 19.
[3] Quoted in B. Trinder, 'Industrialising towns, 1700–1840', in P. Clark (ed.), *CUHB*, Volume 2: *1540–1840* (Cambridge, 2000), p. 805.
[4] G. Nicholson, *The Cambrian Traveller's Guide and Pocket Companion* (Stourport, 1808, 2nd enlarged edition, 1813), p. 602.

volumes of smoke continually rising from the numerous and extensive works that are established here, render many parts unpleasant, if not insalubrious, even to those who live at some distance'.[5] The growth of metal smelting in the town undoubtedly polluted the atmosphere and harmed the health of some of Swansea's inhabitants but, as the well-documented history of legal actions in the 1830s and 1840s shows, the leading industrialists of the region were never fully held accountable. Research into the records of these unsuccessful prosecutions has, nevertheless, done much to enshrine a view of industry as fundamentally detrimental to the quality of urban life in Swansea.[6]

This environmentally focused view of Swansea's experience of industrialization, however, is problematic on a number of different levels. Firstly, it devotes too much attention to copper smelting as the town's dominant industry. Phrases such as *King Copper* and *Copperopolis* imply that nineteenth-century Swansea was a one-industry town and underplay the degree of diversity which, as this chapter will show, was an important characteristic of its economy in the first half of the nineteenth century. Secondly, the attention which historians have devoted to the impact of industry in the early nineteenth century has, to some extent, obscured the much longer history of industrial development in the Swansea region. The character of the town was not suddenly and radically altered by fast-paced industrial growth in the way that other parts of south Wales were. In this respect, interpretations of Swansea's industrialization have, perhaps, been unhelpfully influenced by patterns of development elsewhere in south Wales. In the iron towns of Monmouthshire and Glamorgan and, later, the eastern end of the coalfield, industrial growth was rapid and engulfing. Output of coal from Aberdare parish, for example, rose from 177,000 tons in 1844 to over 2,000,000 tons in just twenty years.[7] The charting of dramatic expansion in the iron and coal industries, and the accompanying images of urbanization in Merthyr Tydfil and the Rhondda, have thus dominated histories of industrial south Wales.[8]

---

[5] J. Feltham, *Guide to the Watering and Sea-bathing Places* (London, 1806), p. 396.
[6] R. Rees, 'The great copper trials', *History Today*, 43, no. 12 (1993), 38–44.
[7] J. Williams, *Digest of Welsh Historical Statistics*, Volume 1 (Cardiff, 1985), p. 341.
[8] For example, M. Atkinson and C. Baber, *The Growth and Decline of the South Wales Iron Industry, 1760–1880: An Industrial History* (Cardiff, 1987); D. Egan, *Coal Society. A History of the South Wales Mining Valleys, 1840–1980* (Llandysul, 1987); C. Williams, *Capitalism, Community and Conflict: The South Wales Coalfield, 1898–1947* (Cardiff, 1998).

Swansea's experience has not only been overshadowed, but subsumed into the general picture of south Wales as a single industrial region in which iron, then coal, were the dominant players. Its particular experience of industrial growth, with the expansion of the non-ferrous sector and the effect that this had on the urban environment, has not occupied a prominent place in Welsh industrial history.[9] Recent contributions to the historiography of British industrialization, however, have made the case for a greater appreciation of the varying rates of growth in different industrial sectors.[10] In this context, there is a case for viewing south Wales as two distinct industrial regions, east and west, in which patterns and rates of growth were quite different. In the western region, centred on Swansea, a slower, more incremental style of industrialization was the norm and, as a result, the experience of urban growth in this part of Wales was distinctive.

Thirdly, and most significantly for the purposes of the current analysis, studies of the harmful effects of industry on the town have not been counterbalanced by notice of the considerable advantages which Swansea derived from its industrial expansion. Industrial growth, especially in the first two decades of the nineteenth century, helped rather than hindered the town's rising pretensions as an urban centre. In this period Swansea grew in status as a town. The capital brought to the area by incoming entrepreneurs, the trading and commercial links forged with suppliers and customers, both domestic and foreign, and the growing influence of the town over a widening region, all added to Swansea's already confident urban identity. By 1830 the fact that this bustling resort could also claim to be an industrial heavyweight gave a further boost to its urban identity. The new town directory published in that year proclaimed that Swansea 'may truly be called the metropolis of Wales, not only from its size, but from its charming situation and extensive trade'.[11] It was a formidable combination.

Although Swansea's economic growth is most often associated with copper, the root of its expansion as an industrial town can more accurately be attributed to its abundance of coal. By the end of the eighteenth century, Swansea was already the most significant

[9] See, for example, W. E. Minchinton (ed.), *Industrial South Wales: Essays in Welsh Economic History* (London, 1969).
[10] For example, M. Berg, *The Age of Manufactures. Industry, Innovation and Work in Britain, 1700–1820* (Oxford, 1985).
[11] *Matthews's Swansea Directory for the Year 1830* (Swansea, 1830), pp. 5–6.

coal port on the south Wales coast, shipping a total of 244,976 tons in 1799 compared with just 18,375 tons by its nearest rival, Newport,[12] and an estimated 12,000 tons from Llanelli.[13] The Swansea figure alone in that year was almost twice that of total coal shipments from south Wales as a whole fifty years earlier.[14] Moreover, coal was having an important shaping effect on the town. A 1802 guide connected the 'increase of the trade of Swansea' with 'the various mines of coal and culm in the neighbourhood'.[15] By 1822 there were some fifteen merchants dealing in coal-stone, coal or culm operating in the town[16] and the influence of the leading coal industrialists, especially the Morris family, on the evolving residential and demographic structure of the town was profound. The population of Morriston, to the north of Swansea, where much of the labour force of the Morris's coal empire was located, reached some 3,000 by the early 1830s.[17]

Two specific features of the coal found in the neighbourhood of Swansea were of interest to industrial entrepreneurs. Firstly, the bituminous coals found in this sector of the coalfield were particularly suited for use in ore-smelting furnaces. Secondly, the coal seams lay very close to the shore. These factors combined to make the area a promising location for the expansion of metal smelting and were the key attractions for many of the incoming investors. According to the historian of Vivian and Sons, the town's largest smelting firm, it was the availability of cheap coal supplies from the nearby collieries belonging to John Morris that led John Vivian to establish his first smelting works in the town in 1809.[18] Similar enticements prompted one of the Vivians' main rivals in the trade, Pascoe Grenfell, to relocate from St Helens, Lancashire, to Swansea in 1812.[19] Agreements over the supply of coal were prominent in all of the early leases

[12] Figures abstracted from Williams, *Digest*, Volume 1, pp. 318–31.
[13] M. Symons, *Coal Mining in the Llanelli Area*, Volume 1: *The Sixteenth Century to 1829* (Llanelli, 1979), p.257.
[14] J. Williams, 'The coal industry, 1750–1914', in G. Williams and A. H. John (eds), *GCH*, Volume V, p. 157.
[15] *The Swansea Guide: containing such information as was deemed useful to the traveler through the counties of Glamorgan and Monmouthshire* (Swansea, 1802), p. 18.
[16] *Pigot's London Provincial Directory* (London, 1823).
[17] I. G. Jones, 'The city and its villages', in R. A. Griffiths (ed.), *The City of Swansea. Challenges and Change* (Stroud, 1990), p. 82.
[18] R. Toomey, *Vivian and Sons, 1809–1924. A Study of the Firm in the Copper and Related Industries* (London, 1985), p. 13.
[19] Rees, *King Copper*, p. 14.

secured by the smelters in the district. The Morris and Lane partnership, which leased a smelting site at Landore in 1717, agreed with the landowner, Thomas Popkin, to pay £13 per annum for thirty-one years, and to receive all of their coal from him over the same period at a fixed price.[20] Other factors, such as the development of canal networks, particularly the Swansea valley canal from the 1790s, and the establishment of the harbour commission in Swansea in 1791, provided further encouragement to would-be entrepreneurs seeking an advantageous location for smelting. It was this combination of available coal and improving transport networks at the beginning of the nineteenth century which led, according to a local man, George Grant Francis, to 'a great disposition to construct works and invest capital in connection with copper smelting'.[21]

Copper smelting, however, was a capital intensive industry. When the Vivians' Hafod works was established in 1809, it required a £50,000 capital investment.[22] In the mid-nineteenth century even the smallest works was said to require £45,000 in order to be viable, compared with just £10,000 for a small colliery.[23] Added to this was the problem that it often took time for returns on these investments to be realized. Robert Morris found himself having to reassure his partner, Thomas Lockwood, that 'the copper trade, in which the money employed underwent so many transmutations before it was returned, requires a stronger faith than most other trades'.[24] The copper smelters, then, had to be men of substance, with sufficient capital at their disposal to survive the financial rigours of their early years in business. Significantly, none of Swansea's leading copper smelters became the subject of the kind of 'rags to riches' mythology that attached itself to industrialists in other sectors, but instead they were typical of the 'business middle class' which formed the real backbone of Britain's industrial entrepreneurship in the early nineteenth century.[25]

[20] UWSA, Morris 1, 'A history of the copper concern, 1717–1730'. Historical notes and memoranda by Robert Morris junior, relating to Robert Morris senior's copper-smelting works in Swansea (1774), p. 4.
[21] G. G. Francis, *The Smelting of Copper in the Swansea District of South Wales* (2nd edition, London, 1881), p. 133.
[22] Toomey, *Vivian and Sons*, p. 187.
[23] P. R. Reynolds, 'Industrial development', in G. Williams (ed.), *Swansea. An Illustrated History* (Swansea, 1990), p. 33.
[24] UWSA, Morris 1, 'History of the copper concern', p. 8.
[25] F. Crouzet, *The First Industrialists. The Problem of Origins* (Cambridge, 1985), p. 99.

Although recent research on south-west Wales has focused attention on levels of local enterprise in industrial and economic expansion,[26] the kind of investment levels required in copper smelting necessitated finance from outside the area. The development of smelting in Swansea from the early decades of the eighteenth century was primarily driven by newcomers to the town.[27] For wealthy entrepreneurs with money to invest, the growing copper industry at Swansea was an inviting prospect. Some of the earliest individuals to seize the opportunity to invest came from Bristol. This is not surprising. With its long-established role as a market and distribution centre for south Wales and the south-west of England, Bristol was known as the 'metropolis of the west' and it lived up to its billing in the early eighteenth century, performing a 'pump-priming' function in the Swansea copper industry.[28] John Lane and Thomas Coster were two Bristol men who provided early capital for expansion. Coster had a family background in non-ferrous smelting in Bristol and in metal mining in Devon.[29] Lane, meanwhile, had no specialist industrial knowledge. Trained as a doctor, he participated in the Swansea smelting industry as a financier, in partnership with smelters like Robert Morris at Landore.[30]

The success of these early entrepreneurs was in part responsible for attracting new waves of inward investment. By 1784, the Glamorgan smelters were consuming 70 per cent of all the ore raised in Cornwall.[31] The possibility of setting up rival smelting establishments in Cornwall had been tried at Hayle, but abandoned by the end of the eighteenth century as non-viable because of the expense of shipping the required amounts of coal.[32] Consequently, Cornish mining 'adventurers' like John Vivian were lured across

[26] M. D. Matthews, 'In pursuit of profit? Local enterprise in south-west Wales in the eighteenth century' (unpublished Ph.D. thesis, University of Wales Swansea, 1998).

[27] D. O. Evans, 'The non-ferrous metallurgical industries of South Wales and Welshmen's share in their development', *Transactions of the Honourable Society of Cymmrodorion* (1929–30), 1–37. Despite its title, this article confirms the non-Welsh origins of the leading players in this industrial sector.

[28] W. E. Minchinton, 'Bristol – metropolis of the West in the eighteenth century', *Transactions of the Royal Historical Society*, 5th ser., IV (1954), 69–89.

[29] R. O. Roberts, 'The White Rock copper and brass works near Swansea, 1736–1806', in R. Denning (ed.), *Glamorgan Historian*, Volume 12 (Barry, 1981), p. 137.

[30] UWSA, Morris 1, 'History of the copper concern', p. 3.

[31] Williams, 'The coal industry, 1750–1914', p. 159.

[32] R. O. Roberts, 'The development and decline of the non-ferrous metal smelting industries in south Wales', in W. E. Minchinton (ed.), *Industrial South Wales, 1750–1914. Essays in Welsh Economic History* (London, 1969), p. 126.

the Bristol Channel with a view to securing a share in some of the benefits being reaped by the smelters receiving their ores. Vivian was a member of the Cornish Metal Company, founded in 1785 in order to act on behalf of the Cornish mines in the ore markets,[33] and also a partner in the Cornish Bank at Truro, which helped finance his entry into the smelting industry in south Wales.[34] Other prominent Cornish families which followed similar routes into the smelting industry in the Swansea district were the Foxes of Falmouth, the Grenfells of Penzance and the Williams family of Scorrier, near Redruth.

Other significant groups of investors were prompted by similar motives. By the 1780s the Birmingham brass trades had become important purchasers of copper, consuming around one thousand tons annually.[35] Like their counterparts from the Cornish mining industry, they were anxious to exert some measure of control over the smelting trade and feared the influence that a small, geographically concentrated group of producers might exert over the market price of copper. An anonymous 'inhabitant of Birmingham' gave voice to these fears in 1790, urging the metal manufacturers of the town to 'call to your recollection what you have suffered from the fluctuation in the price of copper' and to act in concert to protect their own interests.[36] Setting up in business alongside the established Swansea smelters was one way of securing a greater say in the production and price of the smelted copper. As a result, a group of new smelting firms was established on the Tawe in the 1790s, including the Birmingham Mining and Copper Company, the Crown Copper and Spelter Company and the Rose Copper Smelting Company.[37]

The motives which prompted the other major player, the Anglesey solicitor and copper mine owner, Thomas Williams, to throw his hat into the ring and enter the copper-smelting industry in Swansea were broadly similar. Although, by 1779, he already had a smelting works in Ravenhead, south Lancashire,[38] the increasing

[33] UWSA, Yorkshire Imperial Metals (YIM), A1, Abstract of Agreement for establishing the Cornish Metal Company, 1 September 1785.
[34] Toomey, *Vivian and Sons*, p. 196.
[35] Roberts, 'Development and decline', p. 122.
[36] UWSA, YIM, A14, 'Observations on the copper trade by an inhabitant of Birmingham and its neighbourhood' (1790).
[37] R. O. Roberts, 'Enterprise and capital for non-ferrous metal smelting in Glamorgan, 1694–1924', *Morgannwg*, XIII (1979), p. 59.
[38] J. R. Harris, *The Copper King. A Biography of Thomas Williams of Llanidan* (Liverpool, 1964), p. 37.

concentration of the industry in the Swansea area in the 1780s led him to seek a foothold there, first taking over the Upper Bank works, around 1782, and later the Middle Bank works by 1787.[39] Like many of the Cornish investors, he was then in a position to supply these works with his own ores. Middle Bank works, for example, was supplied with large quantities of ore from his Mona Mine in Anglesey throughout the 1780s.[40]

The net result of these developments was an increase in the industrial power of the growing copper-smelting fraternity, centred on Swansea. The scale of the inward investment meant that the town soon became generally acknowledged as the focal point of the British copper-smelting industry. According to one recent business historian, it was 'the most highly concentrated major British industry in the eighteenth and nineteenth centuries'.[41] Considerable influence could be wielded from a position of such unrivalled industrial might. The Swansea smelters were able, for example, to effect more convenient arrangements for ore sales, or 'ticketings'. The Welsh smelters operating in the eighteenth century had always been obliged to attend these 'ticketings' in Cornwall, at Truro or Redruth, or to send agents there in person to act on their behalf. Robert Morris at Landore had always found this to be a problem as 'my coming is inconvenient, and when I come the sellers know I must buy and hold up the ore'.[42] By the early nineteenth century, however, with so much of the copper-ore market bound up with the smelting developments in the Swansea area, additional ticketings were hosted in Swansea itself to handle sales of non-Cornish ores. From 1804 onwards, and more frequently from 1815, representatives from the smelting works and mines gathered fortnightly at the Mackworth Arms to dine and bid for ores.[43] By the 1830s, when increasing quantities of foreign ores were being imported into Britain, these commercial gatherings had taken on a 'truly international' flavour,[44] with many of the new Latin American mining companies represented.

---

[39] Ibid., p. 180.
[40] UWSA, Grenfell C2, Raw Material Records, Anglesey Mona Mine Copper Account Book.
[41] E. Newell, '"Copperopolis": the rise and fall of the copper industry in the Swansea district, 1826–1921', *Business History*, XXXII, no. 3 (1990), 77.
[42] UWSA, Morris 1, 'History of the copper concern', p. 14.
[43] Newell, '"Copperopolis"', 81.
[44] E. Newell, 'The British copper ore market in the nineteenth century with particular

With such a geographically concentrated group of industrialists, collective agreements for the promotion of their shared interests were also feasible. The main instrument for this was the Copper Trade Association which was dominated by the Swansea smelters and through which they tried to define and defend their collective interests. Although riven by internal disputes, most clearly evidenced when the Vivians withdrew from the first Association in 1829 over the issue of output policy,[45] the Copper Trade Association benefited the Swansea smelters. In the first half of the nineteenth century in particular, its activities helped to increase the differential between the prices of ore and smelted copper, to the advantage of the smelting interest.[46] It also helped to counter levels of collaboration among some of the ore producers. In 1787, Thomas Williams had assumed control of the Cornish Metal Company on behalf of the ore producers of Anglesey and Cornwall combined, so that 'the disposal of all the copper raised in Cornwall and Anglesey [would be] in one hand'.[47] In response, the Swansea copper smelters had no choice but to act collectively to ensure that their influence in the marketplace was not lost.

The position of industrial pre-eminence which Swansea had attained by the early decades of the nineteenth century was remarkable because it had been achieved without any of the classic features of industrial take-off that characterized expansion in other manufacturing sectors.[48] The origins of growth long pre-dated, for example, the late eighteenth-century expansion of the Welsh iron industry centred on Merthyr Tydfil. Located in the western section of the south Wales coalfield, coal mining in Swansea dated back to medieval times. The first copper-smelting venture in the region was the establishment of the Mines Royal Company at Aberdulais, near Neath, in 1584.[49] In Swansea itself, the Llangyfelach works, established by the Bristol physician, Dr John Lane, dated from 1717, and

reference to Cornwall and Swansea' (unpublished D.Phil. thesis, University of Oxford, 1988), p. 124.

[45] Toomey, *Vivian and Sons*, pp. 325–7.

[46] L. Valenzuela, 'Challenges to the British copper smelting industry in the world market, 1840–1860', *Journal of European Economic History*, 19 (1990), 666–74.

[47] UWSA, YIM, A10, Proposal for a new agreement with the Anglesey companies, 1787.

[48] For a discussion of the concept of industrial 'take-off', see D. Whitehead, 'The English industrial revolution as an example of growth', in R. M. Hartwell (ed.), *The Industrial Revolution* (Oxford, 1970), pp. 3–27.

[49] L. Ince, *Neath Abbey and the Industrial Revolution* (Stroud, 2001), p. 12.

by the middle of the eighteenth century additional smelting sites had sprung up at Melincryddan, Landore and White Rock.[50] Thanks to these early developments, the south Wales smelters were already producing half of all Britain's copper by 1750.[51]

New markets for copper emerged in the late eighteenth and early nineteenth centuries. John Vivian, writing in his capacity as deputy governor of the Cornish Metal Company in July 1786, predicted that 'the flourishing state of our manufactories and the prospect of a general use of copper in all the navies of Europe afford a comfortable hope of increased consumption'.[52] New uses for copper included the production of domestic utensils and the manufacture of coins. The customers of the south Wales smelters included Matthew Boulton in Birmingham, who used copper for the manufacture of coinage. The applications of copper in industry, noted by John Vivian, included the manufacture of new products for industrial processes such as print rollers and steam engines.[53] The importance of marine applications also became apparent as copper was increasingly used for sheathing the hulls of ships.[54] As a result of these new markets and the increased demands for copper, the output from the smelters grew from under 1,000 tons in the early eighteenth century to 7,000 tons in the early nineteenth.[55]

These steadily rising output levels were achieved by means of an increase in the smelting capacity of the Swansea furnaces. If there was a transformation of any kind in copper smelting in the early years of the nineteenth century, it was in the extent of operations. The new works, opened at Landore in the 1790s and at Hafod in the first decade of the next century, introduced a new scale of smelting, with two-storey furnaces designed for extra capacity.[56] This drive towards maximizing output was a deliberate policy on the part of the town's leading smelters and was in part a response to increasing levels of competition in the industry concentrated in the vicinity of Swansea. Already by the first decade of the nineteenth century, the

[50] R. O. Roberts, 'The smelting of non-ferrous metals', in Williams and John (eds), *GCH*, Volume V, pp. 86–7.
[51] Toomey, *Vivian and Sons*, p. 5.
[52] UWSA, YIM, A9, 'Observations on the Metal Company', 18 July 1786.
[53] Roberts, 'The smelting of non-ferrous metals', p. 48.
[54] Reynolds, 'Industrial development', p. 33.
[55] Roberts, 'Development and decline', p. 125.
[56] S. R. Hughes, *Copperopolis: Landscapes of the Early Industrial Period in Swansea* (Aberystwyth, 2000), pp. 28–9.

trade seemed set to become dominated by a few large-scale players. Charles Nevill estimated in 1805 that twelve Welsh copper companies were smelting, between them, some 2,020 tons of copper per week, and that within this group there was already a two-tier structure emerging, with three of the firms, Crown, Rose, and Williams and Grenfell, each easily exceeding 200 tons a week.[57] By 1820 there were some thirteen copper works operating within a twenty-mile radius of the town of Swansea.[58] Profitability depended on the throughput of ores in the furnaces being 'sufficiently large enough to generate economies of scale'.[59] John Vivian's son, John Henry Vivian, writing in 1829, suggested that bulk production was the only way to succeed in such a climate: 'All that I see to be done is to carry on our concern on as large a scale as we can manage with our own capital.'[60]

The difference in scale resulting from this new emphasis on bulk production was evident in just a few years. By the 1840s, the Vivians' Hafod works consisted of ninety-five furnaces and calciners and was capable of smelting over 1,000 tons of copper ore per week, producing a weekly copper output worth some £9,000.[61] Bulk output, crucially, gave the smelters greater flexibility over price, and the ability to sell at a cheaper rate than one's neighbour was all important in securing a firm place in the market. In this climate, price wars were inevitable. As early as 1814, for example, John Vivian was on the defensive, accused by the rival Grenfell firm of selling below the proper price.[62] Such tactics were not unique to the copper industry in early nineteenth-century Britain. Textile manufacturers operating at the lower-grade end of the market also found that bulk output and cheap sales were the key to staying ahead of the competition.[63]

Yet the growth of production in the copper sector was steady rather than seismic. Compared with iron output in south Wales, which rose from 34,000 tons in 1796 to 525,000 in 1840,[64] the

---

[57] NLW, Nevill A, 20, Letter from C. Nevill to R. Nicholl, 27 September 1805.
[58] Figure abstracted from Roberts, 'The smelting of non-ferrous metals', pp. 86–91.
[59] Newell, '"Copperopolis"', 77.
[60] UWSA, YIM, A20, Extracts from Vivian letters and documents, 1829.
[61] Ibid., A26, Statement, c.1845–46.
[62] Ibid., A20, Extracts from Vivian letters and documents, March 1814.
[63] L. Miskell and C. A. Whatley, '"Juteopolis" in the making. Linen and the industrial transformation of Dundee, c.1820–1850', *Textile History*, 30, no. 2 (1999), 186.
[64] P. Jenkins, *A History of Modern Wales, 1536–1990* (London, 1992), p. 221.

performance of the copper smelters of Swansea and district appears modest. The two sectors, however, had little in common. The copper works were small enterprises. Quality rather than quantity was the main requirement as far as the recruitment of labour was concerned; by 1770 the entire workforce of the south Wales non-ferrous sector is estimated to have been only around 500.[65] There were no major innovations in production techniques of the kind that transformed output levels in the iron industry from the 1790s. The 'Welsh method' of smelting copper in coal-fired reverberatory furnaces, in which the ore and fuel were kept separate, had come into use in south Wales before 1700,[66] long pre-dating the main period of technological advance in other industries.[67] Once in common use, this smelting process remained largely unchanged, and as a result the industry's growth was not characterized by sudden surges in output.

Improvements and new technologies, where they were introduced, were applied to increase efficiency or quality in particular areas of production. In 1816, John Henry Vivian was in communication with W. E. Sheffield of London, seeking permission to use his patent air conductor for the treatment of copper ore in the furnace, on payment of £400.[68] Other widely adopted technologies included the introduction of steam power in copper rolling. One commentator has suggested that this innovation first appeared at the Taibach works of the English Copper Company in 1803,[69] although more recent assessments date the general development of steam-powered rolling mills to the 1820s.[70] There was also experimental innovation in the production of new metal alloys. John Henry Vivian commenced spelter production in 1835 and G. F. Muntz patented his own version of a copper-zinc alloy developed at his Swansea works.[71]

---

[65] Roberts, 'Development and decline', p. 133.
[66] Toomey, *Vivian and Sons*, p. 277.
[67] N. Von Tunzelmann, 'Technology in the early nineteenth century', in R. Floud and D. McCloskey (eds), *The Economic History of Britain since 1700*, Volume 1: *1700–1860* (Cambridge, 1994), pp. 271–98.
[68] UWSA, YIM, F1, Patents, 13 May 1816.
[69] J. Rowlands, 'Essay on the history of Cwmavon', in *Aeron Afan: sef y cyfansoddiadau buddugol yn Eisteddfod Iforaidd Aberafan, Mehefin 23 1853: Idan nawdd y Burdd Iforaidd* (Caerfyrddin, 1855), p. 19.
[70] Hughes, *Copperopolis*, pp. 36–7.
[71] Toomey, *Vivian and Sons*, pp. 288–90.

Perhaps the most pressing problem which the smelters looked to new technologies to solve was the question of how to reduce the sulphurous copper smoke given out by their furnaces as a by-product of the smelting process. It was a problem which occupied John Henry Vivian from as early as 1812, and it was for his efforts in this sphere that he was made a Fellow of the Royal Society. The quest to reduce emissions, however, was a costly and difficult one which continued to occupy his son, Henry Hussey Vivian, in the second half of the nineteenth century. Not until the adoption, in the mid-1860s, of Gerstenhöffer's new furnace, described by Henry Hussey as a 'novel and beautiful invention', was any real progress made.[72]

Historians have remained largely sceptical of the efforts of the Swansea smelters to make their industry cleaner. Even Vivian and Sons' sympathetic chronicler, Toomey, points out that they were more likely to have been motivated by an anxiety to avoid costly legal claims against them over the effects of copper smoke than by purely environmental considerations.[73] Other historians have doubted their levels of success, claiming that by the 1820s pollution from the smelters was affecting the town to such an extent that it was causing the gentry to move 'upwind' of the copper smoke.[74] Contemporary opinion within the town, however, was rather different. The corporation made a point of expressing its satisfaction at the efforts being made by the leading smelters to restrict emissions, indicating that the problems of pollution were a small price to pay for such a source of wealth and prosperity to the town. In March 1823, they sent a copy of a resolution to the Vivians, saying that:

> It is the opinion of this corporation that the prosperity and welfare of the town of Swansea and its neighbourhood is mainly supported by the extent to which the copperworks situated near this town are carried on and this corporation think it right to take the present opportunity to express the high satisfaction they feel at the success that has attended the spirited and scientific exertions of Messrs Vivian and Sons in counteracting any inconvenience that may have at any time arisen to any individuals from the great issue of smoke from the furnaces at use in different copperworks.[75]

---

[72] Francis, *The Smelting of Copper in the Swansea District*, p. 153.
[73] Toomey, *Vivian and Sons*, pp. 285–6.
[74] Reynolds, 'Industrial development', p. 37.
[75] WGAS, B/S Corp, B9, 7 March 1823.

The reference made to the situation of the copperworks, 'near this town', is particularly significant. Carried inland from the smelting works, which were themselves situated upriver from the coast, the copper smoke had much less effect on the town of Swansea than it did on the lower Swansea valley, which became synonymous with pollution. In assessing the impact of industry on Swansea's urban development, it should be noted that it was the agricultural hinterland and the northern fringes of the town, rather than the central commercial district, which bore the brunt of pollution. The claimants against the smelters were principally farmers, who suffered damage to crops and cattle. It was part of the argument employed by the members of the Swansea Commercial Society, in their objections to the routing of the new Carmarthenshire road outside the town, that the proposed route would be 'amidst the smoke arising from the copper works situated higher up the said river' and 'at a considerable distance from the mercantile and trading part of the town'.[76]

These geographical factors have sometimes been overlooked in historical portrayals of Swansea as a town blighted by industrial pollution. In fact, the town itself showed little sign of being engulfed by industry in the early years of the nineteenth century. Some central areas, such as the commercial core of Wind Street, had experienced a degree of deterioration by mid-century. Here, the gardens to the rear of street-fronting properties were gradually infilled with smaller dwellings and non-residential premises such as bonded stores, pigsties, a dyers' shed and a candle factory.[77] Such developments were a common feature of expanding towns throughout Britain, as population growth and the spread of business and retail premises put pressure on urban space. Heavy industry in Swansea, however, was confined to the outskirts of the town. Prestige residential areas on the Burrows, the lower slopes of Mount Pleasant and the sea-facing terraces of Uplands remained attractive to the upper middle classes, who were not yet persuaded in large numbers that a better standard of living could be had at a greater distance from the town centre.[78] Other towns, where large-scale manufacturing operations were more centrally located,

[76] WGAS, RISW, GGF, B7, Swansea Commercial Society Minutes, 27 April 1827.
[77] J. C. M. Rees, 'Evolving patterns of residence in a nineteenth-century city: Swansea, 1851–1871' (unpublished Ph.D. thesis, University of Wales Swansea, 1983), p. 160.
[78] Ibid., pp. 162–3.

had experienced middle-class departure to outlying suburbs by 1840.[79]

The upper echelons of Swansea society were given an injection of wealth and personnel by the arrival of industrial entrepreneurs from the eighteenth century onwards. The newcomers, with their established business and financial backgrounds, were not so very different in terms of status from the lesser gentry and landowners of the region who traditionally made up the local elite. Friendships and bonds between the two groups were forged with relative ease and can be detected in the interlinking social and marriage patterns between key individuals. Lewis Weston Dillwyn, the heir to the Penllergaer estates, and John Henry Vivian became life-long friends and political allies. Griffith Llewellyn, of Baglan Hall, meanwhile, married Madelina, daughter of copper smelter Pascoe St Leger Grenfell.[80] Singleton Abbey and Sketty Hall, the homes of John Henry Vivian and Lewis Weston Dillwyn respectively, became important focal points in the town for the social lives of the elite. The assimilation of leading industrialists into the upper ranks of urban society was not so easily achieved in some other manufacturing districts;[81] in Swansea it epitomized the way in which the town's traditional functions were complemented, rather than compromised, by industrial development in the first half of the nineteenth century.

Even the tourist trade derived some indirect benefits from industrial growth. Nowhere is this better illustrated than in the operation of the new Swansea to Oystermouth tramroad. Established by Act of Parliament in 1804, with the blessing of Swansea corporation and the support of shareholders drawn from the ranks of the landowners, industrialists, tradesmen and professionals of the town, the tramroad was intended to 'open a communication with several extensive limestone quarries, coal mines, iron mines and other mines, whereby the carriage and conveyance of limestone, coal, iron ore, and other minerals and commodities will be greatly facilitated'.[82] By 1807, however, it was also – uniquely – conveying

---

[79] M. Reed, 'The transformation of urban space, 1700–1840', in Clark (ed.), *CUHB*, Volume 2, pp. 639–40.

[80] T. Nicholas, *Annals and Antiquities of the Counties and County Families of Wales* (London, 1872), p. 635.

[81] See, for example, L. Miskell, 'Civic leadership and the manufacturing elite, c.1780–1850', in L. Miskell, C. A. Whatley and B. Harris (eds), *Victorian Dundee. Image and Realities* (East Linton, 2000), pp. 51–69.

[82] *An act for making and maintaining a railway or tramroad, from the town of Swansea, into the parish of Oystermouth, in the county of Glamorgan*, 29 June 1804.

passengers in a horse-drawn carriage along the rails. The line, which ran along the seashore through Blackpill and Clyne to the village of Mumbles, provided a popular scenic excursion and a novel attraction for fashionable visitors to the town. One tourist described his ride and his fellow passengers:

> The car is intended to carry sixteen persons and runs on a railway drawn by one horse. The distance is five miles from Swansea Turnpike to the Mumbles. We had ten persons with us and myself and companion, the only gentlemen. Among the ladies were two very pretty, delicate girls, apparently only visiting for their health at Swansea. I was very much pleased with my ride being all along the sands on the railway before mentioned, the scenery being grand particularly Oystermouth Castle and the bay of Swansea.[83]

This mineral tramroad thus became the world's first passenger railway and symbolized the successful coexistence of industry and fashionable leisure in Swansea in the early decades of the nineteenth century.

All the signs in Swansea, then, were of a town that had incorporated, rather than been swamped by, industrial growth. This was as evident in the town's early nineteenth-century economic profile as anywhere else. Although it was the growth of copper smelting that was the most marked economic development in the region from the eighteenth century onwards, there was far more to Swansea's economy than this. In addition to its close association with the non-ferrous sector, Swansea also had strong links with the iron industry, and the careers of a number of industrialists and entrepreneurs in the town reflected the connections between the two sectors.[84] James Palmer Budd, for example, who came to Swansea in 1825 as an assistant to John Henry Vivian at the Hafod copper works, later developed interests in the iron industry in the district when he joined the Ystalyfera ironworks and, whilst there, patented a method of using waste gases in the hot blast process.[85] There was even greater variety in the range of commercial and retail businesses in the town. The analysis of occupations of over 2,000 householders in Swansea, compiled by the local statistical society in the 1830s, illustrates this variety (see Figure 3.1). By the early decades of the

---

[83] T. Lloyd, 'The diary of a visitor to Swansea and Gower in 1821', *Gower*, 34 (1983), 12–13.
[84] For a fuller discussion of this issue, see L. Miskell, 'Separate spheres'? Rethinking the history of the metalliferous industries in South Wales', *WHR*, 21, no. 2 (2002), 249–70.
[85] Atkinson and Baber, *Growth and Decline*, p.42.

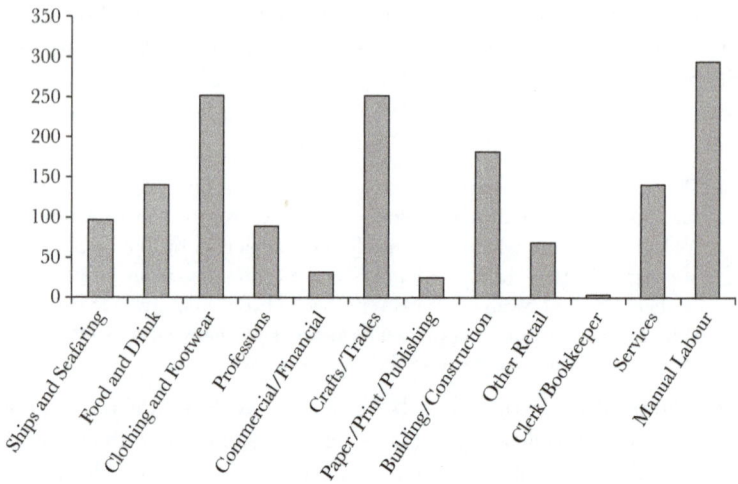

Figure 3.1 Occupations of Swansea householders, 1838

nineteenth century a large retail sector, a flourishing construction industry, a broad range of skilled crafts and flourishing publishing, professional and commercial sectors had grown up in the town.

The ships and seafaring category in Figure 3.1 included some 76 shipbuilders and ships' carpenters and mariners, testifying to the importance of the harbour to the town's economy in this period. Amongst the food and drink retailers were 78 grocers and the clothing sector included 152 shoemakers. Within its professional ranks, the town possessed seventeen solicitors and thirty ministers of the gospel. Seven accountants and five bankers joined the merchants and factors in the commercial sector, and the small but significant paper and publishing contingent included ten booksellers and thirteen printers. The craft and trade sector included a huge range of skilled workers, from the sixty-eight potters employed at the town's two earthenware manufactories, to the piano maker, gunsmiths, silversmiths and jewellers, and the basket makers, curriers and dyers. In the construction trade there were some sixty masons and an additional three specialist marble masons, and the service sector included eighty-eight lodging-house keepers as well as a dentist, an optician and four livery-stable keepers.

The strength of the retail and commercial sector in the town was underpinned by the establishment of the Swansea Commercial

Society at a meeting at the Mackworth Arms hotel in 1824. Its original committee members included the coach-maker, John Francis, the banker John Voss, the ironmonger John Edmond, and David Griffiths, the currier.[86] Through this society, the town's tradesmen expressed their views to the municipal authorities, and occasionally to Parliament, on matters directly affecting their collective interests. In November 1824, for example, they lobbied improvement commissioner, Henry Sockett, over the issue of the planned new market, recommending to him their favoured site.[87] In April 1827, they resolved to support the petition submitted to Parliament by the inhabitants of the town, objecting to the proposed route of a new road from Briton Ferry to Carmarthenshire which was planned to pass 'nearly close to the town of Swansea but on the opposite side of the River Tawe, without passing through the town'; this would have the effect of 'depriving the inhabitants of Swansea of all the benefits which now arise from its being a thoroughfare'.[88] In the 1830s they were writing to George Clive, the poor law commissioner for Wales, to offer their opinion on the size of the proposed new poor law union district.[89]

The importance of the retail and trade sectors to Swansea's economy, and the influence their representatives exerted in the town have not always been fully acknowledged. Some of the most recent accounts of the town have continued to present the 'copperopolis' image,[90] at the expense of a broader appreciation of Swansea's economic diversity. Even the attempt of a local historian neatly to summarize the industrial profile of the town as the 'three cs': coal, copper and chemicals,[91] underestimates the breadth of its industrial and commercial life. By contrast, earlier commentators were well aware of its abundance of trades and manufactures. Charles Wilkins, writing in 1903, commented that: 'Swansea possesses one great advantage over colliery towns, tinplate towns and agricultural towns in the number and variety of its industries.'[92]

[86] WGAS, RISW, GGF, B7, 2 March 1824.
[87] Ibid., 2 November 1824.
[88] Ibid., 27 April 1827.
[89] TNA: PRO MH32/12, 31 October 1837.
[90] Hughes, *Copperopolis*; Newell, '"Copperopolis"', 75–94.
[91] N. L. Thomas, *The Story of Swansea's Districts and Villages*, Volume 2 (Swansea, 1969), p. 72.
[92] C. Wilkins, *History of the Iron, Steel, Tinplate and other Trades of Wales* (Merthyr Tydfil, 1903), p. 392.

Wilkins's observation was a shrewd one. He quite rightly acknowledged that Swansea's industrial strength and diversity gave the town an important edge over other urban centres. This was especially so because the scope of its economic power-base was not confined to Swansea itself. The south Wales copper-smelting region extended west into Carmarthenshire as far as Llanelli, east across Aberafan as far as Taibach and inland into the Neath and Swansea valleys. By the early decades of the nineteenth century, this was becoming one of Britain's most highly concentrated industrial districts.[93] Although many of the earliest copper-smelting ventures in the area had been based in Neath, with the Mines Royal Company operating there from 1584 and Sir Humphrey Mackworth's Melincryddan works from 1695, the trend thereafter was westward as entrepreneurs clamoured to take advantage of Swansea's growing coal industry and its harbour and canal facilities. By the beginning of the nineteenth century, copper was no longer being smelted in Neath borough,[94] but Neath Abbey, just outside the town, was becoming an increasingly important and diverse industrial site in its own right. Two new copper works built near the Mines Royal site on the banks of the river Neath were operating by the late 1790s.[95] Iron production also developed there, with the Neath Abbey Iron Company operating from 1792, and a number of new collieries were sunk to provide easily accessible fuel supplies.[96]

To the east, industrial developments were underway on Thomas Mansel Talbot's lands at Margam, near the parish of Aberafan. A portion of his estates was first leased to industrial entrepreneurs in 1757 and thereafter Mynydd Bychan colliery was opened, tramroads built and work begun on the construction of a new copper works at Taibach in 1770.[97] Talbot was particularly excited by the prospect of this latter development and wrote from Milan in 1771 that 'no transaction with regard to my affairs ... will rest more deeply engraved in my breast than the great and important establishment of the British Copper Company'.[98] Further developments

[93] The extent of the 'Swansea region' is described in S. R. Hughes and P. Reynolds, *A Guide to the Industrial Archaeology of the Swansea Region* (Swansea, 1988), p. 3.
[94] C. Trott, 'Copper industry', in E. Jenkins (ed.), *Neath and District. A Symposium* (Neath, 1974), p. 143.
[95] L. Ince, *The Neath Abbey Iron Company* (Eindhoven, 1984), p. 16.
[96] For futher details, see L. Ince, *Neath Abbey and the Industrial Revolution* (Stroud, 2001).
[97] R. Morgan, *A History of Taibach to 1872*, translated by A. L. Evans (Port Talbot, 1987), pp. 5–7.
[98] NLW, Penrice and Margam Muniments (2), L1, 293, 12 October 1771.

took place a few miles inland at Cwmafan, where Samuel Fothergill Lettsom built a blast furnace in 1819. Taken over by the Vigurs and Smith partnership of the Ynysygerwyn tin-plate works a year later, this went on to become the site of a new integrated works for iron, copper and tin-plate manufacture, purchased by the English Copper Company in 1841.[99] Likewise, in the Tawe valley, north of Swansea, for a distance of some fifteen miles collieries, iron and tin-plate works grew up, along with a string of settlements including Clydach, Pontardawe, Ystradgynlais and Aber-craf.[100] Further west, the area around Llanelli had considerable potential for industrial development. Its coal resources began to be exploited in earnest from 1750 on, through the efforts of Chauncey Townsend, Sir Thomas Stepney and others.[101] Then, from the mid-1790s onwards a further phase of expansion began with the arrival of another group of entrepreneurs including Alexander Raby and the commencement of copper smelting there in 1805 by the Birmingham manufacturer, Charles Nevill, who was attracted to the area because of 'the very superior quality of coal in that neighbourhood [and] the abundant resources that surround it'.[102]

Swansea, however, was very much the industrial and commercial focus of this burgeoning industrial district. Other industrial areas of Britain had much less clear-cut 'capitals'. The Black Country, for instance, was 'a cohesive cluster of urban localities'.[103] A number of key towns such as Wolverhampton, West Bromwich and Dudley provided various urban services and facilities but none was dominant, perhaps because of the close proximity of Birmingham which exerted so much influence over the area.[104] In Swansea, the grafting of industrial expansion onto an already well-developed urban infrastructure gave the town a distinct edge over the other urban centres emerging in its vicinity. Not only was there a growing concentration of works along the Tawe river, but also an increase in commercial activity associated with the copper trade. The hosting of ticketings at Swansea gave the town a function as the centre of commercial

[99] Rowlands, 'Essay on the history of Cwmavon', pp. 39–48.
[100] Jones, 'The city and its villages', pp. 84–5.
[101] Symons, *Coal Mining in the Llanelli Area*, pp. 16–17.
[102] NLW, Nevill A, 20, Letter from Charles Nevill, 1 November 1804.
[103] R. Trainor, *Black Country Elites. The Exercise of Authority in an Industrial Area, 1830–1900* (Oxford, 1993), p. 40.
[104] G. C. Allen, *The Industrial Development of Birmingham and the Black Country, 1860–1927* (London, 1966), p. xv.

activity for the copper trade of the region. The influence of the Swansea-based smelters was widely felt throughout the district. In 1838 the Vivians took over the copper works at Taibach, near Aberafan, formerly run by the Governor and Company of Copper Miners in England. A decade later, they opened a colliery nearby at Morfa to supply the works with fuel.[105] Swansea men were also prominent in the management of smelting works throughout the district. Phillip Jones of Swansea was the longest-serving manager for the English Copper Company at Taibach, and after the Vivian takeover, John Henry Vivian had his brother-in-law, Robert Lindsay, installed as manager there in 1838.[106] Swansea also enjoyed the distinction of being the dominant port in the region in the early decades of the nineteenth century. Despite the opening of new docks at Llanelli in 1836 and Aberafan in 1837, which was described by one commentator in the 1840s simply as 'an out port of the port of Swansea',[107] it continued to outstrip its neighbouring ports in the shipping of copper ore and coal for most of the 1830s. It was also keeping its nose in front of the growing ports further east in the Bristol Channel. The 1837 figures for coastal shipments of coal, which were much more significant than foreign shipments in the 1830s, show that Swansea was shipping 491,960 tons, compared with Newport's 480,472 and Cardiff's 169,348.[108] These rival ports had made great advances since the late eighteenth century, but they had yet to overhaul Swansea's early lead.

The town inevitably exerted a pull on the surrounding districts, where the range of shops and services was much more limited. It was to Swansea Grammar School, for example, that Charles William Nevill was sent to begin his education in the 1820s.[109] The town of Llanelli, where the Nevill family's industrial interests were based, and which owed much of its early nineteenth-century growth to them, remained firmly in Swansea's shadow, its population increasing from a little over 2,000 to almost 8,500 in the half-century after 1801.[110] In Neath, the loss of momentum in copper

[105] Morgan, *History of Taibach*, pp. 13–16.
[106] M. Phillips, 'The copper industry in the Port Talbot district', *Transactions of the Aberafan and Margam District Historical Society*, 6 (1933–4), 93–6.
[107] UWSA, YIM, A26, Statement *c.*1845–6.
[108] C. Wilkins, *The South Wales Coal Trade and its Allied Industries from the Earliest Days to the Present Time* (Cardiff, 1888), p. 62.
[109] H. M. Jones, *Llanelli Lives* (Llandybïe, 2000), p. 105.
[110] Williams, 'The economic development of Swansea and of the Swansea district to 1921', *Social and Economic Survey of Swansea and District*, 4 (Cardiff, 1940), p. 166.

smelting to Swansea meant that the population of the town grew only marginally in the first two decades of the nineteenth century.[111] Assessed in the early 1830s as part of the administrative changes brought about by the new Reform Act, Neath was found to have around twenty resident burgesses and a population principally made up of labourers from the various works in the vicinity. It was also noted that 'the proportion of poor houses to good ones is very high'.[112] Further east, Aberafan's urban growth had also been limited. In the early 1830s the parish of Aberafan had 125 houses, of which only 11 had a rateable value of £10 or above, and its offices of portreeve, alderman and sergeant at mace were said to be 'at present filled by mechanics and publicans who can hardly read or write and who do not appear themselves to know the limits of the borough'.[113] The subordinate position of these neighbouring towns relative to Swansea is reinforced by comparing the total rateable values of their property in this period. Table 3.1 shows that, by this measure also, Swansea stood out as an urban centre of importance.

It was Swansea's more mature commercial and retail functions, as well as its industrial growth in the first few decades of the nineteenth century, which set it apart from the wider industrial district as a whole, and marked it out as the dominant urban centre of the region. Official recognition of the range of towns that fell within Swansea's urban orbit was expressed most clearly in 1832 with the passing of the new Reform Act, which redrew the lines of parliamentary representation in Britain. The old parliamentary division of Cardiff Boroughs, to which Swansea had been one of seven contributory boroughs since the Acts of Union, was broken up, and a new Swansea District was created with twice the electorate of the new, modified Cardiff division. The new Swansea District comprised Swansea town, Aberafan, Kenfig, Neath and Loughor.[114] With the exception of Llanelli, which lay beyond the county boundary and remained part of the Carmarthenshire seat, the new parliamentary district closely mirrored the industrial region which had developed over the preceding half-century, and confirmed Swansea's place as its administrative and urban focus.

---

[111] From 2,502 to 2,823. See Williams, *Digest*, Volume 1, p. 63.
[112] WGAS, RISW, GGF, F32, Neath.
[113] Ibid., F28, W. Wylde, 'Notes on Aberavon'.
[114] R. Grant, *The Parliamentary History of Glamorgan, 1542–1976* (Swansea, 1978), pp. 45–6.

Table 3.1 Annual rateable value of property in selected Glamorgan towns, 1826

Town	Rateable value (£)
Merthyr Tydfil	19,837
Cardiff	12,730
Cowbridge	1,844
Neath	6,220
Aberavon	779
Brombil and Margam	2,453
Swansea	20,247
(Total for Glamorgan)	(325,220)

Source: Compiled from NLW, Vivian 2, L23, Abstract of the annual value of all the rateable property in the County of Glamorgan, 10 January 1826 (Cardiff, 1826).

The boundaries of the town itself were also redrawn to take account of the industrial developments that had reshaped it during the first three decades of the nineteenth century. The new parliamentary borough, created in 1832, included the expanding industrial areas to the north and east of the town, along the banks of the river Tawe. St John's, St Thomas and Morriston were included, so that the extent of the town was expanded from just 230 acres to 5,400 acres.[115]

It was not merely within the immediate district that the effects of Swansea's development as an industrial and urban centre were felt. The emergence of the town as a copper-smelting centre and as an important coal port heightened its profile throughout the Bristol Channel and into the West Country, the west Midlands and further afield. The trading connections it developed in this period were extensive. The 1823 *Swansea Guide* boasted that it 'furnishes constant intercourse with London, Bristol, Cornwall and Ireland, and its trade is extended to eighty-two ports in the kingdom'.[116] Connections with the West Country had traditionally been strong. The north Devon coast, separated from Swansea only by a thirty-mile stretch of water, was an importer of Gower limestone long

[115] Jones, 'The city and its villages', pp. 80–1.
[116] *The New Swansea Guide, 1823* (Swansea, 1823), p. 27.

before it began receiving shipments of coal from the area's collieries.[117] Swansea's success as an early coal port owed much to the expansion of copper mining in Cornwall in the second half of the eighteenth century. From only 7,000 tons in the 1740s, output from the Cornish metal mines spiralled to 50,000 by 1800 and 145,000 by the late 1830s. Coal was needed to power the steam equipment increasingly used for exploiting the metal mines to ever increasing depths and for smelting the metal from the ore that was raised. An important two-way trade was thus established between south Wales and Cornwall which underpinned the industrial development of both regions. As the economic historian John Williams has observed, 'The development of the copper industry thus strengthened the long-standing importance of Swansea and Neath whilst these ports naturally also served as the outlets for the back-shipment of coal to the Cornish copper mines.'[118] These strong connections with the south-west reveal the extent to which Swansea, by the end of the eighteenth century, already had in place a well-established trading orbit, separate and distinct from the towns of the Welsh iron belt.

The close links with the West Country fostered increased migration as well as trade. Cornwall and Devon not only furnished Swansea with some of its most successful entrepreneurs; they also provided an important source of labour for the town. From the early 1820s, access to Swansea from the south-west was improved with the launch of twice-weekly sailings of the Glamorgan and Bristol steam packets between Swansea and Ilfracombe. The 1851 census recorded that some 8.2 per cent of adults in the Swansea population had been born in Devon.[119] For them Swansea seemed 'a boom town',[120] offering a wide range of employment prospects and a flourishing urban environment. Other sources of in-migration were detected by the local statistical society, which conducted a survey into the birthplaces of Swansea inhabitants in 1838. It found that, 'To every 100 householders that are natives of Swansea, there are 185.08 natives of other places.'[121] These 'other places' comprised

[117] F. V. Emery, 'Contact between north Devon and south Wales in the 1840s', *Devon and Cornwall Notes and Queries*, 27, no. 8 (1957), p. 198.
[118] Williams, 'The coal industry, 1750–1914', p. 160.
[119] Emery, 'North Devon and south Wales', p. 199.
[120] See comments of Alys Grenfell on her ancestors' migration to Swansea in J. Grenfell Hill (ed.), *Growing up in Wales, 1895–1939* (Llandysul, 1996), p. 104.
[121] *Annual Report of the Council of the RISW, 1838–9* (Swansea, 1839), p. 89.

not only the West Country, but also rural Wales and the west Midlands. Connections with the metal manufacturing town of Birmingham, in particular, grew stronger in the first few decades of the nineteenth century. A number of the Swansea smelters corresponded regularly with Matthew Boulton at his Soho works, although the opportunity of a more enduring link between the Boulton family and the town of Swansea was lost when his niece, Mary Mynd, turned down a proposal of marriage from the architect, William Jernegan.[122]

These patterns suggest that, although the south-west was still an important part of Swansea's trading and migratory networks, industrial growth had begun to redefine the town's relationship with Bristol and the dynamics of the urban hierarchy in that region. The traditional 'metropolis of the West' was no longer the sole focus of Swansea's trading and commercial connections. Neither was it any longer automatically considered to be the most convenient communications route to key English towns. In March 1827, Lewis Weston Dillwyn wrote to John Henry Vivian detailing a range of transport improvement ideas, and put forward the view that 'the present communication with Bristol is quite sufficiently good and that we had better direct our attention to a communication with London through Merthyr and Abergavenny which would be about sixteen miles shorter and avoid the passage'.[123] The Bristol Channel corridor was, by this time, only one part of a wider geographical network in which Swansea was forging connections and spreading its influence.

As the copper trade evolved, these connections extended overseas as the industrial elite of Swansea developed business links with foreign smelters and ore producers. The metalliferous regions of northern Europe supplied many of the skilled managers and specialist workers required for the development of copper-smelting works in Swansea, and it was to the Continent that some of Swansea's leading copper smelters looked for their industrial education. John Henry Vivian and Henry Hussey Vivian both studied mineralogy, geology and metallurgy at the University of Freiburg, which provided them with the broad range of practical and scientific knowledge required to run the Hafod works successfully.[124]

---

[122] T. Lloyd, 'The architects of Regency Swansea', *Gower*, 41 (1990), 58–62.
[123] NLW, Vivian 1, A254, L. W. Dillwyn to J. H. Vivian, 6 March 1827.
[124] L. A. Cook, 'The Vivians of Cornwall', *Minerva*, 4 (1996), 23.

Moreover, they drew on the contacts established while at university in Freiburg to recruit experts such as G. B. Hermann, a German chemist, to work at Hafod. Flemish and Walloon copper workers were employed in the town in the eighteenth century, and Belgians were engaged to ensure the smooth running of the Silesian furnaces introduced for the smelting of zinc.[125] The increasing availability of foreign copper ores in the 1830s and 1840s, particularly from Chile and Cuba, further widened the town's trading and commercial networks. One contemporary estimate put the quantity of foreign ore imported into Swansea in the year from 9 August 1842 to 8 August 1843 at 64,098 tons, a figure equal to the amount of domestic ore being used.[126] As a result of this trade, close links developed between Swansea's smelting houses and overseas ore suppliers. C. P. Grenfell, for example, became chairman and director of a new company formed in 1835 to exploit the Cobre Mines in Cuba.[127] New entrants to the Swansea smelting industry were also attracted from overseas ore-supplying areas, notably Charles Lambert, a Chilean smelter and mine owner who built a new works at Port Tennant, to the east of Swansea, in 1852 and married into a prominent Swansea merchant family.[128]

The experience of industrialization in the Swansea area in the late eighteenth and early nineteenth centuries was thus different, in a number of key respects, from the expansion of the iron belt and the eastern portion of the south Wales coalfield later in the nineteenth century. As one historian has pointed out, change in the Swansea metalliferous region resembled a gradual 'intensification' rather than a 'sudden transformation' of production and output.[129] This gradual, incremental pattern of growth had a less disruptive effect on the established forms of economic and commercial activity in the town, particularly the development of the coastline for sea bathing, than might otherwise have been the case. Far from displacing its other functions as a resort town and a place of polite entertainment for local gentry, industry took its place alongside these other characteristics in the first half of the nineteenth century and was regarded as an additional sign of the town's flourishing wealth and importance. Partly this was a consequence of the

[125] Roberts, 'The smelting of non-ferrous metals', pp. 63–4.
[126] *The Times*, 11 August 1843.
[127] Valenzuela, 'Challenges to the British copper smelting industry', 661.
[128] 'Pyrites', *The Copper Trade. Swansea, 1860–1914* (Edinburgh, n.d.), p. 7.
[129] Reynolds, 'Industrial development', p. 30.

geographical location of the major smelting works on the northern and eastern fringes of the town, leaving the coastal strip and the commercial and residential centre relatively untainted by heavy industry and its accompanying pollutants. As a result, despite successive decades of industrial development, Swansea's bay continued to prove attractive to summer visitors, the local elite continued to find desirable residential dwellings in the town, and contemporary commentators continued to characterize Swansea as a healthy and wholesome place. *Pigot's Provincial Directory* of the early 1820s described it as 'not only pleasant but extremely healthful' and 'much resorted to by company for sea bathing', as well as noting the 'immense mines' and manufactories in its vicinity.[130] Even in the late 1850s, directories were still referring to Swansea as 'the resort of company for sea bathing' and praising its 'picturesque scenery', its 'beautiful bay' and its 'delightful promenades'.[131] Leisure and industry seemed set to coexist.

Although copper smelting was the most important growth sector, placing Swansea on the industrial map and stimulating the development of the local coal industry, it was far from being the only expanding part of the economy. The varied range of small-scale manufactures and trades, commercial and professional occupations and services that developed in the town in the first few decades of the nineteenth century set Swansea apart from neighbouring urban centres as a more diverse and fully developed urban economy. Significantly, contemporaries never applied 'shock city' descriptions to Swansea's experience of urban growth as they sometimes did to the larger industrial cities of England, such as Manchester.[132] Within Wales, Swansea fits less well into the 'frontier' imagery which has been applied to some parts of the industrial south in the throes of economic and demographic expansion.[133] It never attracted comparison with fast-growing American cities as did Cardiff, which was described in the late nineteenth century as the 'Chicago of Wales'.[134] Instead, the sense in Swansea was of a town that had absorbed, rather than been absorbed by, industry.

[130] *Pigot's London Provincial Directory, 1822–23.*
[131] *Slater's Royal National and Commercial Directory and Topography of the Counties of Gloucester, Monmouthshire and North and South Wales* (London, 1858–9), pp. 121–2.
[132] See, for example, S. Marcus, *Engels, Manchester and the Working Class* (London, 2nd edition, 1985).
[133] G. A. Williams, *When was Wales?* (London, 1985), ch. 9, 'The Frontier Years'.
[134] J. Davies, *Cardiff. A Pocket Guide* (Cardiff, 2002), p. 48.

Swansea reaped some important benefits from becoming a major industrial centre in this period. Incoming investors brought substantial capital into the area and forged links with the traditional merchant and gentry elites. The town emerged as the capital of a wider metalliferous district stretching west to Carmarthenshire and east past Aberafan. Moreover, the links it established outside the immediate region, with ore-supplying districts of Cornwall, north Wales and, later, South America, with metal-smelting areas of northern Europe and with metal manufacturers in the Midlands, raised Swansea's profile to a new level and introduced an element of cosmopolitanism into its evolving urban identity. The industrial development of the town helped it to emerge from Bristol's shadow as an important urban centre in its own right and had a direct bearing on the shaping of that urban environment. The success with which the early copper smelters of the district managed to expand their production and establish themselves at the centre of a highly concentrated industry brought a new sense of confidence to the town. It was this sense of economic achievement and industrial importance that provided the platform on which was built a self-confident urban image of Swansea as not only the capital of an industrial region, but also as the metropolis of Wales by the middle of the nineteenth century.

IV
'THE CONTENT AND COMFORT OF THE WORKMEN': THE SWANSEA POPULACE AND SOCIAL RELATIONS

By 1841 Swansea was a town with industry, but not an industrial town. Its population in the census of that year was recorded as 16,787 inhabitants, but a further 9,394 lived in the parish of Llangyfelach to the north.[1] Geographically remote from the commercial and residential core, it was here that much of the industrial development associated with the copper industry took place. Still further up the Tawe valley, parishes like Ystradgynlais and Llan-giwg expanded as the Swansea valley canal stimulated the local coal trade.[2] In the town itself, far greater numbers of people were engaged in the retail, craft and service sectors than in industrial occupations, reflecting the traditional importance of the town as a market centre as well as more recent economic developments such as the growth of summer tourism and the expansion of pottery production. It is possible, then, to view early nineteenth-century Swansea as a place that kept its industry at arm's length. While in the town centre individual initiative and corporation money were being channelled into the development of bathing facilities and recreational venues for fashionable visitors and local gentry, the growth of labouring populations employed in the expanding copper and coal trades was largely confined to the surrounding parishes.

Few of the industrialists whose capital was invested in the copper works and collieries resided in these districts. John Morris moved from Clasemont, the house designed for the family in the 1770s by John Johnson, to Sketty Park, west of the town centre and with views over the bay, in the first decade of the nineteenth century. There he was a neighbour of the Vivians, who chose to distance themselves from their copper works at Hafod, residing instead at Marino, the villa which was later rebuilt as the centre of the Singleton Park estate. On the other hand, the Grenfells lived at Maesteg House in Kilvey, in relatively close proximity to their

---

[1] 1841 Census of Great Britain.
[2] H. Thomas, 'The industrialisation of a Glamorganshire parish', *National Library of Wales Journal*, 19 (1975–6), 194–228.

copper works.[3] But in general it appeared as though there was geographical as well as social distance between employer and worker in nineteenth-century Swansea. Culturally there was distance too. The linguistic and religious differences between the largely English industrialists and their predominantly Welsh-speaking workforces seemed to epitomize the divergent interests of the two groups. Even climatic conditions apparently reinforced the divide. It was over the homes of the labouring population of the northern districts that the copper smoke hung in ever greater quantities as the industrialists sought to increase production. According to Henry de la Beche's 1845 health report, only one day in every three or four was it blown seawards, towards the town and the homes of the industrialists, professionals and retailers. Visitors and observers in the early nineteenth century were quicker to claim what local medical opinion would not: that the growing levels of industrial pollution had a detrimental affect on the health of the working population. Feltham's 1806 guide to watering and sea-bathing places described the 'sickly looks and the dissipated habits of the workmen' in Swansea,[4] and the *Morning Chronicle*'s correspondent in the town in 1849 came to similar conclusions: 'Their countenances are sallow and their persons dessicated, wiry and thin. Breathing an air largely impregnated with arsenic and sulphur, it could scarcely be otherwise.'[5]

Evidence of a working population that experienced all of the problems, but none of the benefits, of Swansea's expansion in the first half of the nineteenth century is thus not difficult to find. Moreover, such a view of the Swansea worker's lot chimes with the predominant image of the Welsh industrial working classes that emerges from social histories of other parts of south Wales. Turbulent workplace relations, social dislocation and frequent industrial protest have been the staple diet of nineteenth-century Welsh industrial history, with Merthyr the undisputed capital of the 'disturbed districts'. Much of the history of the changing economy and society of south Wales in the first half of the nineteenth century has been the history of protest and social unrest. From the Rebecca

[3] P. R. Reynolds, 'Industrial development', in G. Williams (ed.), *Swansea. An Illustrated History* (Swansea, 1990), p. 37.
[4] J. Feltham, *Guide to the Watering and Sea-bathing Places* (London, 1806), p. 396.
[5] J. Ginswick (ed.), *Labour and the Poor in England and Wales*, Volume 3: *South Wales – North Wales* (London, 1983), p. 195.

riots against the tolls levied on the growing numbers of turnpike roads bisecting the Welsh countryside, to the threats and intimidation practised by the Scotch Cattle in the Monmouthshire iron belt, historians have charted the sometimes desperate attempts of workers to retain an element of control over the changing environment around them.[6] The more coordinated activities of the Merthyr rioters who raised the red flag of protest in 1831, and of the Chartists who marched on Newport eight years later,[7] represented the outright rejection, by industrial workers, of the social hierarchies that had grown up in their society and the gulf in wealth and influence between themselves and the commercial and capitalist classes which gained most from the proceeds of industrial development.

Although this well-documented unrest earned south Wales in general a reputation for disturbance and tumult in the 1830s and 1840s, the Swansea region has figured little in this story of Welsh industrial protest. The copper-smelting districts of the Tawe, Neath and Afan valleys had no equivalent of the Scotch Cattle who operated in Monmouthshire's iron towns in the 1820s and '30s. At flashpoints of tension in other towns, such as at Merthyr Tydfil in 1816, Swansea volunteers were dispatched to help quell the disorder.[8] The Rebecca rioters were also kept at bay. Although neighbouring Carmarthenshire was the epicentre of their activities, they never ventured beyond the fringes of Swansea where the town authorities kept a close watch on their movements. Neither did Swansea ever become a centre of Chartism. One historian has calculated that there were no more than twelve Chartists in Swansea and its neighbouring towns at the height of the movement in the late 1830s,[9] although a more recent study estimated Swansea branch membership of the National Charter Association in 1842 at over fifty.[10] The anti-immigrant tensions, particularly directed

---

[6] D. Williams, *The Rebecca Riots: A Study in Agrarian Discontent* (Cardiff, 1955); D. J. V. Jones, 'The Scotch Cattle and their black domain', in idem, *Before Rebecca. Popular Protests in Wales, 1793–1835* (London, 1973), pp. 86–113.

[7] D. J. V. Jones, *The Last Rising: The Newport Chartist Insurrection of 1839* (Cardiff, 1999); G. A. Williams, *Merthyr Rising* (London, 1978).

[8] *The Times*, 22 October 1816.

[9] P. S. Thomas, 'Industrial relations. A short study of the relations between employers and employed in Swansea and neighbourhood from about 1800 to recent times', *Social and Economic Survey of Swansea and District*, pamphlet 3 (Cardiff, 1940), p. 25.

[10] R. Wallace, *Organise! Organise! Organise! A Study of Reform Agitation in Wales, 1840–1886* (Cardiff, 1991), p. 40.

towards the Irish, that regularly punctuated social relations in the iron towns, especially at times of economic strife, were only fleetingly evident in Swansea. Even historians who have adopted a bleak view of the working conditions endured by Swansea's copper workers admit that industrial relations in the town in the first half of the nineteenth century were generally good. Ronald Rees, for example, argues that: 'In spite of defections, occasional confrontations and strikes, relations between copper masters and copper men were generally cordial until the last quarter of the nineteenth century.'[11]

Swansea's experience of social relations does not entirely correspond with the wider picture of tension and disturbance in industrial south Wales and cannot be properly understood in that context. Instead, a rather different question needs to be asked of Swansea from the one which historians of Wales have traditionally posed: why was there so little unrest, rather than so much? In posing this question, the intention is not to reject outright the 'conflict thesis' which has formed such a prominent strand in modern Welsh history.[12] The 1830s and 1840s were undoubtedly turbulent times in south Wales, but the picture was not a uniform one across the region. The failure of tensions to ignite in Swansea as they did elsewhere suggests the need for a more locally adjusted understanding of social relations – one which pays greater heed to the presence of pockets of stability among the wider areas of disturbance.

The nature of the urban and industrial setting of Swansea was crucial in shaping its different experience. Although there was an environmental price to pay for the increase in copper smelting and its effects on the health and habitat of the populace, there is evidence to suggest that industrial and urban growth was less problematic and more manageable in Swansea than was the case elsewhere and that this helped to create a climate in which social relations were more stable. An evenly paced rate of population growth in the first half of the nineteenth century helped Swansea to avoid some of the more severe problems of overcrowding and ill health suffered by other, faster-growing industrial towns. In turn, this rendered the presence of various migrant groups, attracted to

[11] R. Rees, *King Copper. South Wales and the Copper Trade, 1584–1895* (Cardiff, 2000), p. 59.
[12] K. O. Morgan, 'Consensus and conflict in modern Welsh history', in D. W. Howell and K. O. Morgan (eds), *Crime, Protest and Police in Modern British Society. Essays in Memory of D. J. V. Jones* (Cardiff, 1999), pp. 16–41.

Swansea through the town's long-standing role as a trading port, less contentious than was the case in other large port towns where they were closely associated with poor living conditions and disease.[13] In Swansea, the lack of an obvious period of urban crisis in these years helped to create an atmosphere in which the various immigrant groups present by the second quarter of the nineteenth century could enjoy relatively tranquil relations. Moreover the important, but not dominant, position of industry in the local economy was also significant. Although the town was furnished with employer-built housing, schools and religious establishments in the first half of the century, its mature retail sector rendered unnecessary the unpopular 'truck' shops, which were to be found elsewhere in industrial south Wales. In short, a number of key features of Swansea's urban and industrial growth had an important impact on the living conditions and social relations of the populace in the first half of the nineteenth century.

Still only around half the size of Merthyr Tydfil, but some 6,000 or so inhabitants larger than both Cardiff and Newport, Swansea was Wales's second most populous town in 1841, as it had been in 1801. In the intervening decades, Swansea's population growth had generally been less rapid than that of these other Welsh towns, owing to the more measured pace of industrial growth described in chapter III. A rate of increase of between one-fifth and one-quarter in each of the first three decades of the nineteenth century, dipping just below this between 1831 and 1841, was steady but unspectacular. In contrast, Newport, albeit from a much smaller base, more than doubled in size in the first decade of the nineteenth century and sustained a rate of growth almost twice that of Swansea's in each decade up to 1841. Cardiff, boosted by the increased trade brought from the interior by the Glamorganshire Canal from the mid-1790s, grew at a faster rate than Swansea from 1811 onwards. Merthyr Tydfil's already rapid growth as an iron town since the 1780s continued, with the exception of the decade from 1821 to 1831. The significance of population growth rates for shaping social relations has not been extensively explored in a Welsh context, but the work of Patrick Joyce on factory culture in Lancashire and the West Riding is instructive here. He noted a 'link between population

[13] N. Evans, 'Comparing immigrant histories: the Irish and others in modern Wales', in P. O'Leary (ed.), *Irish Migrants in Modern Wales* (Liverpool, 2004), p. 156.

Table 4.1 Population growth in four south Wales towns, 1801–41

Town	1801	% Growth	1811	% Growth	1821	% Growth	1831	% Growth	1841
Cardiff	1,870	23	2,457	30	3,521	43	6,187	38	10,077
Merthyr Tydfil	7,705	30	11,104	36	17,404	12	22,083	36	34,917
Newport	1,135	51	2,346	41	4,000	43	7,062	32	10,492
Swansea	6,099	25	8,196	20	10,255	24	13,694	18	16,787

Source: Population figures from J. Williams, *Digest of Welsh Historical Statistics*, Volume 1 (Cardiff, 1985), pp. 63-4.

stability and the onset of social calm' which produced differing degrees of class harmony in the various towns of Lancashire and the West Riding, in accord with their particular experiences of industrial and demographic growth.[14] More rapid population growth inevitably made the experience of urbanization a more difficult and disruptive one for large sections of the population, not least because it placed a strain on some of their most basic necessities such as housing, water and sanitation.

As Swansea evolved rather than mushroomed into a major industrial centre in the first half of the nineteenth century, local leaders and populace alike had a little more time to adapt to the expansion of urban life than did their counterparts in faster-growing textile and iron towns. The period after municipal reform, in particular, saw a number of changes to basic services such as water, refuse collection and sanitation which brought tangible improvements to living conditions. In 1836 the town council approved the setting up of a company to 'construct water works which shall afford a sufficient supply of pure and wholesome water to the town'.[15] In Welsh terms this was an early development which came about with none of the argument and rancour that accompanied debates over water supply elsewhere.[16] It also brought Swansea into line with developments throughout Britain at a time when almost all towns were entrusting their water requirements to private companies.[17] In the

---

[14] P. Joyce, *Work, Society and Politics. The Culture of the Factory in Later Victorian England* (London, New Brunswick, 1980), p. 103.

[15] WGAS, B/S Corp, B10, Council Minute Book, 1835–1844, 9 June 1836.

[16] J. W. Pritchard, 'Water supply in Welsh towns, 1840–1900: control, conflict and development', *WHR*, 21, no. 1 (2002), 44–47.

[17] J. A. Hassan, 'The growth and impact of the British water industry in the nineteenth century', *Economic History Review*, 38 (1985), 531–47.

same year the town council took advantage of new powers under the Municipal Corporations Act to assume the functions of the paving commission, an event which one historian has described as 'of singular importance to the municipal history of Swansea'.[18] Although it continued to meet as a separate body, the new commission, made up of elected council members, was more accountable than its predecessors whose members had served for life. Other initiatives included, in 1847, the building of a new police station after the council's police committee concluded that 'the present station house is entirely unfit and ill-suited to the purposes for which it is intended'.[19]

These measures clearly brought benefits to the town. An 1849 directory commented on 'the streets being wide, clean, well-paved and lighted by gas',[20] but significant problems remained. G. T. Clark's report on the sanitary state of the town in 1850 made it clear that many of these early nineteenth-century initiatives to improve living conditions had been woefully ineffective. Swansea's paving commissioners noted amongst his findings the conclusion that:

> The mortality of Swansea town as compared with that of its own registration district is high, especially the infantile mortality, nor is there any reason to attribute this to want of food or to distress peculiarly affecting Swansea...That in the opinion of the medical men this mortality is connected with the great deficiency of water supply and want of drainage and of proper paving in the courts and alleys and with a filthy condition of the ... lower classes and the presence of numerous open cess pools.[21]

Clark's findings influenced the critical comments of the *Morning Chronicle*'s correspondent on the sanitary condition of the town. He concluded that: 'To a person accustomed to the compact and even pavements, the well-kept roads, and the sufficiently lighted streets of an equal-sized English town, Swansea appears a neglected and filthy place.'[22] Large sections of the population who lived in areas that lay beyond the immediate scope and concerns of the improvers did not acquire adequate paving, lighting and other services. The

---

[18] T. Ridd, 'The development of municipal government in Swansea in the nineteenth century' (unpublished MA thesis, University of Wales Swansea, 1955), p. 107.
[19] WGAS, B/S Corp, B11, Council Minute Book, 1844–52, 14 June 1844.
[20] *Hunt and Co.'s Directory and Topography for the Cities of Gloucester and Bristol and the towns of Carmarthen, Kidwelly, Laugharne, Llanelly and St Clears* (London, 1849), p. 144.
[21] WGAS, B/S Corp, F2, Paving Commissioners' Minute Book, 1843–1850, 26 November 1849.
[22] Ginswick (ed.), *Labour and the Poor*, p. 176.

sanitary needs of the suburbs of Landore and Morriston, in particular, received scant attention as commissioners charged with responsibility for organizing paving and refuse collection concentrated their meagre resources on improving the more central areas of the town.[23] Likewise, water provision lagged far behind need. Only about 470 out of 3,369 homes were connected with water by 1845, the remainder continuing to have to bring their own supplies from wells or water carts.[24] The consequence of these deficiencies was that Swansea's working classes remained vulnerable to some of the worst hazards of urban life throughout the first half of the nineteenth century. Spates of epidemic disease continued to claim lives, as in 1849 when a new cholera outbreak resulted in 262 deaths.

In reality, there were few towns in Britain in which water supply, sanitation and health were not ongoing problems for the authorities throughout the second quarter of the century. Although Swansea may have had its difficulties in these spheres, other towns, where these problems were exacerbated by more rapid demographic growth, fared much worse. It would be difficult, for example, to perceive anything like the same level of 'urban crisis' in early nineteenth-century Swansea as there was in Glasgow in the same period; there the population rose by 30 per cent in the decade after 1801, and by a further 46 per cent from 1811 to 1821, overwhelming the medieval infrastructure of the town.[25] Similarly, smaller towns like Bradford, where demographic growth in response to industrialization was very rapid – increasing by 43,000 from 1801 to 1841 – found it much more difficult to manage sanitation, health and street conditions.[26] Moreover, alongside other towns in Wales, Swansea compared favourably. Heavier cholera death-tolls in 1849 in Cardiff, where 396 people died, and in Merthyr Tydfil, where there were 1,682 fatalities, suggest that conditions there were distinctly worse.[27] The Swansea populace, then, fared rather better than the inhabitants of faster-growing towns where efforts to provide key facilities were rapidly outpaced by the growth of population.

[23] Ridd, 'Development of municipal government', p. 92.
[24] G. Roberts, 'The municipal development of the borough of Swansea to 1900', *Social and Economic Survey of Swansea and District*, Pamphlet 1 (Cardiff, 1940), p. 38.
[25] T. M. Devine, 'Urban crisis', in idem and G. Jackson (eds), *Glasgow*, Volume 1: *Beginnings to 1830* (Manchester, 1995), pp. 406–7.
[26] T. Koditschek, *Class Formation and Urban Industrial Society. Bradford, 1750–1850* (Cambridge, 1990), pp. 108–12.
[27] G. P. Jones, 'Cholera in Wales', *National Library of Wales Journal*, 10 (1957–8), 293.

As well as expanding at a more manageable rate, Swansea also had a very different worker-employer dynamic compared with other industrial towns in south Wales, and this too had an important bearing on social relations in the early nineteenth century. In particular, the smaller workforces, the high levels of specialist skills required of the workers and the evolutionary pattern of growth in the copper-smelting industry compared with iron manufacture, placed Swansea's industrial workforce on a rather different footing from that of their counterparts in the ferrous sector. The skill level required in the workforce was an especially distinctive feature of the copper-smelting industry. According to the leading historian of the Welsh non-ferrous sector, 'skilled personnel appear to have been about a quarter of the total number employed in the copper establishments in the early and middle decades of the nineteenth century'.[28] This was in contrast to the situation in the iron industry where modest numbers of highly skilled puddlers formed a small minority in a workforce requiring high levels of unskilled labour to operate the furnaces and coke ovens.

The need for skilled workers was a constant preoccupation of employers in the copper industry. The difficulties of recruiting and retaining skilled workers were magnified by the concentration of smelting works in such a small geographical area around Swansea. In the summer, skill shortages could become particularly acute as workers left the hot and uncomfortable conditions of the smelting furnaces to help with the harvest. Charles Nevill of the Llanelli copper works wrote to his partners in 1806 to inform them that: 'From the fineness of the weather, the harvest here is universally begun and in consequence [we] experience such a temporary scarcity of workmen as to be obliged to stop a part of the calciners.'[29] In starting up new smelting works, many of the early nineteenth-century Swansea smelters had to look to mainland Europe for the recruitment of skilled furnacemen, refiners and agents; again in the 1840s, when zinc smelting was introduced into the area using Belgian and Silesian furnaces, employers looked to these countries to recruit their core of skilled hands.[30]

---

[28] R. O. Roberts, 'The smelting of non-ferrous metals', in G. Williams and A. H. John (eds), *GCH*, Volume V: *Industrial Glamorgan* (Cardiff, 1980), p. 62.
[29] NLW, Nevill A, vol 20, C. Nevill to W. Savill and J. Guest, 14 August 1806.
[30] Roberts, 'The smelting of non-ferrous metals', p. 64.

With a much bigger sector of the metal-manufacturing industry located nearby in the iron districts of Glamorgan and Monmouthshire, the copper smelters were acutely aware that their skilled workers might look to the ironworks for employment if conditions of work and pay in the copper works were not to their liking. In 1820, G. N. Grenfell wrote to Josiah John Guest at Dowlais, drawing Guest's attention to:

> a list of workmen who have struck for an increase of wages and have left the smelting works of Messrs Williams, Grenfell and Co, to which house I belong, without due notice, and to request that you will not receive them into your employment as this may be an inducement for them to return to their work here.[31]

Grenfell's last comment provides a telling indication that the copper smelters could not afford the luxury of dismissing or writing off workers who went absent without leave. With little hope of replacing their skills, the best that could be hoped for was that they might fail to find work elsewhere and so return to their posts.

Employers in the copper-smelting trade generally went to great lengths to avoid reaching the position in which Grenfell found himself in 1820. The value they placed on their skilled labour was reflected in workplace relations. Ronald Rees notes that employers in the copper industry were 'more inclined than other owners to yield to demands for higher wages'.[32] Certainly there is a case for seeing relations between workers and key industrial employers as characterized more by harmony than by hostility, at least until the second half of the nineteenth century. One contemporary observer claimed that 'strikes are a very rare occurrence indeed. The son succeeds his father in the works and lives his time out without apprehension of change or discomforts.'[33] From the early eighteenth century, employers became accustomed to offering added incentives as a means of securing the loyalty of their most skilled men. Such incentives often took the form of housing provision. In 1726, Robert Morris found himself struggling to keep the copper works at Landore viable after the bankruptcy of his partner, John Lane. In the face of overtures from a rival smelter, James Griffiths, to his head copper-man, William Bevan, Morris went on the offensive. 'To

[31] GRO, Dowlais Company Letterbooks, D/DG 1820 (1) 471, G. N. Grenfell to J. J. Guest, 29 August 1820.
[32] Rees, *King Copper*, p. 57.
[33] W. R. Lambert, 'Some impressions of Swansea and its copperworks in 1850', S. Williams (ed.), *Glamorgan Historian*, Volume 5 (Cowbridge, 1968), p. 210.

prevent him departing ... [I] was obliged to engage to set about rebuilding his house ... He is certainly a good servant and I will not part with him if it can be helped.'[34]

By the late eighteenth and early nineteenth centuries, Morris's successors in the copper-smelting industry were using the lure of workers' housing on a much grander scale. In about 1750 his descendant, John Morris, built the well-known castellated tenement on the hill above Morriston to accommodate up to forty workers and their families. While the residents of 'Morris Castle' were mainly colliers, Morriston itself was a planned industrial suburb, inhabited by workers from the nearby Forest copper works as well as the local collieries. Laid out on a grid pattern by William Edwards, by 1796 it consisted of 141 houses and over 600 residents.[35] By the time Walter Davies commented on it, for his report on the agriculture and domestic economy of south Wales in 1814, its inhabitants had increased to 1,100, sufficient to warrant the description of 'a neat little town'.[36] This was a very early, and rare, example of planned workers' housing in south Wales, where the initial growth of many of the larger industrial towns like Merthyr Tydfil was more often haphazard and uncoordinated.[37]

Later industrialists continued this tradition of providing workers' housing. The village of Trevivian was the Vivians' version of Morriston, built to house workers in the Hafod copper works. By 1845 they already had some sixty cottages in the vicinity of the works and they continued to use housebuilding as a recruitment tool in the 1850s at times of labour shortage.[38] These houses provided their occupants with a degree of space and comfort at an affordable rent. The *Morning Chronicle*'s correspondent, who commented in detail on Swansea in the course of his letters on south Wales which were printed in the newspaper in 1850, gave a favourable description of the houses in Trevivian:

---

[34] UWSA, Morris 1, 'A history of the copper concern 1717–1730', Historical notes and memoranda by Robert Morris junior, relating to Robert Morris senior's copper smelting works in Swansea (1774), p. 51.

[35] J. M. Davies, 'The Morris family and Swansea', *Gower*, 5 (1952), 28–30.

[36] Quoted in H. Carter, *The Towns of Wales. A Study in Urban Geography* (Cardiff, 1965), p. 300.

[37] J. B. Lowe, *Welsh Industrial Workers' Housing, 1775–1875* (Cardiff, 1977), p. 51.

[38] R. R. Toomey, *Vivian and Sons, 1809–1924. A Study of the Firm in Copper and Related Industries* (London, 1985), pp. 152–3.

They are of two classes – one having two rooms below and two above stairs, for which the rent is 1s. 6d. per week; the other having two good rooms, a parlour, kitchen, and a passage on the ground floor, and three rooms upstairs – one for the parents, another for the sons, a third for the daughters – a most judicious and praiseworthy arrangement. These let for 2s. a week. The kitchen floor is of brick; there is in the fireplace a good range and an oven; the parlour is boarded and the rooms are lofty and sufficiently lighted ... A complete sewerage has lately been added to these most comfortable and convenient dwellings. I saw in the houses I entered the same wealth of furniture, the same love of display, and the same neatness and cleanliness which I spoke of as characterising the workmen's cottages in the ironworks ... Not only at these but at all the copper works, the men are allowed a certain quantity of coal for household use, cost free. This is a great boon to them.[39]

Each house was also equipped with a small patch of garden, a privy, pigsty and coal-hole. At Margam, too, workers were accommodated in employer-built housing. By the 1840s the Vivians owned around 100 worker cottages, built on land leased from C. R. M. Talbot.[40] Housebuilding continued and by the late 1860s there were some 282 Vivian-owned houses occupied by workers in the Morfa colliery and Margam copper works.[41]

The contribution of employers to the housing stock in Swansea in the first half of the nineteenth century has been almost entirely overlooked in local studies of the town's working-class residential sector, which offer an unremittingly grim picture of living conditions,[42] and in broader-based studies of industrial housing in Wales.[43] In fact, the willingness of the town's employers to engage in housebuilding on an extensive scale probably helped to ease the problem of accommodating the growing population of Swansea in the first half of the nineteenth century as well as to foster good relations with the workforce. Local health and sanitary inspectors reported that the town was free of some of the more acute problems of overcrowding and poor housing stock that afflicted other expanding industrial towns. Henry de la Beche, in his report on the

[39] Ginswick (ed.), *Labour and the Poor*, pp. 196–7.
[40] UWSA, YIM, A26 Statement, *c*.1845–6.
[41] R. Morgan, *A History of Taibach to 1872*, trans. A. L. Evans (Port Talbot, 1987), p. 40.
[42] B. Morris, 'Swansea houses: working class houses, 1800–1850', *Gower*, 26 (1975), 53–61; C. J. Bevan, 'The rise and fall of Back Street. A study of workers' dwellings in Swansea, 1803–1879' (unpublished local history dissertation, University of Wales Swansea, 1991). One important exception to this is S. R. Hughes, *Copperopolis. Landscapes of the Early Modern Industrial Period in Swansea* (Aberystwyth, 2000), pp.155–210.
[43] Lowe, *Welsh Industrial Workers' Housing*.

sanitary state of the town in the 1840s, found that the average number of occupants per house changed little over the first four decades of the nineteenth century, from 5.1 to 5.3. His findings were reinforced by the observation of a local doctor who claimed that:

> Another main-spring of health is the occupancy of distinct houses by each family. The practice of cottage building prevails at Swansea to an extent seldom witnessed in the manufacturing districts of England, and as a natural consequence we seldom find more than one family located in each house. We have nothing of what is so common in other crowded districts, tenements, comparatively large, containing three, four or even six different households, to the manifest detriment of the independence, comfort, cleanliness and health of all ... An obvious consequence of this separate occupancy, and one constituting an important sanatory [*sic*] feature, is that our dwellings are not over-crowded.[44]

De la Beche also learned that cellar dwellings, in which living conditions were perhaps most hazardous, were not to be found in Swansea. Dr George Gwyn Bird informed him that: 'I am not aware of there being any cellar residences in this place, nor can I on inquiry learn that any portion of the inhabitants dwell in such places.'[45] Even the Irish quarter of the town, known locally as Greenhill, was devoid of this sort of accommodation. One study of residential patterns in that part of Swansea concluded that it 'was not the housing nadir of the town, being free of back-to-backs and courts and relatively well provided with privies'.[46]

The provision of good-quality employer-built accommodation was by no means unique to Swansea. Elsewhere in industrial south Wales, employers were responsible for constructing some of the better-quality housing available to the working classes. The iron masters were particularly active on this front, employing very large workforces in areas where existing housing provision was limited. In Dowlais, for example, where the workforce numbered around 6,000, the Guests built some 600 cottages in the 1840s.[47] In some other parts of industrial Britain, however, employer-housing was less common. Dundee's rapid expansion as a centre for linen manufacture after 1780 came about largely without the provision of

---

[44] H. de la Beche, *Report on the Sanatory Condition of Swansea* (London, 1845), p.134.
[45] Ibid., p.132.
[46] J. C. M. Rees, 'Evolving patterns of residence in a nineteenth-century city: Swansea, 1851–1871' (unpublished Ph.D. thesis, University of Wales Swansea, 1983), p. 182.
[47] K. Sullivan, '"The biggest room in Merthyr": working-class housing in Dowlais, 1850–1914', *WHR*, 17, no. 2 (1994), 159.

housing by leading manufacturers. There, industrialists employed a predominantly low-waged, female workforce in making a low-cost product and did not face the same difficulties of attracting and retaining skilled workers as did their counterparts in Swansea. Moreover, they recognized that rents on any worker housing provided would have had to be set low in order to be affordable and would thereby have reaped little in the way of profits.[48] In terms of their access to affordable housing of a decent standard, Swansea's industrial workers fared better than some of their counterparts elsewhere in Britain and, in the context of industrial south Wales, they were at least as well provided for as were the more numerous employees in the iron belt.

The same was true of educational provision for Swansea's industrial workers. The copper smelters provided good-quality schooling for their employees' children in purpose-built premises run by trained teachers. Pascoe St Leger Grenfell's schools in Kilvey, established in 1806, were funded by a deduction of 1d. per week from the workers' wages and, along with John Guest's schools at Dowlais, have been described in a recent account of Welsh educational history as the best examples of works' schools in south Wales.[49] The establishment of John Henry Vivian's works' schools at Hafod for boys, girls and infants came rather later, in 1847. The fact that they opened just in time to receive a visit from the inspectors carrying out their investigations into the state of education in Wales was probably more than coincidental. The hasty timing of the schools' opening was not lost on the visiting inspector, who noted that 'The master ... had arrived only the day before my visit, and was wholly engaged in the process of organization. Indeed the carpenters were still at work, and the apparatus not fixed.'[50] Yet, at least one historian of education in industrial Wales has pointed out that Vivian's contribution to local educational provision, and that of his wife Sarah who started a small girls' school in St John's parish in 1825 and a model dame school in the grounds of Singleton Abbey,[51] long

---

[48] E. Gauldie, B. Lenman and C. Lythe, *Dundee and its Textile Industry, 1850–1914* (Dundee, 1969), p. 80.

[49] G. E. Jones and G. W. Roderick, *A History of Education in Wales* (Cardiff, 2003), pp. 60–1.

[50] PP 1847 XXVII, pt. 1, Reports from the Commissioners on the State of Education in Wales, p. 360.

[51] T. Evans, 'Elementary schools in Swansea in the nineteenth century' (unpublished MA thesis, University of Wales Swansea, 2003), pp. 3–4.

pre-dated the 1847 inquiry.[52] Further investment continued thereafter. By the time of the *Morning Chronicle* reporter's visit three years later, Vivian had also appointed a female teacher:

> I here found the governess and a circle of infants kneeling at prayers. It was a touching and beautiful sight. I obtained the following particulars relative to this department of the schools. The governess, a very intelligent and, I should say, efficient teacher, is from the Home and Colonial Training Establishment. Infants from two to seven years of age are here educated. The average attendance is 110 ... The infants are taught reading, spelling, the rudiments of natural history, and singing. To these excellent schools there are attached convenient lavatories and spacious playgrounds, furnished with swings for girls, and gymnastic poles for boys. There are also commodious houses for the masters and mistresses, and gardens attached.[53]

In terms of education and housing, Swansea's copper smelters ensured that their workers were provided with facilities on a par with the best of the iron district. When it came to the question of pay and social status, however, the copper men were widely believed to do better. One historian of the south Wales copper trade has claimed that: 'On the industrial social scale copper workers were a full notch above colliers and iron workers.'[54] Rates of pay varied for the different grades of worker employed in the copper industry. In 1850 it was estimated that the lowest labourer took home about 12*s*. a week, the calciner 15*s*. and other grades of workmen more, up to the foreman refiner who could expect to earn as much as 48*s*. per week.[55] These rates of pay compared favourably with the earnings of men in the iron industry. In Dowlais labourers earned 10*s*. a week, puddlers 20*s*. and rollers 25*s*.[56] They were also comparable with rates of pay in other, non industrial trades such as printing. The average minimum weekly rate for compositors in Cardiff in 1850, for example, was 21*s*.[57]

The same was not true of the few women employed at the copper works, where opportunities for female employment were few and decreasing by the middle decades of the nineteenth century. At Hafod works, the *Morning Chronicle*'s correspondent was told that

---

[52] L. W. Evans, *Education in Industrial Wales, 1700–1900* (Cardiff, 1971), p. 125.
[53] Ginswick (ed.), *Labour and the Poor*, pp. 197–8.
[54] Rees, *King Copper*, p. 58.
[55] Lambert, 'Some impressions of Swansea and its copper works in 1850', p. 210.
[56] Ibid., pp. 36–7.
[57] J. Williams, *Digest of Welsh Historical Statistics*, Volume 1 (Cardiff, 1985), p. 187.

tasks such as slag-trimming, once performed solely by women, were now the work of boys. The few who were employed there carried out duties such as wheeling ore in barrows and loading trams with clay:

> I saw there women, dressed in the linsey-woollen garments of the country, loading and wheeling the ore in barrows to the bottom of an incline, worked by steam, up which the barrows were drawn to the platform of the calcining furnaces. I questioned one of these women. She wore a red and white Welsh plaid woollen gown, gathered up behind, black petticoats, sleeves of blue cotton and a white apron, a neat cap and jaunty Welsh hat. She was thin, sallow and smoke-dried, and at one time she must have been handsome. She said, 'I have been working here these 15 years. We work 9 hours a day but not by night. We earn 9s. a week.' Another of them told me the work agreed pretty well with their health.[58]

Once in employment, copper workers' income was subject to fewer fluctuations caused by disputes or market variations than were the earnings of other industrial workers. In the climate of general industrial depression after the Napoleonic Wars, colliers and iron workers in the Monmouthshire and Glamorgan valleys stopped work as their employers attempted to impose wage reductions against a background of rising food prices.[59] Comparable disturbances failed to take hold in Swansea despite widespread hardship among the labouring poor of the town; indeed, Swansea cavalry were sent to Merthyr Tydfil to help to restore order there.[60] The relative passivity of Swansea workers on this occasion may have been a consequence of the more stable conditions in their industry. The measures adopted by the principal Swansea smelters to regulate the market for copper went some way towards guarding against the kind of fluctuations in price with which manufacturers in the iron industry had to contend. This did not mean that disputes were unknown in the Swansea region or that workers in general were more predisposed than their counterparts in the iron districts to submit to their employers' will. Rather the difference was one of approach. With its longer-established tradition of industrial employment, Swansea had early experience of worker collective action, such as the attempt, in 1806, by employees at Grove's ropeworks in the town to force a wage increase. By the 1830s and 1840s

[58] Ginswick (ed.), *Labour and the Poor*, p.191.
[59] Jones, *Before Rebecca*, pp. 69–85.
[60] Thomas, 'Industrial relations', p. 18.

a number of craft workers' societies were in existence, providing workers with an organizational structure by which to make wage demands and coordinate strike action, the most notable instance of which came in 1853.[61] Like the coalfield district of the north-east of England, with its even longer history of industrial labour, there had developed in the Swansea region a tradition of labour organization, precluding the need for more militant outbursts of the kind that erupted in the iron towns.[62]

In June 1831, while Merthyr Tydfil was in the grip of a workers' uprising, Swansea workers showed a willingness to negotiate with their employers and, as a result, the town remained free of violent confrontations. Lewis Weston Dillwyn recorded in his diary on Tuesday, 7 June that 'Sir John Morris's colliers marched into town and behaved very well', although he later took the precaution of detaining a detachment of the cavalry in town while the colliery districts remained unsettled.[63] Magistrates and deputy lieutenants at Swansea examined what measures might be taken to preserve the peace and wealth of their town, though more through fear that the Merthyr insurgents might make their way towards the coast than in anticipation of a similar uprising in Swansea:

> In the event of the rioters bending their lawless course towards this town (at present in a rather defenceless state) it would strengthen the dependence of the civil authorities if a small ship of war could be obtained ... and also if applied to, to receive on board any treasure that the branch bank of England may be desirous of shipping for security.[64]

The fears of the authorities proved unfounded and the town received no such visitation, but while tensions continued to simmer elsewhere in south Wales, nervous Swansea officials remained poised on a knife-edge. On 22 January 1840, just two months after the Chartist march on Newport, Lewis Weston Dillwyn recorded in his diary on 22 January:

> Sent for to Swansea in the afternoon by Colonel Jones and the Reverend Samuel Davies who were frightened out of their wits by the non-arrival of the

[61] Ibid., pp. 17–18, 29–33.
[62] For further discussion of this comparison, see N. Evans, 'Patterns of protest and regional labour implantation in South Wales and the North-East of England, 1780–1950', *Tijdschrift voor Sociale Geschiedenis* (1992), 212–30.
[63] H. J. Randall and W. Rees (eds), 'Diary of Lewis Weston Dillwyn', *South Wales and Monmouth Record Society*, 5 (Newport, 1963), p. 69.
[64] TNA: PRO HO44/24, Letter from W. Jones, G. Tennant, N. Cameron and L. W. Dillwyn, to the command office of HM ships, Milford, 5 June 1831.

mail coach which ought to have arrived yesterday evening and they supposed that the detention must have arisen from some Chartist outbreak. It seemed obviously more from the violence of the storms.[65]

On this occasion, once again, their heightened level of concern proved unjustified and the mail coach arrived unscathed at 8 o'clock that evening.

Swansea likewise escaped lightly during the period of tension that accompanied the severe economic depression in 1842. Wage reductions and strikes in other industrial districts of south Wales were accompanied by increased Chartist activity and fears of widespread disorder.[66] In Swansea, however, the mayor wrote reassuringly to the Home Office of his readiness to 'resist the entrance into this town of any riotous multitude', stating that, 'I am however pretty confident that no such attempt will be made as we have very few Chartists or other disaffected or discontented people amongst us.'[67] Indeed, Swansea remained trouble-free until, in the summer of 1843, the copper men decided to resist the imposition of a wage reduction in response to a fall in the market price of manufactured copper. Workers from Swansea and Neath joined forces and the ensuing strike attracted extensive coverage in the local and national press. *The Cambrian* reported on the size of the reductions: 'slagmen, formerly earning 30s. a week, are now reduced to 22s. 6d.; metal smelters from 36s. to 26s. 3d. ... ore smelters from 36s. to 27s. 6d.'[68] The newspaper's sympathies lay firmly with the employers:

> The masters endeavour to keep on their hands during bad times, and ask them to consent to a small reduction in their wages ... We say such a workman, in such a state of trade, has no right to complain. It is true that he works hard, but he must not forget that even his diminished wages are a great contrast to those received by any agricultural labourer in the country.[69]

The Times sent a correspondent to the town and his reports were equally critical of the usually highly paid and fairly treated workers:

> It is admitted that they are required to work in very unequal temperatures, and that therefore they ought to receive high wages; yet on the other hand, the

---

[65] G. Gabb (ed.), *Mr Dillwyn's Diary* (Swansea, 1998), Wednesday, 22 January, p. 60.
[66] H. Jordan, 'The 1842 General Strike in south Wales', *Our History*, Pamphlet 75 (n.d.), pp. 1–23.
[67] TNA, PRO HO 45/265, Letter from Richard Aubrey, 22 August 1842.
[68] *The Cambrian*, 5 August 1843.
[69] Ibid., 18 August 1843.

present depressed price of copper has caused so ruinous a loss to the masters, that the workmen might, I think, reasonably consent to the proposed reduction, and would be still receiving 22s. and 23s. per week on the average.[70]

The critical nature of the comment levelled at the striking copper men was no doubt influenced by the recent industrial discontent and by the fact that their protest coincided with an intense bout of anti-tollgate activity by Rebecca rioters in Carmarthenshire and Glamorgan, which was exhaustively reported in the local press in the summer of 1843. In August, at the height of the copper workers' dispute, the Rebeccaites were on the outskirts of Swansea where, in defiance of a strong police and military presence, 'the Tycoch gate – half a mile distant from the town of Swansea, was levelled to the ground unobserved'.[71] After this experience, the authorities in the town became more alert to the threat, and when the Pontarddulais gate was similarly threatened by Rebeccaites in September, a number of leading local men, including Dillwyn's two sons, joined forces with the police and managed to deter them.[72] In such apparently volatile circumstances, the striking copper workers found little sympathy for their cause, and after five weeks of stoppages they had no option but to return to work at the reduced wage rate.[73]

Despite claims by some historians that the 1843 strike heralded the end of paternalism and the beginnings of a polarization between worker and employer in the copper industry,[74] it is difficult to conceive that such trends would have been evident at the time. Public demonstrations of affection for leading employers were common in the copper districts, just as they were in the towns of the iron belt, and workers seemed undeterred from displaying their loyalty by the experience of industrial dispute. Thousands reportedly turned out in September 1845, for example, to celebrate the marriage of Louis Vigurs, whose family had been involved in the running of the Cwmafan copper works for a decade. *The Cambrian* reported that:

> All business was entirely suspended, groups were seen in their holiday attire from an early hour, and happy excitement gave way to the toils of the day.

[70] *The Times*, 11 August 1843.
[71] *The Cambrian*, 5 August 1843.
[72] Gabb (ed.), *Dillwyn's Diary*, Wednesday, 6 September, Thursday, 7 September 1843, p. 62.
[73] *The Cambrian*, 4 September 1843.
[74] Thomas, 'Industrial relations', p. 27.

About 5 o'clock the happy couple arrived at Aberavon where they were loudly cheered by the assembled thousands ... after receiving the hearty congratulations of all parties at Aberavon, they drove up to Cwmavon House. Again the cheers of thousands rent the air.[75]

Similar scenes were witnessed in the same area in 1852, when the English Copper Company returned to take possession of the Cwmafan works after a spell of four years under the control of the Bank of England. Locals celebrated what they saw as a return to more secure employment and the return of a respected and esteemed employer. Mr Morgan, draper of Aberafan, presented an address to the company on behalf of the assembled thousands:

> We, the agents and workmen of your establishment and other inhabitants of this valley, feel bound by every sense of obligation and gratitude to tender our heartfelt congratulations on your taking possession of this your extensive and important property ... We feel that our interests are inseparable from yours, and that in these days of keen competition in our manufactures, it behoves us to give you our best services.[76]

In Swansea itself, the strike of 1843 apparently did little to sour permanently worker–employer relations. In August 1850 workmen from the copper works at Kilvey lined up alongside Mr Grenfell's three sons for a game of cricket. They comprehensively defeated a team led by Starling Benson by an innings and thirty-eight runs and *The Cambrian* observed that 'all parties (winners and losers) seemed to enjoy thoroughly their day's pastime in this manly game'.[77] John Henry Vivian's popularity in the town also seemed remarkably robust. Four years after the 1843 strike *The Times* commented on his position of strength as parliamentary representative for Swansea Boroughs, describing him as 'all powerful, his native business-like habits and great interest rendering him a fitting – perhaps the only fitting representative ... it appears to us absolutely futile to attempt to oust Mr Vivian'.[78] His unopposed return to parliament in successive elections between 1832 and 1852 was formally endorsed by a modest electorate of around 1,500, but the public demonstrations of approval that accompanied his successes indicate that support for him as Swansea's representative at Westminster went much deeper. At the time of his first election in 1832, a celebratory procession

---

[75] *The Cambrian*, 12 September 1845.
[76] Quoted in *The Cambrian*, 14 May 1852.
[77] *The Cambrian*, 23 August 1850.
[78] *The Times*, 10 May 1847.

through the town was organized by local coach-maker and leading reform campaigner, John Francis.[79] *The Cambrian* reported that 'the member was most enthusiastically cheered and no language can adequately express the unanimity and harmony which all seemed anxious to evince'.[80] Thereafter it became traditional, on the occasion of Vivian's unopposed elections to parliament, for him to be carried in triumph through the streets of Swansea on a golden chair, to the delight of cheering crowds.[81] This ritual 'chairing' of the victorious candidate was an important aspect of popular participation in elections, representing what one historian has called a communal 'coming together' after the divisions of the election contest.[82] At Swansea, however, where Vivian's successes went uncontested, there were no real divisions to heal. Rather was the chairing the main opportunity for a demonstration of communal endorsement of his election.

The status which Vivian derived from his position as MP was reinforced by his highly visible public profile in the town, where he held numerous positions on public bodies including the town council and the harbour commission, as well as in charitable institutions. Other copper smelters in the region were similarly prominent in the lives of their localities. Richard Janion Nevill, who ran his family's industrial concerns in Llanelli for forty-eight years, played a similarly prominent role in town life. Credited by one historian as being the man who 'developed the town of Llanelli', he became high sheriff and a county magistrate and was renowned for his attention to his employees' welfare, providing schooling and midwifery services and importing flour for sale at low cost during periods of shortage.[83] In December 1847 he was presented with a piece of silver plate 'from the working men alone, as a testimony of the opinion they entertained of the worthy gentleman in all the relations of life but especially as a master'.[84]

These sorts of demonstrations of loyalty and deference by workers towards their employers were significant but not unusual in

[79] S. Thomas, 'J. Francis, coach-maker', *Minerva*, 2 (1994), 32.
[80] *The Cambrian*, 15 December 1832.
[81] W. W. Price, *Biographical Index of W. W. Price, Aberdare* (Aberystwyth, 1981), vol. 28, p. 15.
[82] F. O'Gorman, 'Campaign rituals and ceremonies: the social meaning of elections in England, 1780–1860', *Past and Present*, 135 (1992), 91.
[83] H. M. Jones, *Llanelli Lives* (Llandybïe, 2000), pp. 100–1.
[84] *The Cambrian*, 10 December 1847.

industrial south Wales, and they should not disguise the fact that there was a substantial cultural gulf separating masters and men. In Wales the gulf was made especially deep by the linguistic divide between the English-speaking, immigrant industrialists and their workforces. Most commentators agree that there was a linguistic distinction in Swansea between the town centre, where knowledge of English was widespread, and the settlements on the northern industrial fringes of the town, including Morriston and Landore, where Welsh was the language of everyday communication.[85] Unfortunately, these phenomena are difficult to map given the paucity of reliable statistical evidence on language patterns in the town in this period. There are no data equivalent, for example, to the statistics collected in the 1840s by G. S. Kenrick, manager of the Varteg ironworks, on the language spoken in Merthyr Tydfil, Blaenafon and Pontypool.[86] The Swansea Statistical Society did not systematically attempt to gather information on language in the course of its surveys of the town between 1837 and 1839. Its analysis of religious accommodation, however, tends to confirm the impression of the town centre as predominantly English speaking, showing that only six of the nineteen places of worship identified conducted their services exclusively in Welsh.[87]

The comments of employers in the copper works and collieries of Swansea and its environs offer further evidence of the linguistic divide between industrial workers and the commercial and business elite. In most of the copper works, collieries and ironworks in industrial south Wales for much of the nineteenth century, Welsh was overwhelmingly the language of the workplace. When asked about the extent to which his workers understood English, Pascoe St Leger Grenfell commented that their knowledge was 'very limited. Many of the workmen speak none at all, and those that do scarcely understand anything beyond the common routine phrases applying to their own peculiar station.'[88] Despite the provision of schooling, all

[85] N. Evans, 'Immigrants and minorities in Wales, 1840–1990: a comparative perspective', *Llafur*, 5, no. 4 (1991), 6; M. Peres Le Roy, 'Decline of the Welsh language in the Swansea region' (unpublished MA thesis, University of Wales Swansea, 1989), pp. 26–7.

[86] D. Jones, *Statistical Evidence Relating to the Welsh Language, 1801–1911* (Cardiff, 1998), pp. 217, 324.

[87] *Annual Report of the Council of the Royal Institution of South Wales, 1838–39* (Swansea, 1839), p. 90.

[88] PP 1847 XXVII pt. 1, Report of the Commissioners on the State of Education in Wales, p. 487.

knowledge of English seemed to evaporate when they entered the workplace. One employer commented that 'they go into the collieries or the ironworks, and in four or five years you would never believe that one of them had ever entered an English school'.[89]

Religious affiliation was another facet of this cultural gulf. Nonconformist denominations gained ground fast in Swansea, especially in the first decade of the nineteenth century and again in the 1820s, and it was in the working-class suburbs such as Morriston, Landore and Llansamlet that most of their adherents were won.[90] Such was the success with which they met the religious needs of Swansea's growing industrial population that the town became known as 'the mecca of Welsh Nonconformity'. It was not until the late 1830s that the established Church made a concerted effort to redress the growing religious imbalance in the town.[91] Prominent employers took a leading role in the provision of new Anglican places of worship, some of which were located in the outlying industrial suburbs. John Llewelyn contributed £2,000 for a new church building in Gorseinon in 1839 and Riversdale William Grenfell was responsible for founding All Saints, Kilvey, in 1842.[92] Other new Anglican establishments dated from the same period, including Trinity Church, Swansea, built in 1843, and St John's, Clydach, consecrated in 1847.[93] The Swansea employers, however, were not insensitive to the different needs of their workers. The Vivians, who contributed conspicuously towards Anglican religious accommodation in the region, including St Paul's Church in Sketty and St Paul's Church, Aberafan, were careful not to offend Nonconformist sensibilities. They and their fellow Swansea smelters never refused Nonconformist chapel sites to workers in the town.[94] Likewise, the Grenfells, although they were churchmen, made their works' schools at Kilvey non-denominational as a concession to their predominantly Nonconformist workforce.[95]

[89] Letter from James Shaw of the Cwmafan works, *The Times*, 10 September 1879.
[90] D. G. Evans, 'The growth and development of organised religion in the Swansea valley, 1820–1890' (unpublished Ph.D. thesis, University of Wales Swansea, 1977), pp. iv–v.
[91] One exception to this was St John's chapel of ease built by John Morris in Morriston in 1802.
[92] E. C. Williams, 'The Nonconformist movement in industrial Swansea, 1780–1914' (unpublished M.Phil. thesis, University of Wales Swansea, 1993), pp. 220–1.
[93] I. G. Jones, 'Denominationalism in Swansea and District: a study of the Ecclesiastical Census of 1851', *Morgannwg*, 12 (1968), 84.
[94] Hughes, *Copperopolis*, p. 290.
[95] Jones and Roderick, *History of Education in Wales*, p. 61.

Elsewhere, employers who were seen as less tolerant were heavily criticized. In Cwmafan, John Biddulph, during his time as proprietor of the works on behalf of the Bank of England, rebuilt St Michael's Church and reportedly clashed with local Nonconformists who accused him of interfering with their religious liberties.[96] These sentiments were not shared, however, by the Roman Catholic population of the neighbourhood, predominantly Irish immigrants, whose priest wrote to Biddulph at the end of his tenure to thank him for:

> the urbanity, kindness and uniform liberality which they have experienced from yourself ... Invariably have I heard them speak of the fairness with which they have been treated both nationally and religiously:– the fact of their being born in a sister Ireland was never an obstacle to their obtaining employment and their religious feelings were never disturbed by any official interference.[97]

If relations between masters and men were generally good, despite the cultural and social divide, this was a consequence not only of the esteem in which the leading industrialists in the copper sector were held, but also of their employment of effective and skilful managers who did much to ensure that workers' needs were met. Robert Lindsay, brother-in-law of John Henry Vivian, looked after the Vivians' affairs at the Margam works when they took over from the English Copper Company in 1838. Trusted and experienced managers like Lindsay were essential to the smooth running of the workplace. Right up to his death in the summer of 1853, the Vivians continued to seek his advice on operational matters,[98] and he also played an important role in maintaining harmonious workplace relations. It was Lindsay who persuaded the family to build an isolation hospital during a cholera epidemic in the town.[99] The managers, far more commonly than the owners of the works, were of Welsh origin. During the English Copper Company's period of ownership of the Margam works, a Swansea man, Phillip Jones, became manager. Described by one contemporary writer as 'the first Welshman to hold a position of importance in the company', he presided over a period of expansion at the works and in the

---

[96] M. Phillips, 'The copper industry in the Port Talbot district', *Transactions of the Aberafan and Margam District Historical Society*, VI (1933), 105.
[97] UWSA, St David's Priory, (37) C.
[98] UWSA, YIM, Vivian Papers, K5. Henry Hussey Vivian to Robert Lindsay, 3 June 1853.
[99] Phillips, 'The copper industry in the Port Talbot district', 97.

provision of housing for workers.[100] He was also responsible for starting a copper works' school at Taibach in 1830.[101] English-born managers, too, occasionally achieved a strong rapport with the copper workers. George Dyer, who was employed at the Cape Copper Works in Briton Ferry and later at Margam, was one example of a manager who learned to speak Welsh for more effective communication with the employees.[102]

Such men played an important part in the maintenance of good relations between the copper smelters and their men in the first half of the nineteenth century; they were also helped, in no small measure, by the absence of the sort of grievances which were a major cause of tension in the ironworks and colliery communities. Of particular significance here was the absence of truck shops. The 'truck' system, of company-owned retail outlets where workers could obtain credit or exchange tokens for goods, was 'originally a human necessity in an isolated district'.[103] By 1830, however, the abuses of the system, which kept workers in thrall to their employers between pay days, were becoming evident and concerted opposition was mounted in Parliament in the form of an anti-truck bill introduced in the Commons by a Staffordshire MP. In some localities, industrialists took the initiative themselves to abandon truck shops once a sustainable retail system had developed to support the local community. In Cwmafan, for example, the company shop was abolished under Mr Mowatt's management in the late 1840s.[104] The Swansea copper industry, however, remained free of the system. *The Times* correspondent who reported on the 1843 strike commented that, 'to the credit of the copper masters they have not adopted the abominable truck system'.[105] The Bank of England branch in the town was also unwilling to conduct business with such establishments, objecting to them on a combination of social and financial grounds:

> The Bank cannot countenance an establishment conducted upon such principles. The purchases made by such shops should be with ready money and for ready money prices, otherwise the workmen, instead of being benefited, must

[100] Morgan, *History of Taibach*, p. 10.
[101] L. A. Cook, 'An examination of the social impact of the Vivians on Swansea, 1809–1894' (unpublished Ph.D. thesis, University of the West of England, 1997), p. 197.
[102] Roberts, 'The smelting of non-ferrous metals', p. 65.
[103] Williams, *Merthyr Rising*, p. 38.
[104] Phillips, 'The copper industry in the Port Talbot district', 104.
[105] *The Times*, 11 August 1843.

be greatly injured. Besides this it is likely to give occasion to a false system of credit and this the Bank must on principle oppose.[106]

In terms of employers' shaping of industrial communities, this was perhaps the most significant way in which the Swansea copper district differed from the other growing industrial areas. The absence of truck shops from all but the outlying colliery districts of the upper Swansea valley meant that the working-class population of the town was spared a major industrial grievance. It was also an important indicator of the extent to which industrial relations could develop differently in different urban environments. The absence of truck in Swansea symbolized the less dominant position of industry in the town. As one historian has plausibly suggested, 'the semi-urban environment of the lower Swansea valley made it unnecessary to provide company shops'.[107] In other words, the fact that the town was a well-developed urban centre prior to the expansion of copper smelting from the early eighteenth century onwards, instead of a previously 'isolated district' with no established retail sector, meant that truck shops were unwarranted. This point appears all the more evident when the economic characteristics of Swansea are compared with those of other Welsh towns.

As the 1841 Census figures for Swansea show (see Figure 4.1), employment in the town itself was far from dominated by industrial occupations.[108] Small-scale craft production and the service sector each accounted for over one-fifth of the employed population resident in the town, outstripping the corresponding proportions for Cardiff and Merthyr. Swansea also had a comparatively large retail sector. In 1841 there were 99 grocers, 63 butchers, 175 tailors, 191 dressmakers and 318 bootmakers and shoemakers to provide for its food and clothing needs. The market place, housed in a 'large and commodious' building, provided ample supplies of foodstuffs, including 'butter, poultry, fish and meat, besides other articles of almost every description' and attracted shoppers from a wide hinterland on the main market days of Wednesday and Saturday.[109]

---

[106] BoEA, C148/7 Swansea 2. Private Letters from London, 1829–34, 5 December 1829.

[107] Hughes, *Copperopolis*, pp. 291–2.

[108] Note that the figures used in the 1841 census occupational abstracts, on which this analysis is based, were for Swansea town, which excluded Morriston where large numbers of employees in industrial occupations lived.

[109] *Pearse's Swansea Directory* (Swansea, 1856), p. 6.

124 'THE CONTENT AND COMFORT OF THE WORKMEN'

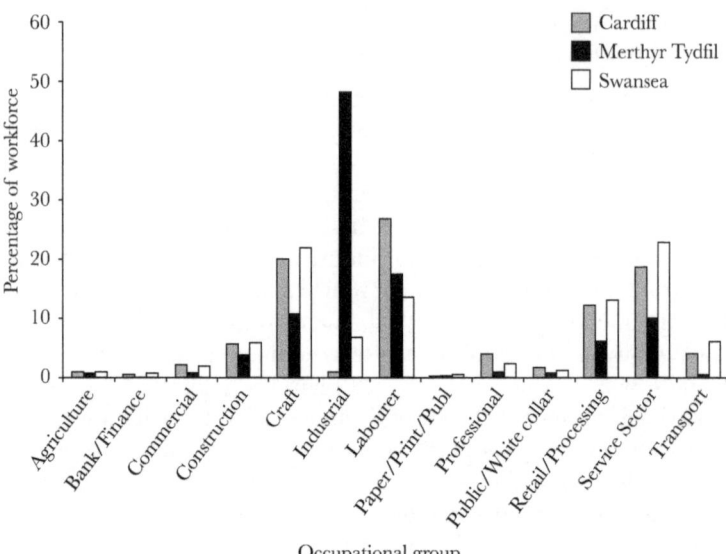

Figure 4.1 Comparison of occupations in Cardiff, Merthyr Tydfil and Swansea, 1841

Opened in 1830, this extensive retail space, measuring 344 feet long and 213 feet wide, had been built by the corporation with the significant assistance of former portreeve, Calvert Richard Jones, who gifted a piece of land on which to site it.[110] Small wonder, then, that truck shops were surplus to requirements in a town where retail provision was so extensive. Swansea's established urban infrastructure cushioned the effects of industrial growth, creating less opportunity – and need – for the employer to dominate all aspects of his workers' lives, and more chance that a balanced set of social relations would develop.

As well as avoiding some of the major social tensions manifested in other south Wales towns in the 1830s and 1840s, Swansea also remained comparatively free of the sorts of anti-immigrant disturbances which periodically surfaced in areas of industrial and demographic growth in Wales and elsewhere in Britain in the middle decades of the nineteenth century. In-migration had played

[110] WGAS, B/S Corp B9, 15 October 1827; N. L. Thomas, *The Story of Swansea's Markets* (Swansea, 1965), pp. 21–3.

a large part in fuelling population growth in Swansea since the middle of the eighteenth century, when industrial and commercial developments in the vicinity began to exert a drawing-in effect.[111] Jewish residents were present in the town by the early decades of the eighteenth century and were numerous enough to require the lease of their own burial ground by 1768.[112] Likewise, the arrival of Irish migrants long pre-dated the famine years and, partly because of this, Swansea was seen as a promising location for the establishment of a new Catholic mission in south Wales as early as 1808.[113] By 1851 some 43 per cent of the 31,461-strong population of Swansea borough had been born elsewhere. Some 1,333 were from Ireland, but most of the incomers were short-distance migrants from neighbouring towns or nearby rural areas. Just over 3,000 were from elsewhere in Glamorgan while 2,581, or 8 per cent, came from Carmarthenshire. Swansea's close connections with the south-west of England also continued to be reflected in migration streams, with a 4 per cent Devonshire-born contingent.[114]

The migrants made their mark on the residential complexion of the town, arranging themselves largely according to place of origin in different housing areas. Migrants from rural Wales, for example, most commonly settled in the industrial districts immediately north of the centre, such as at Morriston, Cwmbwrla and Plasmarl, where they obtained work in the local collieries and smelting works.[115] English migrants were more often found in the central districts of the town, while the greatest concentration of Irish-born residents was located in the Greenhill area, close to the Vivians' Hafod works. Separate patterns of religious practice were also evident in the first half of the nineteenth century. Information gathered by the Swansea Statistical Society in the 1830s on places of worship clearly reflects this. Many Cornish and Devonian migrants attended the Wesleyan Methodist chapel in Goat Street, built in 1789. The Roman Catholic population, mainly Irish migrants, had its own church in Nelson Terrace from at least 1815, and the small Jewish

---

[111] C. R. Anthony, 'Seaport, society and smoke: Swansea as a place of resort and industry, c.1700–1840' (unpublished Ph.D. thesis, University of Leicester, 2002), p. 103.

[112] N. Saunders, *Swansea Hebrew Congregation, 1730–1980* (Swansea, 1980), p. 29.

[113] G. Spencer, *Catholic Life in Swansea. The Centenary of St David's Church, Swansea, 1847–1947* (Swansea, 1947), p. 12.

[114] *1851 Census. Population Tables*, Volume 2 (London, 1854), p. 892.

[115] I. G. Jones, 'The city and its villages', in R. A. Griffiths (ed.), *The City of Swansea. Challenges and Change* (Stroud, 1990), p. 87.

contingent was catered for by a synagogue capable of accommodating up to eighty worshippers, founded in 1818.[116] The distinct identities of these different groups survived well into the twentieth century. One descendant of Cornish migrants recalled of her childhood in Swansea in the 1920s:

> We saw a lot of relatives. And only mixed with other Devonian or Cornish families: those whose grandparents or parents had come over to Swansea in the last century. The Welsh went to their own chapels. We didn't think of ourselves as Welsh at all, although our parents had been born in Wales.[117]

The presence of these migrant groups with their own traditions of religious observance and their distinctive residential patterns was largely trouble-free. In a port town with trading connections throughout Britain, Ireland and mainland Europe, there was a long tradition of contact and communication with 'outsiders'.[118] More important than this, however, was the fact that some of the social and economic problems which caused anti-immigrant tensions to flare up in other towns were less acute in Swansea. Rates of death from epidemic disease, for example, were lower than elsewhere in Wales, and, significantly, the de la Beche report on health in the town in the mid-1840s made no direct link between public health risks and immigrant minorities. This was particularly important in the case of the Irish, who were vilified elsewhere for importing epidemic diseases into Welsh towns. Crucially for Swansea, the burden of dealing with refugees from the Irish famine crisis largely fell elsewhere. By the late 1840s, when the famine exodus was at its height, Swansea had been overtaken by Cardiff and Newport as the major coal ports on the south Wales coast and, as a result, it was these towns which bore the brunt of the arrivals of destitute Irish on the returning coal ships.[119]

In the absence of such pressures, there were few overt signs of anti-Irish hostility in Swansea. One former priest in the district recollected that: 'I found in Greenhill an absence of bigotry

---

[116] WGAS, RISW, Swansea Statistical Survey (SSS) 12, Description of the amount of religious accommodation and instruction in the town of Swansea, 1 January 1839.

[117] Alys Grenfell of Swansea (born 1912), quoted in J. Grenfell-Hill (ed.), *Growing up in Wales, 1895–1939* (Llandysul, 1996), p. 117.

[118] For details, see J. R. Alban, 'The wider world', in Griffiths (ed.), *The City of Swansea*, pp. 114–29.

[119] F. Neal, 'South Wales, the coal trade and the famine refugee crisis', in O'Leary (ed.), *Irish Migrants in Modern Wales*, pp. 9–33.

amongst the Welsh people and a good understanding between them and their Irish neighbours. A Catholic priest was received everywhere with respect, and often with welcome.'[120] The work of one of his predecessors, Fr Charles Kavanagh, did much to underpin these good relations. As well as occupying an important position in the local Irish community, Kavanagh moved in respectable circles in the town, for example as a member of the scientific society, and he won friends and admirers throughout Swansea for his work in tending the sick – Catholic and non-Catholic alike – during the cholera epidemic in 1849.[121] Town leaders cooperated readily with Catholic priests over requests for leases of land on which to construct new church buildings,[122] and in general there seems to have been an acceptance of the Irish as integral members of the community.

Yet their presence in Swansea was not entirely without its tensions. Boisterous behaviour on St Patrick's Day had long been a source of annoyance. One late nineteenth-century commentator recalled that: 'So much has been said and deservedly so in past years, of the scenes of vicious indulgence on the part of the inhabitants of Greenhill which have followed these annual outings in honour of St Patrick, that the orderly inhabitants of the town have been led to view them with something of aversion.'[123] The predominantly Irish area of Greenhill was evidently viewed as a trouble spot by local police. As early as 1839 the town council was directing them to 'be on alert at the ensuing Greenhill fair',[124] and in 1842 the mayor of Swansea felt concerned enough to alert the Home Office to the 'excited state of the poor Irish here, occasioned by the murder of one of their countrymen in this town'.[125] On this occasion no trouble erupted, but more serious anti-Irish disturbances surfaced twice among the workforce at the Rose Copper Works in Swansea, in July 1827 and May 1828. On the latter date, a concerted attempt was made to drive Irish workmen away and Lewis Weston Dillwyn felt compelled to alert the cavalry.[126] But these appear to have been the only occasions when Swansea figured as a venue for the kinds of

---

[120] J. W. Richards, *Reminiscences of the Early Days of the Parish and Church of St Joseph's Greenhill, Swansea* (Swansea, 1919), p. 7.
[121] WGAS, D/D WCR 123, biographical information on Charles Kavanagh.
[122] See, for example, WGAS, B/S Corp, B10, 3 November 1836; 10 May 1839.
[123] *The Cambrian*, 19 March 1875.
[124] WGAS, B/S Corp, B10, 10 May 1839.
[125] TNA, PRO HO 45/265, letter from R. Aubrey, 22 August 1842.
[126] Gabb, *Mr Dillwyn's Diary*, Thursday, 22 May 1828, p. 90.

anti-Irish hostilities experienced with relative frequency elsewhere in industrial Wales between the 1820s and 1880s.[127]

Whatever the precise combination of factors which kept anti-immigrant tensions and other types of disturbances at bay, their relative absence can be seen as indicative of a general sense of economic security and stability among the population of Swansea for whom the benefits of life in a town of growing importance and prosperity may have outweighed the problems. Evidence of the range of people who prospered to some degree as the wealth and status of the town grew can be seen in the development of the Swansea Savings Bank. Established in 1827 with just 73 depositors and a balance of less than £1,000, by 1848 there were almost 2,500 savers on the books, with a total of £81,329 in their accounts. The bank was particularly popular with tradesmen, mechanics and industrial workers. Some 25 per cent of its account holders in 1848 were classed as 'mechanics', such as weavers, tailors and shoemakers. A further 14 per cent were copper men and colliers and, significantly, at least 20 per cent were women, including dressmakers, female servants, nurses, charwomen and widows.[128] The savings of these women together accounted for a little under one-fifth of the total money deposited with the bank. Moreover, it was married, as well as single, working women who were saving money. In 1848 it held accounts for two female friendly societies: the 'wives of colliers' held a balance of £332 and the 'wives of workmen' a balance of £109.[129] By these means, women in Swansea, both married and single, were taking advantage of the opportunities afforded them in the developing town to earn, save and invest their money in their own and their families' future financial security.

As well as the provision of financial facilities for working-class men and women, Swansea developed other institutions in the first half of the nineteenth century, aimed specifically at meeting their needs. In 1826 a Tradesmen's and Mechanics' Institute was founded in the town with the object of instructing working men in 'the principles of the arts they practise and in the various branches of science and useful knowledge'.[130] By 1851 there were some 700

---

[127] P. O'Leary 'Anti-Irish Riots in Wales, 1826–1882', *Llafur* 5, no. 4 (1991), 29.
[128] Ginswick (ed.), *Labour and the Poor*, p. 180.
[129] Ibid., p. 182.
[130] Swansea Central Library, (SCL), SW2126, 'Introductory Discourse on Swansea Tradesman's and Mechanic's Institute by J. H. Moggridge', 7 December 1826.

such institutions in the country with an estimated 120,000 members.[131] Swansea was not one of the earliest towns in Britain to found a mechanics' institute, but it was in the first mass wave, from the mid-1820s onwards, and it had the distinction of being one of the first institutions of its kind in Wales.[132] Located in the town's Goat Street, it organized lectures and operated its own library, thereby giving working-class users an alternative to the town's subscription libraries as an access point to reading material.[133] Records of attendance and of the classes held at the Swansea Mechanics' Institute do not survive, but the experience of other similar institutions in the town was that members wanted to be provided with amusement as well as educational opportunities. The Swansea Literary Improvement Society of Working Men, which was in existence by the 1840s, ran classes in such subjects as arithmetic, elocution and vocal music, but found it necessary:

> to combine amusement with instruction, and believing that the absence of some kind of pleasurable excitement of this kind has tended to alienate members of the working classes from the pursuit of knowledge, have attached classes for the practise of the noble games of drafts and chess. The committee furthermore consider that the restrictive character of the libraries of 'mechanic's institutes' have been a feature fatal to their prosperity... With this impression they have thrown open their library to the admission of works of fiction.[134]

As this society's 'modest intake of membership' illustrated,[135] the facilities and opportunities offered by these working-class institutions were taken up by a relatively small proportion of the town's working population. The alternative outlets for popular leisure activities in the growing town were perhaps too numerous for them to compete effectively. By 1839 there were 144 hotels, inns, public houses and beer-houses serving the growing population. Likewise in

---

[131] S. Shapin and B. Barnes, 'Science, nature and control: interpreting mechanics' institutes', *Social Studies of Science* 7, no. 1 (1977), 33.

[132] G. W. Roderick, 'Educating the worker. The mechanics' institute movement in south Wales', *Transactions of the Honourable Society of Cymmrodorion* (1991), 162. Smaller Welsh towns also followed the trend, including Neath, where a mechanics' institute was established in 1843.

[133] E. Rees and G. Walters, 'Swansea libraries in the nineteenth century', *Journal of the Welsh Bibliographical Society*, X (1966–71), 47.

[134] WGAS, RISW, GGF, F14, Report of the Swansea Literary Society of Working Men, January 1851.

[135] Ibid.

the summer months, Swansea's bathing facilities, though principally aimed at fashionable visitors and local gentry, also proved popular with working-class residents, not only from the town itself but also from elsewhere in industrial south Wales. It was noted in the mid-1840s that

> numbers of persons from the interior, including many of the men engaged in the iron works and Merthyr Tydfil, with their wives and families, come annually to bathe in the sea at Swansea, the sandy coast being favourable for the purpose, and many in the town avail themselves of the opportunities thus afforded.[136]

So popular was the beach by the mid-1820s that supervision of bathing activities was required, and in 1824 the corporation had to direct two constables to make daily visitations during the bathing season to prevent 'indecent exhibitions'.[137]

Although the popular use of recreational areas may have raised occasional concerns among the authorities, it indicated that the town was far more than just a place of work for its working-class inhabitants. It was also where they shopped, ate, drank, conversed, acquired news, met and mingled, learned and found amusement. Through successive decades in the first half of the nineteenth century, Swansea gradually became better equipped to meet all of these needs. Undoubtedly early nineteenth-century urban life was hard, here as elsewhere. George Clark's 1850 report on sanitary conditions, with its graphic descriptions of the continuing problems of disease, refuse and inadequate water and drainage facilities, leaves little doubt that Swansea, along with many other growing urban centres, struggled to find ways to keep its streets and houses healthy and habitable. Yet this was not the whole story. Early nineteenth-century Swansea was an attractive urban centre enjoying increasing status and prosperity on the back of its role as a world centre for non-ferrous smelting. Its central streets at least were well flagged, cleansed and lighted and had a look of urban civility about them. Its smart town-centre shops with their 'showy elevations and stylish plate glass fronts', and its well-supplied covered market made it an attractive retail centre for residents and visitors alike. Its relatively diverse economic sector offered employment opportunities for men and women in a range of occupations, with an opportunity to

---

[136] De la Beche, *Report on the Sanatory Condition of Swansea*, p. 133.
[137] WGAS, B/S Corp, B9, 30 August 1824.

earn good wages and even to save a little from their weekly income. Without the sudden demographic surges experienced in other towns, or the traumatic swings in economic conditions felt in the iron and coal sectors, the growth of industry and population in Swansea felt controlled and manageable. Copper workers especially, their skills highly valued by their employers, enjoyed good workplace relations, and with one of their most respected employers, John Henry Vivian, elected parliamentary member for the town from 1832 onwards, there was a sense that their interests were being represented at the highest level.

There was an underlying sense of security – economic and social – in Swansea in these decades as elites and populace each derived benefits from the growing range of facilities for improved leisure, education, health and hygiene with which the town was furnished. Contemporaries urging striking copper smelters back to work during the dispute of 1843 seemed to know that ultimately their sense of commonality with the employers would outweigh their sense of opposition. This view of a town in a general state of harmony seems a far cry from the 'pressure cooker' images normally applied to social relations in south Wales in this period. Swansea was not typical of the region, but neither was Merthyr Tydfil. The general reality was more complex. Swansea's relative stability throughout the period of Rebecca and the Merthyr and Newport uprisings owed as much to its mature urban identity as it did to its particular brand of steady economic and demographic growth. That this produced a set of social relationships different in character from those in other parts of south Wales, where industrial and population expansion was more rapid, should come as no surprise. Urban society in south Wales was developing many different faces.

V
'CUTTING EACH OTHER'S THROATS BY OUR UNHAPPY DIVISIONS': LOCAL GOVERNMENT IN THE POST-REFORM ERA

If social relations among the Swansea populace were relatively tranquil compared with the situation in other Welsh towns in the 1830s and 1840s, the same cannot be said of local government in the period. Among Swansea's urban leaders a number of serious rifts opened in these years which had a disruptive effect on local government and delayed the implementation of key improvements. Given the relative absence of factionalism among the town's governing elites in earlier periods,[1] this disunity in the decades after municipal reform is perhaps surprising. The election of the first reformed town council in January 1836 was greeted with popular approval and a good deal of optimism in the town. There was, it seemed, every reason to suppose that Swansea's newly elected urban leaders would accomplish much more than their predecessors in the arena of urban improvement. In reality, though, the municipal reforms of 1835 placed added problems before the eighteen newly elected councillors, as well as increasing their powers. The decades immediately following the reform were characterized by dispute and stagnation in a number of key areas of urban administration. The result, at least in some aspects of urban life, was that Swansea's early lead over other Welsh towns was compromised rather than consolidated.

It was not until the passing of the Municipal Corporations Act in 1835 that any attempt was made to introduce a 'system' of local administration to British towns.[2] The Act brought an end to the reign of the old, self-elected bodies with their narrowly defined remit of managing the property of the borough and protecting their own rights and privileges from erosion. In their place the new household franchise gave the towns elected councillors with, potentially, a much wider range of powers. Liberal reformers were

---

[1] See above, chapter 1.
[2] D. Fraser (ed.), *Municipal Reform and the Industrial City* (Leicester, 1982), pp. 2–4.

propelled into local government posts for the first time. Municipal boundaries were also redrawn, in some cases bringing additional large swathes of land and people within the jurisdiction of the new bodies. Far-reaching though these changes appeared, a number of town studies have shown that, in reality, the reforms rarely brought abrupt transformations to the operation of local government.[3] In Bristol, for example, it was noted that 'In certain ways the 1835 Act produced remarkably little change',[4] and in Southampton, the town's historian warns that 'Too much must not be made of the reform of the municipal administration in 1835 as a dividing point.'[5] In practice the reformed town councils could only extend their activities into new areas of local government, such as street improvement, harbour management and policing, where the various commissioners and trustees, previously responsible for these matters, were willing to surrender their powers. As a result, the new councils were often seen as being little different from the old corporations.[6]

There was still great scope for variation in the make-up and performance of different local government institutions up and down the country. While in Glasgow, town council membership attracted the 'wealthiest and worthiest citizens' including many of the city's leading manufacturers,[7] Dundee's equivalent body was tainted with a reputation for financial mismanagement and corruption and, as a result, it was not until the second half of the nineteenth century, and not without some difficulty, that the town's more prominent and successful businessmen and industrialists could be persuaded to stand for election to its ranks.[8] We know very little of how Welsh towns fared during and after this key period of municipal reform. A number of histories of local government were produced in the early decades of the twentieth century, but few shed much light on Wales. The Webbs' monumental nine-volume study

[3] See, for example, J. Prest, *Liberty and Locality. Parliament, Permissive Legislation and Ratepayers' Democracies in the Nineteenth Century* (Oxford, 1990), p. 19.
[4] G. Bush, *Bristol and its Municipal Government, 1820–1851* (Bristol, 1976), p. 210.
[5] A. Temple Patterson, *History of Southampton, 1700–1914*, Volume 1: *An Oligarchy in Decline, 1700–1835* (Southampton, 1966), p. 161.
[6] Prest, *Liberty and Locality*, pp. 18–19.
[7] I. Maver, 'Glasgow's civic government' in H. Fraser and I. Maver (eds), *Glasgow*, Volume 2: *1830–1912* (Manchester, 1996), p. 443.
[8] L. Miskell, 'Civic leadership and the manufacturing elite, *c.*1780–1850', in L. Miskell, C. A. Whatley and B. Harris (eds), *Victorian Dundee. Image and Realities* (East Linton, 2000), pp. 51–69.

of local government institutions over two centuries focused specifically on English towns.[9] F. H. Spencer's *Municipal Origins* used some Welsh examples, but coverage of Wales was by no means comprehensive.[10] In Scotland, by contrast, the fledgling new journal, *Scottish Historical Review*, was devoting generous space to the history of municipal government in the burghs.[11] In Wales there was no comparable work in the same period and, even later, efforts were rather sporadic.

The main contribution on Swansea's nineteenth-century municipal history remains an unpublished MA thesis completed in 1955.[12] Its author, Tom Ridd, concluded that in Swansea, as in other British towns, there were strong elements of continuity alongside the changes brought about by the Municipal Reform Act.[13] Ridd's research provides a useful starting point from which to analyse how the institutions of local government operated in practice, and how their work affected the development of the town. Unlike Cardiff, where the second marquess of Bute exerted a decisive influence in local government, there was no single, dominant figure or overwhelming interest group imposing its will in Swansea in the immediate post-reform period. Instead, a number of individuals drawn from the town's diverse range of economic sectors sought to contribute to the decision-making process in local government. After the years of dominance over town affairs by the duke of Beaufort's steward, municipal leaders in this era tried to do things by consent and consultation. By these means they achieved much in combating the day-to-day problems of urban life, but when it came to bigger projects requiring a longer-term, strategic approach, it proved more difficult to gain consensus and turn goodwill into concerted action. It was in these areas that Swansea was disadvantaged compared with rival Welsh towns where there were fewer disparate interests to unite and a more obvious driving force to carry

[9] S. and B. Webb, *English Local Government from the Revolution to the Municipal Corporations Act* (London, 1906–29).
[10] F. H. Spencer, *Municipal Origins. An Account of Private Bill Legislation relating to Local Government, 1740–1835* (London, 1911).
[11] J. D. Marwick, 'The municipal institutions of Scotland', *Scottish Historical Review*, 1, no. 2 (1904), 123–35; T. Keith, 'Municipal elections in the royal burghs of Scotland, II: from the union to the passing of the Scottish burgh reform bill in 1833', *idem*, 13, no. 51 (1916), 270–8.
[12] T. Ridd, 'The development of municipal government in Swansea in the nineteenth century' (unpublished MA thesis, University of Wales, 1955).
[13] Ibid., p. 106.

things forward. The area of urban development in which these problems were most evident was the harbour. Ultimately, it was delay and disagreement in this sphere that sealed Swansea's fate within the wider Welsh urban hierarchy.

The road to municipal reform in Swansea was a relatively smooth one. The old corporation, though it exhibited many of the hallmarks of a typical, self-elected local government body, was not an object of great loathing in the town. The commissioners on municipal corporations had found much to criticize in its activities, and its report in 1834 held up many of the less scrupulous aspects of its work to public scrutiny. There were irregularities, for instance, in the collection of quayage, market and wharfage tolls. The 'all prevailing' influence of the duke of Beaufort's steward over the appointment of aldermen and portreeves was commented on, as was the inadequate provision of policing in the town.[14] Yet while the Swansea body shared many of the limitations of other, unreformed corporations, it did not exhibit the kind of abuses and corrupt practices of which some other self-elected bodies were guilty. In Coventry, for example, the commissioners found that the corporation was guilty of attempted vote-fixing at election time, when large numbers of new burgesses, who could be relied upon to support the existing order, were sworn in.[15] At Leicester, financial corruption tainted corporation practices as large portions of town lands were sold off to aldermen and councillors at rates well below their market value.[16] The Swansea corporation not only avoided some of these dubious practices, but it also managed, in its last few years at the helm, to make a number of conciliatory moves towards greater inclusiveness in local government. More financial control, for example, was devolved to the burgesses of the town in March 1834 when:

> It was resolved unanimously that future portreeves be respectfully requested to surrender all their claims for dues and tolls to the burgesses in consideration of their receiving a specific sum ... to be voted by the burgesses out of their own funds for the maintenance of the dignity of the office of portreeve.[17]

---

[14] WGAS, SL2 2/3, Report of the Commissioners on Municipal Corporations in England and Wales: Swansea (1834), pp. 387–93.
[15] S. and B. Webb, *English Local Government*, p. 438.
[16] Ibid., pp. 479–80.
[17] WGAS, B/S Corp, B9, 12 March 1834.

Table 5.1 Occupations of Swansea burgesses, 1760–92 and 1835

Occupational category	1760–92		1835	
	No.	%	No.	%
Construction	7	7.8	4	4.7
Craft	17	19	7	7.8
Gentleman	22	24.7	7	7.8
Industrial	0	0	2	2.3
Merchant	6	6.7	7	7.8
Military	0	0	4	4.7
Professional	4	4.5	15	17.8
Public Service	0	0	2	2.3
Retail	6	6.7	4	4.7
Transport	10	11.2	11	13
White Collar	2	2.2	2	2.3
Unknown	14	15.7	19	22.6

Source: J. R. Alban, *Calendar of Swansea's Freemen's Records from 1760* (Swansea, 1982).

A few months later it took the belated step of conferring burgess membership upon John Henry Vivian and Lewis Weston Dillwyn, both of whom were MPs by this time, but who had never formally been granted the freedom of the borough. The honour was finally bestowed upon both men in August 1834 in recognition of their 'great and important services' to the borough and the 'great personal respect' with which they were regarded in the town.[18]

Burgess membership in general had broadened considerably since the days when Gabriel Powell kept appointments to a bare minimum. The number of individuals admitted as burgesses had increased from just 35 in 1789 to 53 in 1802 and to 104 by 1833.[19] As the number of burgesses increased, so their occupational profile broadened to reflect the widening range of economic activity undertaken by the middle classes in Swansea. An illustration of this trend can be seen in Table 5.1. By 1835 the ranks of burgesses in Swansea were swelled by a growing number of professionals, who accounted for almost 18 per cent of the total. The number of 'gentlemen' had diminished considerably while industrialists had

[18] Ibid., 8 August 1834. See also Ridd, 'Development of municipal government', pp. 96–7.
[19] J. R. Alban, *Calendar of Swansea's Freemen's Records from 1760* (Swansea, 1982), p. 3.

just begun to make their appearance. Individuals from the craft and retail sectors continued to feature, as did representatives from the transport and construction trades.

These moves towards greater inclusiveness may have been the last-minute acts of a defunct body, but they did help to pave the way for a relatively painless transition to reformed local government in Swansea. The last recorded meetings of the old corporation in the summer of 1835 made little reference to imminent changes. In June it was resolved 'that an open committee of the aldermen and burgesses be appointed to communicate with the member for our borough during the progress of the municipal corporations bill through both houses of parliament'.[20] After the minutes of the final corporation meeting on 28 September 1835, local antiquarian, George Grant Francis, who became a prominent figure in the public life of the town in the middle decades of the nineteenth century, wrote that 'It appears to be very remarkable that no "why" of any kind was made on the great change which took place in the year 1835 on the Corporation Reform Act taking effect.'[21] It seemed that the old guard had decided to go quietly.

Reports in *The Cambrian* depicted the first election to be held in Swansea under the new Municipal Corporations Act as a smooth transition to the new order. It was noted approvingly that 'There did not appear to be any political party feeling whatever manifested as all persons proposed were Reformers, and not the slightest attempt was made to put forward a Tory candidate.'[22] This was not the case in all towns. In Bristol, for example, the Tories managed to retain a hold on the local council in the first municipal elections in 1836.[23] In Swansea a new eighteen-member town council was elected, with nine members representing each of the town's two new wards, upper and lower. Henry Sockett, commenting on the proceedings, was keen to emphasize the elements of continuity that prevailed with the onset of the new regime. The eighteen newly elected council members, he noted, included four men who had previously served on the old corporation. He also expressed the hope that the new body would continue the work of

[20] WGAS, B/S Corp, B9, 18 June 1835.
[21] Ibid., notes made by Grant Francis at the end of the minute book, n.d.
[22] *Cambrian*, 2 January 1836.
[23] S. Poole, 'To be a Bristolian: civic identity and the social order, 1750–1850', in M. Dresser and P. Ollerenshaw (eds), *The Making of Modern Bristol* (Tiverton, 1996), pp. 85–6.

Table 5.2 Swansea's first town council, 1836

_	Lower Ward	_	_	Upper Ward	_
Name	Votes	Occupation	Name	Votes	Occupation
Lewis Weston Dillwyn*	199	landowner/manufacturer	Thomas Walters	241	Grocer/tea dealer
R. M. Phillips*	179	Military rank: major	J. H. Vivian*	231	Copper smelter
S. Benson*	156	Copper smelter	N. Cameron*	219	Coal proprietor
D. Edwards*	154	Unknown	M. J. Michael	218	Corn and flour merchant
Sir J. Morris	139	Industrialist	M. Williams	215	Gentleman
William Martin	123	Unknown	Samuel Jenkins	211	Ironmonger and bar-iron warehouse
John Davies	122	Unknown	David Sanders	205	Military rank: captain
J. Richardson	119	Shipowner	John Grove	192	Merchant
William Moyse	116	Unknown	Richard Aubrey	168	Merchant

Source: *Cambrian*, 2 January 1836.
* signifies alderman

the old corporation which 'had contributed largely towards the improvement of the public edifices of the town'.[24]

Within the ranks of the new councillors, however, there were signs that a significant shift had taken place in the make-up of local government (see Table 5.2). As chapter 1 illustrated, public life in late eighteenth-century and early nineteenth-century Swansea was dominated by a relatively close-knit group of families. This elite was still largely intact in the 1830s. The merchants, surgeons and gentlemen who dominated Swansea's aldermanic ranks in 1802 were little different from their counterparts in 1830. The 1802 body included surgeons Charles Collins and John Roberts, merchants William Grove and William Jones, and gentlemen Rowland Pritchard and Gabriel Powell.[25] In 1830 Charles Collins was still there and was joined by another surgeon, Thomas Edward Thomas. The Grove family continued to be represented, this time by Thomas and John, both merchants. This pattern of higher status

[24] *The Cambrian*, 2 January 1836.
[25] *Swansea Guide: containing such information as was deemed useful to the traveller through the counties of Glamorgan and Monmouthshire* (Swansea, 1802), p. 19.

occupational groups, such as professional, commercial and independent income earners filling the upper echelons of local government, seems to have been a common feature of public office in the region. In Neath, too, it was typically doctors, solicitors and industrialists who occupied the senior posts of mayor and alderman.[26] The fact that aldermen were appointed for life was a natural obstacle to change and ensured that traditional membership patterns were perpetuated. Despite the industrial growth of Swansea since the late eighteenth century, there was little sign of a new industrialist presence in the ranks of its local government elite. The sole industrialist representative among Swansea's aldermen in 1830 was Sir John Morris of Sketty Park.[27] Swansea's varied middle class of retailers, craftsmen and tradesmen, along with the industrialists, professionals and merchants and other commercial elites, was thus far from fully represented in the higher ranks of local government in the years prior to municipal reform.

In 1836, however, some of the more prominent names in the industrial and commercial life of the town were immediately elected to the new town council, including John Henry Vivian of the Hafod copper-smelting works and Lewis Weston Dillwyn of the Penllergaer estate and the Cambrian Pottery. Another prominent copper smelter, Starling Benson, also took his place on the new body, as did John Richardson, whose family had moved from Northumberland to Swansea in the 1820s and entered the expanding shipping trade in the town. The professions, merchants and gentlemen who had held sway over the old corporation had thus, to some extent, given way to a new intake of commercial and industrial interest groups. This transition had occurred, according to *The Cambrian*, as a result of popular will rather than aggressive campaigning. Several members of the new body, including Lewis Weston Dillwyn and Colonel Nathaniel Cameron, claimed not to have known that they had been nominated until after the candidates for each ward had been announced.[28] The implication was that they were responding to the public will rather than actively seeking their own advancement.

---

[26] G. Eaton, *From Castle to Civic Centre. A History of Local Government in Neath, c.1100–1972* (Neath, 1975), pp. 71–2.
[27] *Mathews's Swansea Directory for the year 1830* (Swansea, 1830), p. 13.
[28] *The Cambrian*, 2 January 1836.

Whatever their precise motives in taking up council posts, Swansea's new representatives were, in the main, men who were already prominent townsmen in their own right. Seven of them had served as improvement commissioners in Swansea since the passing of the Paving Act in 1809.[29] Cameron, Dillwyn and Grove were magistrates, Vivian and Dillwyn were MPs, and Morris, Vivian, Dillwyn, Phillips and Benson were all harbour trustees. These were, in other words, men of established status and reputation in Swansea. It was the same story in other towns, such as Bristol, where 'men were selected ... because they had already attained success ... and came from the "right and respectable" orders of local society'.[30] In Swansea, the presence of two MPs on the council was especially advantageous when it came to representing the town's interests at a national level. John Henry Vivian acted as an effective intermediary between the local council and Parliament throughout negotiations over issues such as postal services and the routing of transport links between south Wales and London.[31] Thus, the presence of Vivian and Dillwyn on the town council in these years reflected more than their reputations locally. These were men who also had standing at Westminster and a range of contacts there which they could use when local petitions required support. They bridged the all-important divide between central and local government and helped the council to present its petitions and requests in the most effective way.

As well as bringing some of the key figures from commercial and industrial life in Swansea onto the town council, the municipal reform also greatly extended the area over which they exercised jurisdiction. St Thomas's and St John's parishes had both been incorporated within Swansea for the purposes of the new parliamentary boundaries drawn up under the 1832 Reform Act.[32] In 1835 these boundaries, with the addition of Morriston, were adopted as the municipal borough, with the result that the authority of the new town council extended over a much larger area and population than ever before. The new municipal borough had some 18,884 inhabitants, of whom just over 5,500 lived outside the 'town and franchise' in outlying villages to the north and east of the town

---

[29] WGAS, D/Dxjk, Acts of Parliament Relating to Swansea, 1791–1822. The original commissioners named in the 1809 act included Lewis Weston Dillwyn, John Davies, John Grove, Samuel Jenkins, Sir John Morris, David Sanders and Michael Williams.
[30] Bush, *Bristol and its Municipal Government*, p. 27.
[31] See, for example, WGAS, B/S Corp, B10, 8 January 1841.
[32] I. G. Jones, 'The city and its villages', in R. A. Griffiths (ed.), *The City of Swansea. Challenges and Change* (Stroud, 1990), p. 82.

centre.[33] For all the claims that municipal reform brought little change, this was a real departure. At one stroke it brought within the new council's jurisdiction areas which were 'almost exclusively occupied by copper works, collieries ... and the houses connected with these establishments' and which had previously been without any kind of local legislation regulating the paving, watching and lighting of their streets.[34]

Perhaps the most significant signal of change, however, was the amalgamation of the paving commission with the new council. In February 1836 the paving commissioners met to 'assign, transfer and set over unto the body corporate of the borough of Swansea, all the powers, rights and authorities vested in us'.[35] The right to take over the functions of the improvement commissions was available to local councils under the Municipal Corporations Act, but in many towns the powers were not immediately utilized, either because commissioners resisted the change or because there was no desire on the part of the council to acquire them.[36] In Swansea there were signs of resistance from some quarters. Henry Sockett, stalwart of the old commission, resigned in 1833 before the handover took place, but other than this there was little minuted comment from either body about the implications of the change. Tom Ridd, nevertheless, concludes that the merger was 'an event of singular importance to the municipal history of Swansea'.[37] The remit of the new council henceforth extended into areas of urban administration well beyond the limited range of its predecessor.

Armed with its new powers and its considerably enlarged jurisdiction, the newly constituted council in Swansea set about its duties with some vigour in 1836. Many of its early resolutions had the feel of a 'new broom' about them. Within six weeks of its election, the council had already carried out a review of the value of town property and rights to salaries, grants and votes of money traditionally enjoyed by town officers. As a result of the latter, annual payments to church vicars were discontinued, as were the £10 yearly

---

[33] PP 1837 XXVIII, Report of the Commissioners Appointed to Report and Advise upon the Boundaries and Wards of certain Boroughs and Corporate Towns.
[34] Ibid.
[35] WGAS, B/S Corp, F1, Paving Commission Minute Book, 1809–43, 3 February 1836.
[36] Prest, *Liberty and Locality*, p.18.
[37] Ridd, 'Development of municipal government', p. 107.

payments to twelve senior burgesses.[38] The council also gave early signs of its intention to tackle some of the bigger problems facing the town. In February a committee was established to look into the question of supplying the town with water, and in June it was resolved to give 'every support and assistance' to Mr William Smith who had been authorized to construct a waterworks in the town.[39] There was also a major advance in the planning of harbour improvements with the passing of a new Harbour Act in July. The new legislation was greeted with great excitement and optimism in the town. The bells of St Mary's church were rung to celebrate the gaining of the royal assent and Nathaniel Cameron, the mayor, who had worked to see the measure though its final stages, was formally thanked by the council for his efforts.[40]

Other ambitious projects dating from this time included the construction of the new guildhall. Although it began life as a modest proposal for alterations and additions to the existing town hall, a council committee, including Vivian, Charles Henry Smith and John Grove, explored the option of building more extensive accommodation from scratch.[41] The result was an elegant classical structure designed by the London architect, Thomas Taylor, and located among Jernegan's Regency terraces in Somerset Place. The council was forced to make repeated pleas to the Treasury for powers to borrow additional funds in order to see the project to completion,[42] but the result was a great success. The town guide published in 1851 described the new building in minute detail and declared it to be 'a magnificent building, and the greatest ornament the town possesses'.[43]

Despite the initial enthusiasm of the new council and its early successes in obtaining a new Harbour Act and initiating the building of the guildhall, Swansea's new leaders soon found the scope of their work severely curtailed by lack of money. A lengthy memorial to the Treasury in 1841 outlined the stark fact that, with an income of just £1,700 from its property and recent expenditure of £20,000 on improvements such as the market, guildhall and

[38] WGAS, B/S Corp, B10, 29 January 1836.
[39] Ibid., 15 February, 9 June 1836.
[40] W. H. Jones, *History of the Port of Swansea* (Carmarthen, 1922), p. 169; WGAS, B/S Corp, B10, 9 November 1836.
[41] WGAS, B/S Corp, B11, 13 September 1844.
[42] Ibid., 9 June 1848, 13 July 1849.
[43] J. Lewis, *The Swansea Guide, 1851* (Swansea, 1851), p. 24.

public rooms, the town was left with a debt of £24,095.[44] The mayor and his council requested the permission of the Treasury Lords to sell off parts of the town lands as a means of raising money for further improvements, but their plea was rejected. Advised instead to seek a reduction of the interest rate on its current debt, the new council found itself working within the same financial constraints as the old corporation and thereby prevented from taking a radically different approach to urban governance. Its zeal to serve the interests of the town and its growing commercial and industrial sector had to be expressed in more modest ways, through declarations of goodwill rather than through practical initiatives of its own. In 1840, for example, it resolved to support the efforts of the inhabitants to improve the Castle Square area,[45] and in 1842 it was resolved to oppose the routing of the London to Swansea mail through Bristol rather than Gloucester, which was considered the more 'natural communication between south Wales and the metropolis'.[46]

Financial constraints were just one of the difficulties that the new council encountered in its quest to put its greater powers into effect. Another, arguably more intractable, problem was how to unite a town of contrasting areas and diverse interest groups behind a single vision of urban development. As several historians have noted, Swansea was topographically diverse and consisted of a collection of disparate settlements and villages which were far from being uniform in character or coherent.[47] The commissioners responsible for delimiting the new municipal wards in 1835 took pains to try to bridge the differences between the commercial core and the outlying industrial areas by creating an upper ward that united the copper works, collieries and their attendant houses with 'a considerable proportion of the town'.[48] But while it was possible to draw the different geographical areas together for administrative purposes, it was less easy to unite the different interest groups within them to pursue the same goals and objectives. The tradesmen,

[44] WGAS, B/S Corp, B10, 8 January 1841.
[45] Ibid., 4 September 1840.
[46] Ibid., 11 March 1842.
[47] See, for example, N. L. Thomas, *The Story of Swansea's Districts and Villages*, Volumes 1, parts 1–3 (Swansea, 1964), and Volume 2, parts 4–8 (Swansea, 1969); Jones, 'The city and its villages', pp. 79–96.
[48] PP 1837 XXVIII, Report of the Commissioners Appointed to Report and Advise upon the Boundaries and Wards of certain Boroughs and Corporate Towns.

copper smelters, coal proprietors and shipping interests all had different concerns and priorities which they wished to see reflected in the urban development of the town, and each body was sufficiently organized to ensure that its views were represented. For its part, the town council was faced with the problem of how to reconcile the wishes of these different parties in its plans for improvement. The scale of the problem was most clearly exposed over the issue of harbour development.

Like many British towns in the early decades of the nineteenth century, Swansea possessed a rather primitive harbour which was coming under mounting pressure from increased volumes of commercial traffic and the growing size of vessels plying between ports. The total number of vessels entering the harbour each year had increased from 2,295 at the end of the Napoleonic Wars to 3,699 by 1835. The tonnage of vessels had risen by an even larger margin: from 153,943 to 237,418 during the same period.[49] The increase in use had not been accompanied by any significant improvement in facilities at Swansea. Despite the passing of the 1791 Harbour Act and subsequent Acts in 1796 and 1804, which had vested the management of the harbour in a body of trustees and provided for the building of piers and a lighthouse, the town still had a basic tidal harbour where vessels were liable to experience considerable delays at low tide.[50] The commissioners who visited to redraw the municipal boundaries observed that 'vessels of considerable burden can enter at high water, although at the ebb of the tide it is left nearly dry'.[51]

By the early 1830s, all interest groups in the town were united in the belief that something needed to be done about the harbour. The increased industrialization of the south Wales valleys, especially the dramatic growth in output of pig iron, from 34,000 tons in 1796 to over 277,600 by 1830,[52] and of coal, about 650,000 tons of which were being shipped from south Wales ports by 1840,[53] meant that there was much at stake for the town that could provide the best

[49] Jones, *History of the Port of Swansea*, p. 363.
[50] Ibid., pp. 132–5.
[51] PP 1837 XXVIII, Report of the Commissioners Appointed to Report and Advise upon the Boundaries and Wards of certain Boroughs and Corporate Towns.
[52] T. Boyns, 'The iron, steel and tinplate industries', in G. Williams and A. H. John (eds), *GCH, Volume V: Industrial Glamorgan* (Cardiff, 1980), p. 149.
[53] J. Williams, 'The coal industry, 1750–1914', in Williams and John (eds), *GCH*, Volume V, p. 165.

harbour facilities for shipment of this mineral wealth. Delays at one harbour might easily induce industrialists to divert their goods to a neighbouring one, with a consequent loss of revenue for the former town. This situation was not unique to south Wales. Elsewhere in Britain, early nineteenth-century plans for harbour improvements gave a competitive edge to patterns of urbanization with, for example, the textile ports of north-east Scotland keeping a close eye on one another's harbour improvement schemes.[54] The close geographical proximity of the port towns on the Welsh side of the Bristol Channel brought the same sense of urgency to harbour-building programmes, and unleashed a flurry of inter-town rivalry which had a major impact on patterns of urbanization in the region.

At the beginning of the 1830s, Swansea was confident that it could see off any opposition. In a plan for harbour improvements put forward in 1831, it was claimed that the town, 'from its geographical position and from the immense mineral wealth of the surrounding district, is well calculated to form an entrepôt for South Wales'.[55] Its author, the engineer Henry Habberley Price of the Rhyddings in Swansea, was the son of Peter Price of Neath Abbey ironworks. Deeply interested in harbour development, he had worked on schemes at Waterford, Cork and Llanelli, and had wider experience of transport networks, having worked for Telford on the Bristol to Milford mail route and, in 1829, on a scheme for straightening the river Tees.[56] In Price's view, a harbour was only as good as its associated transport links. It was important, he pointed out, to promote 'every practicable improvement in communications with the interior, without which no great port can follow up prosperously a foreign commerce'. In Swansea's case this could only mean one thing: a direct rail link with Merthyr Tydfil. Price's plan for Swansea harbour, published in 1831, stated that:

> It is evident that Swansea, which lies almost as near as Cardiff to the great manufacturing district of Merthyr Tydfil, may be united with Merthyr by a railroad taken up the Neath valley as far as Cwm Neath, and thence ascending

---

[54] B. Lenman, *From Esk to Tweed. Harbours, Ships and Men of the East Coast of Scotland* (Glasgow, 1975), pp. 58–75.
[55] WGAS, D/DZ207, Volume of Reports and Correspondence regarding the Harbour, 1794–1847. Plan of H. H. Price, 1 July 1831.
[56] L. Ince, *Neath Abbey and the Industrial Revolution* (Stroud, 2001), pp. 74–5.

gradually the hills and descending into Merthyr by inclined planes, by means of which the produce of the mines of Merthyr might be brought to Swansea at an expense nearly 30 per cent lower than it now costs to take them to Cardiff.[57]

The ambition enshrined in Price's plan was shared by Swansea's harbour trustees, who consulted widely among the foremost harbour engineers of the day to find the best proposal for improving port facilities in the town. Among the plans put forward was one by Thomas Telford who proposed the construction of a 'floating dock' and a new 'cut' in the river Tawe which would provide a navigable passage upriver for larger vessels.

Rather than simply adopt a plan of their own choosing, however, the trustees decided at this point to canvass opinion from all the major interest groups in the town which might be affected by the improvements.[58] It was this process of consultation that revealed how difficult it would be to reconcile the different groups. A meeting of the 'shipping interest', chaired by John Grove, a corporation member and prominent townsman, resolved unanimously that Telford's plan would 'tend to give greater facilities and a new direction to trade'.[59] The following day, the copper companies met, under the chairmanship of John Henry Vivian, and likewise favoured Telford's plan. In addition, they agreed to 'contribute 1d. per ton on all copper ores imported and on copper exported by them' towards the cost of construction.[60] A day later, Vivian was again in the chair at a meeting of the town and neighbourhood on the same subject. Here again it was resolved that 'a floating harbour will extend the trade, enrich the town and neighbourhood and give a new direction and ability to its commerce'.[61] The Swansea Commercial Society, representing the various trades of the town, was also in favour of the project. Under the leadership of the coach-maker, John Francis, it had memorialized the harbour trust as early as 1826, expressing its support for a new harbour, 'as such a measure would, in the opinion of your memorialists ... tend greatly to promote the prosperity and trade of this town'.[62] They also favoured

[57] WGAS, D/DZ207, plan of H. H. Price, 1 July 1831.
[58] TNA, PRO RAIL 877/4, Swansea Harbour Minutes, 29 January 1831.
[59] WGAS, D/DZ207, p. 41.
[60] Ibid., p. 45.
[61] Ibid., p. 46.
[62] WGAS, RISW, GGF, B7, Swansea Commercial Society minutes, 3 March 1826.

the uniform imposition of a tax on all items shipped to and from the port as the best means of paying for the work.[63]

This unanimity, however, was marred by the representatives of the coal trade who met on 3 March 1831 to discuss the plans for a new dock. Principal among them were coal merchant J. D. Berrington of Brynmorgan colliery, and George Tennant, a Neath landowner and coal proprietor, who had single-handedly financed the construction of a canal, completed in 1824, to enable coalowners of the Neath district to communicate more readily with Swansea.[64] Although he endorsed the principle of harbour improvement, Tennant, who had done so much to promote his own plans for improved transport facilities, was not willing to fall in line behind the ideas of the harbour trustees. Neither, crucially, were he and his fellow representatives from the coal trade willing to consent to the imposition of extra taxes to fund the work. They were convinced that harbour dues were 'ill adapted to coals (as a very small increase of charges may wholly shift the course of trade)' and resolved to resist strongly any additional harbour dues on small vessels.[65] The floating dock, as they saw it, would be constructed for the benefit of the importers of ore and, consequently, they should foot the bill. The division between the copper and coal trades could hardly have been more stark. At a further meeting of coal proprietors in January 1832, it was agreed:

> That in the opinion of this meeting that the tax already paid of 4d. per ton on vessels entering this port is very high, as contrasted with the charges which fall on similar vessels in other ports in the channel, and that even the contemplated float is not an improvement sufficient to justify a greater addition than 1d. per ton ... and that no supplementary tax be made.[66]

There was an element of complacency underpinning the attitude of the coalowners. The anthracite coal producers of the Swansea, Neath and Llanelli region were in a particularly buoyant mood in the 1830s and early 1840s, when their product seemed set to become the principal steam-raising coal and, thanks to successful experiments at Yniscedwyn ironworks, to break into the market for

[63] WGAS, RISW, GGF, B7, April 1831.
[64] K. Tucker, *A Scratch in Glamorganshire* (Cilfrew, 1998), pp. 42–66; Jones, *History of the Port of Swansea*, pp. 147–56.
[65] WGAS, D/DZ207, p. 43.
[66] SCL, S87.1, Reports on Swansea Harbour, Meeting of the Coal Trade, 9 January 1832.

iron smelting.[67] At that time they also dominated the London market and saw no reason to anticipate that their position might be weakened by competition from elsewhere. The improvement of port facilities was regarded as unnecessary for the furthering of their predominantly coastal trade:

> Such is the reputation of Welsh coal amongst the public brewers and other great coal consumers in London, and such its acknowledged superiority in steam engines and for various manufacturing purposes ... that nothing more is wanting than a cheap float for the security of large ships in order to place Swansea in full, immediate and successful competition with Newcastle, Sunderland and the best northern ports.[68]

The harbour trustees were dismayed that their consultation process had produced such a division of opinion and they 'viewed with considerable regret the collision of the various interests'.[69] Such was the intransigence of the coal proprietors that it forced the shelving of plans for a new dock. At a meeting of the Swansea Harbour Trustees in February 1832, it was resolved 'that the coal interest, not having come to any definitive arrangement respecting the proportion of tolls to be paid by them, that it is expedient to postpone the bringing in a Bill for the improvement of the harbour until the next session of parliament.'[70] As it transpired, this delay was critical since, by the mid-1830s, a new set of obstacles had appeared, including disputes over land and the exact site for the new dock, thus closing the window of opportunity which had briefly opened and delaying progress for a further decade.[71]

The consequences of these divisions and delays over the harbour were manifold. Frustration mounted among the urban elites who had worked so hard to try to promote the improvement. John Henry Vivian's exasperation spilled over in a letter to the harbour trustees in 1839 in which he lamented that 'a float has been so long under discussion that it has become a subject on which it is impossible to enter without a considerable degree of reluctance ... I almost despair of offering to your notice any remarks.'[72] Along with the

[67] Williams, 'The coal industry, 1750–1914', p. 179.
[68] WGAS, D/DZ207, public meeting of the coal owners of Swansea and neighbourhood, 3 March 1831.
[69] TNA, PRO RAIL 877/4, Swansea Harbour Minutes, 27 January 1832.
[70] WGAS, D/DZ207, meeting of the harbour trustees, 6 February 1832.
[71] For further details of subsequent problems, see Jones, *History of the Port of Swansea*, pp. 169–83.
[72] WGAS, D/DZ207, letter dated 1839.

sense of frustration was the mounting fear that delays at Swansea would result in a loss of status for the town. Vivian observed that 'all the other ports in the channel are being improved and ... we must, to hold our position, improve also'.[73] This was not just paranoia. Along the coast at Cardiff and Newport, ambitious harbour improvement projects were already underway. At Newport, work on a new dock had begun in 1835, almost immediately after the passage of a Harbour Improvement Act in July of that year.[74] In Cardiff, meanwhile, the new Bute West Dock was nearing completion. At the opening ceremony in October 1839, the boost that the new dock had given to Cardiff's urban ambitions was evident for all to see. J. J. Guest MP proclaimed that, 'Bristol has been called the Queen of South Wales, and boasts of her millions, but we shall take some of her trade from her.'[75] A year later, another observer was able to claim that Cardiff was gaining prominence over its rivals as the main shipping outlet for industrial south Wales. 'The Bute Dock', he wrote, 'is setting a proud example as a principal outlet for the mining districts.'[76] The town which Swansea had eclipsed as it rose to prominence as an industrial, commercial, financial and administrative centre during the previous fifty years had suddenly stolen a march in the race for modern harbour accommodation and, with a rail link to Merthyr completed only a few years later, it was at Cardiff rather than at Swansea that Henry Price's vision of an entrepôt for the mineral riches of the south Wales valleys was realized.

Cardiff's experience of undertaking successfully this first major phase of dock building could hardly have been further removed from that of Swansea. While Vivian and his contemporaries struggled to unite the various interest groups in the town behind an acceptable plan for the construction and funding of the harbour, in Cardiff such wrangling over costs and benefits were largely bypassed by the marquess of Bute, who planned, executed and bankrolled the entire enterprise to the tune of over £300,000. At the celebrations in the town to mark the opening of the West Bute Dock, it was acknowledged that such a one-man undertaking was

[73] Ibid.
[74] D. Williams, *John Frost. A Study in Chartism* (Cardiff, 1939), pp. 77–8.
[75] *The Times*, 12 October 1839.
[76] W. H. Smyth, *Nautical Observations on the Port and Maritime Vicinity of Cardiff* (Cardiff, 1840), p. 20.

unusual. 'Neither in this country nor in Europe', remarked one speaker, 'do we ever hear of a single individual undertaking such vast works.'[77] Bute's efforts in Cardiff were compared with the third duke of Bridgwater's canal-building feats in the north-west of England eighty years earlier.[78] Swansea could only look on in envy. 'Be such a Lord Bute in this place,' lamented one commentator in 1846, as the protracted arguments continued.[79]

It was not merely Swansea's standing in relation to rival south Wales ports that was affected by the delays. The issue also cast a long shadow over local government in the town by the early 1840s. It was largely because of lack of progress with harbour improvements that the heady optimism which had greeted the election of the first reformed council in 1836 quickly ebbed away, to be replaced by cynicism and critical comment. An anonymous 'Carol for Christmas 1839' gave vent to some of these sentiments in its first verse, which lamented of 'Abertawe' that:

> Her rulers, so full of mistrust
> Can never complete what's before 'em
> They do nothing but kick up a dust
> Like a Council of great Asinorum.[80]

By this stage, some prominent townsmen were willing to voice their criticisms of the way in which the harbour plans had been handled and, as a result, the divisions in the town were laid bare. William Henry Smith, manager of the Swansea waterworks company, led the charge. In a series of letters to *The Cambrian*, and private correspondence with the harbour trustees in the late 1830s and early 1840s, he gave vent to the mounting frustrations within the town over the lack of progress with the harbour. Smith's complaints are worth examining in some detail for what they reveal about the divisions between different interest groups. In his view, it was the boundary extension of 1836 and the attempt to incorporate large, outlying industrial areas into the administrative framework of the town which had laid the foundations for the conflict and disunity so manifestly demonstrated in the harbour negotiations.

---

[77] *The Times*, 12 October 1839.
[78] H. Malet, *The Canal Duke* (London, 1961).
[79] *The Cambrian*, 30 October 1846.
[80] WGAS, S/L WM3 36, 'A Carol for Christmas 1839. A new song to a very old tune.'

Smith believed strongly that the industrialists with property along the banks of the river, to the north of the town, enjoyed a disproportionate influence over the affairs of the harbour. The various Harbour Acts since 1791 had granted their representatives membership of the Swansea harbour trust as 'proprietory trustees'. As a consequence, men like copper smelter Pascoe Grenfell, coal proprietor John Smith, and other men 'engaged in copper works, potteries, salt works, or any other works and manufactories whatsoever' held positions on the harbour trust.[81] Crucially, the 1836 Harbour Act had increased the number of these proprietory trustees to twenty-four, and at the same time the extension of Swansea's borough boundaries had granted many of them rights as burgesses with influence over the election of the town council representatives on the harbour body. To Smith, this was wholly inequitable. The town-based ratepayers 'can no longer be said to have their interests fairly represented in the harbour trust'.[82] Not only did the industrialists have too strong a voice but, according to William Smith, it was their private interests and jealousies that were 'the chief, if not the only cause, that none of the improvements authorized by the last act have been executed'.[83]

There was evidently a much larger issue at stake here than simply the fate of the new dock. Smith's letters suggest that the administrative and boundary changes of the 1830s, designed to take account of Swansea's industrial and demographic growth during the late eighteenth and early nineteenth centuries, had accentuated divisions in the town and made it more difficult to achieve the kind of support required to secure major improvement measures. In Smith's view, there was only one possible solution to the problem: 'It is high time that the inhabitants of the town should exert themselves and get rid if possible of the dreadful incubus, the connexion with Morriston, oppressing them in the harbour trust and trespassing upon all their borough interests.'[84]

Smith had reason to be embittered. A defeated candidate in the municipal elections in November 1839, he was forced to argue his case from outside the council and the harbour trust. In doing so he utilized the local press to great effect. His missives to *The Cambrian*

---

[81] *A Collection of Acts of Parliament relating to Swansea Harbour, 1791–1901* (Swansea, 1902), p. 3.
[82] *The Cambrian*, 5 October 1839.
[83] WGAS, D/DZ207, letter dated 2 December 1842.
[84] *The Cambrian*, 9 November 1839.

ensured that the conflicts and frustrations of the period were laid bare. In 1843 he even took the step of establishing a second newspaper in Swansea. The *Swansea Journal* pledged itself to provide 'leading articles upon subjects of local importance' and signalled its intent in the very first issue with a page of comment on the doings of the harbour trustees.[85] For some disinterested onlookers, it was all good entertainment. J. W. G. Gutch, former surgeon to the Swansea Infirmary, wrote to his friend, George Grant Francis, from his travels around Britain, pleading for more news of 'what is going on in that little world of scandal and slander' and for reports on 'the whereabouts and wonderful doings of the Swanseaites'. In particular, he wanted to know: 'What is Smith doing? Is his popularity on the wane or was he outmanoeuvred in getting into the council?'[86]

For others, however, the divisions being exposed had more serious consequences. Another writer to *The Cambrian* in 1846 lamented the depth of dispute in the town and warned that 'while we are cutting each other's throats by our unhappy divisions our commercial rivals in neighbouring ports – the natural enemies of our prosperity – are delighted at our proceedings and may be heard on all sides, unable to conceal their satisfaction'.[87] Not until 1848 was the deadlock finally broken. The prospect of the South Wales Railway being extended to Swansea seemed to concentrate minds in the harbour trust, the council and the private interest groups who, in the mean time, had formed their own private dock company with powers to build on a designated site to the south of the town. In 1848 all parties agreed to support the purchase, by the council, of the powers of the dock company, and work eventually began on the long-anticipated 'floating dock' and 'new cut' in September 1849. It had been a protracted and tortuous process. On its completion, the mood was one of relief rather than celebration. One local newspaper reported that:

> No public demonstration was made on the occasion; indeed, the event – all-important as it is to the town and district – was not signalised in any way, beyond the waving of a few banners from some of the adjoining premises, and the hoisting of flags on some of the vessels in the harbour.[88]

---

[85] *Swansea Journal*, 18 January 1843.
[86] WGAS, RISW, E2, Letters from J. W. G. Gutch to Grant Francis, 31 August 1840, 7 December 1840.
[87] *The Cambrian*, 25 December 1846.
[88] *Swansea Herald*, 7 January 1852, quoted in Jones, *History of the Port of Swansea*, p. 191.

What this episode had revealed above all else was just how fractious town politics had become in the few short years since municipal reform. Swansea's urban leaders, it seemed, had not yet come to terms with how to manage their enlarged borough while at the same time ensuring that the views of the various interest groups within it were adequately represented and their needs met. As long as the harbour dispute continued, municipal elections were bitterly contested affairs, particularly in the town's upper ward. The editors of *The Cambrian* noted that 'a contest in upper ward was a matter of course, and inseparable from it were those scenes of strife, excitement and confusion which have rendered this ward famous in the annals of civic warfare'.[89] Moreover, as the town leaders charged with the task of maintaining the condition of the streets found to their cost in the 1840s, the rancour generated by the harbour dispute carried over into other areas of municipal life.

The provision of paving, lighting, water supply and street cleansing had not hitherto been a major political battleground in Swansea as it had been in other towns where improvement commissions sometimes became a focus of anti-corporation sentiment.[90] Prior to municipal reform, the alliance of corporation members and appointed commissioners on Swansea's original paving commission had prevented it from becoming an instrument of opposition to the established local government elite. After the reforms, when the commission's powers were transferred to the new council, financial constraints had prevented the adoption of any radical new approaches to the provision of utilities and sanitary services of the kind which produced acrimony elsewhere. In towns where reformed councils tried to establish municipal water supplies, for example, bitter conflicts ensued over the principles involved.[91] In Swansea, however, the financially constrained council displayed no such ambitions and wholeheartedly supported the creation of a private water company.[92] Similarly, gas for street lighting was supplied privately. By the early 1840s, however, commissioners in Swansea were beginning to wonder whether a more interventionist approach to these services might not prove more lucrative. Towns like

[89] *The Cambrian*, 8 November 1850.
[90] D. Fraser, *Urban Politics in Victorian England* (Leicester, 1976), pp. 91–2.
[91] See, for example, J. E. Callison, 'Politics, class and water supply in Dundee, 1831–1845' (unpublished M.Phil. thesis, University of Dundee, 1985).
[92] WGAS, B/S Corp, B10, 9 June 1836.

Manchester, they noted, generated a significant income from the sale of gas, and so it was believed that a new Act of Parliament, enabling similar powers to be exercised in Swansea, would boost the financial resources available for street improvements in the town.[93] It was W. H. Smith, erstwhile critic of the harbour trust, who, in his capacity as a paving commissioner, was asked to prepare a bill for the better paving and lighting of Swansea, and to conduct a survey of the town for the purpose of fixing a rate.[94]

In the early months of 1844, the prospect of new legislation propelled the issue of street improvement to the front line of public debate in the town for the first time since the late 1780s, when paving had been one of the issues on which reformers within the town attacked Gabriel Powell.[95] Many of the same obstacles that had hindered the harbour improvement scheme were apparent again in this new dispute. While it was widely acknowledged that services like refuse collection, water and gas provision and street paving needed to be improved, opinion was deeply divided as to how this should be achieved and paid for. The prospect of having to bear the costs that legislation might bring was unpalatable to many ratepayers in Swansea, who were already feeling the pinch in the early 1840s. The combination of economic downturn, caused by a depression in the price of manufactured copper in 1843, and the heightened social tensions evident in the widespread strikes and protests of that year, made many ratepayers in Swansea defensive and resentful of proposed change. One of them summed up such sentiments in a letter to *The Cambrian* saying: 'We the ratepayers like to see, more especially in these hard times, how the money we are obliged to pay is disposed of.'[96] Swansea might not have been in the full grip of the 'hungry forties',[97] but the timing was unfortunate.

Moreover, the same critic of the new bill expressed the suspicion that it was largely a result of the commissioners' past failures that new legislation was deemed necessary: 'The recent futile attempt to force a new Act upon us is the natural result of the shameful manner in which their public duties are performed.'[98] A loss of trust in the

[93] *The Cambrian*, 10 February 1844.
[94] WGAS, B/S Corp, F2, 13 November 1844.
[95] See chapter 1.
[96] *The Cambrian*, 3 February 1844.
[97] E. J. Hobsbawm, *Industry and Empire. An Economic History of Britain since 1750* (London, 1968), p. 74.
[98] *The Cambrian*, 3 February 1844.

ability of the commissioners for the streets to carry out their duties effectively was evident. In addition, similar tensions between the town and the newly annexed industrial districts, which Smith had articulated in 1842, surfaced again during debates about the new improvement bill. The inclusion of the industrial areas of Morriston and Llansamlet within Swansea's enlarged municipal boundaries in 1835 had added considerably to the area for which the town council had responsibility, but it had not resulted in a corresponding increase in financial resources for the town, as few of the inhabitants of the additional areas were eligible to pay rates. The information collected by the commissioners who fixed the new municipal boundaries illustrated this quite clearly. Of a total of 923 male ratepayers in the new municipal borough, 808 resided in the old town and franchise and only 115 in the newly absorbed areas.[99] In effect, this meant that the wealth of the town was spread more thinly over a wider area.

When it was eventually passed, the new Improvement Act dealt with this unequal distribution of wealth in a correspondingly unequal way. Instead of attempting to provide the same level of service to the whole area of the town within the municipal boundaries, the Act confined the commissioners' extensive powers of 'management of all the present and future streets' to the smaller area of the 'town and franchise' alone. For the purpose of penalizing people who caused a nuisance or an obstruction in the streets, their jurisdiction comprised 'the whole district within the municipal boundary', but for all other purposes, including the provision of paving, lighting and cleansing, it was the smaller area of the town which was provided for. In an effort to ensure that it was the people deriving benefits from the Act who funded the work of the commissioners, the powers of rating extended to owners and occupiers located within eighty yards of a lamp or adjoining a paved or cleansed street.[100]

The implications of this decision to confine the operation of the Act to the limits of the town and franchise were exposed in the late 1840s when G. T. Clark's report on the sanitary state of Swansea was published. Much harder hitting than de la Beche's earlier survey, Clark's report drew attention to the poor sanitary state of the

[99] PP 1837 XXVIII, Report of the Commissioners Appointed to Report and Advise upon the Boundaries and Wards of Certain Boroughs and Corporate Towns.
[100] SCL, SL X387/7, Swansea Improvement Act 1844.

outlying districts and recommended that the powers available to the council under the 1848 Public Health Act should be applied to the entire borough. However, the commissioners who met to discuss responses to Clark's findings were still influenced by the existing limitations on their activities. While admitting that extending the remit to cover the entire borough was advisable, they concluded that it was 'beyond their province to express any recommendation as to its adoption in the outlying districts'.[101] Local government in Swansea was thus still not reconciled to the full implications of the boundary extensions of the 1830s, and was continuing to operate within a narrowly defined compass.

The post-reform period in local government in Swansea was about turning euphoria into reality. The 'fit and proper persons' who had entered public life in 1836 were faced with the task of satisfying high expectations, and implementing their new responsibilities and meeting a range of demands from different sectors of the town. The perception among some contemporaries was that they fell short of expectations. William Smith, in the face of opposition over his improvement bill, was quick to point out that many of his fiercest critics 'were the first members of the town council, having been borne in on the shoulders of hundreds of the people, they had gone out of office without paying off one fraction of the public debt'.[102] There was a palpable sense of missed opportunity and under-achievement, deriving principally from the delays over harbour improvement, as well as the financial problems facing the town throughout the 1840s. But this sense of lost ground has to be seen in context. Rather than simply reflecting failures by Swansea's urban leaders, the changing circumstances in which they found themselves also have to be borne in mind. The industrial and demographic growth of the previous few decades had come at a price: increased responsibility and greater pressure on slender financial resources. Perhaps it was inevitable that a period of adjustment would be needed.

Significant, too, was the fact that the rest of urban Wales was not standing still. During the first three or four decades of the nineteenth century, Swansea enjoyed a position of almost unrivalled success in south Wales as a bathing resort, a centre for coal shipping and copper smelting, a hub of cultural life and a growing commer-

[101] WGAS, B/S Corp, F2, 26 November 1849.
[102] *The Cambrian*, 3 February 1844.

cial and financial centre. But the clear run which it had enjoyed in most of these spheres could not last for ever. Developments along the coast at Newport and Cardiff in particular meant that Swansea, for the first time in its recent history, faced serious competition as a Welsh urban centre. The loss of initiative to Cardiff over harbour facilities was probably the most significant indicator of this, and its repercussions were felt in other areas of urban life. The first hint that Swansea's recently elevated status as a banking centre might be challenged came in 1842 when, in response to new dock developments, the local Bank of England agent, T. L. Whitehouse, began considering the merits of moving the Welsh branch to Cardiff.[103] Signs of a growing rivalry between the two towns were not slow to follow. In July 1850 the members of Swansea's town council passed a resolution defending themselves against allegations that their mayor, Christopher James, had been less than courteous in his conduct towards his Cardiff counterpart at a recent public breakfast to celebrate the opening of the South Wales Railway.[104] Such tensions, though relatively minor, suggest that the shifts taking place in the Welsh urban hierarchy were being felt by contemporaries operating at local government level.

The response of urban leaders in Swansea to these changes was not to capitulate quietly and to give up the mantle of 'Welsh metropolis' to the up-and-coming towns further east along the Bristol Channel coast. The honeymoon may have been over in terms of Swansea's primacy as a coal shipping port for the south Wales industrial region, but the town still had a trump card up its sleeve which held the key to prolonging its importance for a good while longer; this was its reputation as a centre of urban culture. While other towns had caught up, and even seized the initiative, in the provision of commercial, industrial and transport facilities, no other Welsh town was able to rival Swansea's reputation as an enlightened cultural centre for several decades to come. In view of the ground lost to other ports and trading centres, the cultural status of the town became relatively more important in the 1840s. It was to their cultural institutions, rather than to commercial or municipal enterprise, that Swansea's urban leaders increasingly looked in order to promote their town's urban identity. It was a strategy which met with considerable success.

[103] R. O. Roberts, 'Banking and financial organisation, 1770–1914', in Williams and John (eds), *GCH*, Volume V, p. 378.
[104] WGAS, B/S Corp, B11, 12 July 1850.

VI
'THERE IS A SPIRIT OF INTELLIGENCE ABROAD': URBAN ELITES AND URBAN CULTURE

The year 1835, which saw the much-heralded reform of local government, was also the date of the foundation of an institution which, arguably, was to play a more important role in the shaping of urban identity in Swansea in the middle decades of the nineteenth century than the newly reformed town council. Swansea Scientific Society, soon to relaunch and rebrand itself as the Royal Institution of South Wales (RISW), had a significant overlap in membership with many of the key institutions of local government in Swansea. Some two-thirds of the 1836 town council, for example, were members. As a vehicle for the ambitions and interests of these people, the RISW was the more effective institution. This was not how it was meant to be. In 1836 the Swansea populace showed every sign of being optimistic that their newly elected councillors would provide the leadership that the town needed in order to maintain its status as a principal Welsh urban centre. In reality, however, the delays and disputes which marked discussions over harbour development and improvement legislation in the municipal institutions contrasted starkly with the fortunes of the scientific society, which made great strides in the same period towards establishing for Swansea a reputation as Wales's most enlightened and cultured town. While local government was proving a frustrating experience for many of Swansea's urban elite, science, it seemed, was promoting unity and enlightenment among many of the same people.

There is no mistaking the fact that in the decades following the establishment of its scientific society, Swansea's reputation as a respectable, cultured and intelligent town began to blossom. Guidebooks and directories of the period identified the cultural character of the town and its inhabitants as a key feature distinguishing Swansea from other Welsh towns. According to Hunt's directory and topography, published in 1849, 'the inhabitants enjoy the reputation of great respectability', and 'there is a spirit of intelligence abroad'.[1] The 1851 *Swansea Guide* proclaimed rather bullishly that 'The ancient borough of Swansea ... in point of extent, population and intelligence, has no rival in the Principality.'[2] Slater's directory published seven years later was a little less effusive, but nevertheless stated that 'the inhabitants generally are of great respectability'.[3] In depicting Swansea as a town with a respectable and educated population and as a place of cultural and intellectual refinement, the directories were not simply indulging in local bluster. Their interpretations reflected the unique way in which, in the 1830s and 1840s, the scientific and intellectual interests of some of Swansea's leading inhabitants became a central facet of the town's advancing urban status. To understand why this was so is to enter the cultural world of Swansea's mid-nineteenth-century social elite.

According to one definition, the 'elite' of a town were the 'individuals, from whatever class or stratum, who held leadership posts in the major institutions of the district'.[4] Recent historical research has done much to reveal the significant degree of influence which these people wielded in the shaping of the urban environment.[5] Decisions on all aspects of town life, from the architectural style of buildings to the width of roads, the management of harbours and hospitals to the stock of local libraries and museums, were taken by relatively small numbers of local 'worthies' who, for a variety of reasons, were willing to devote time and energy to such matters.[6] R. J. Morris's research has shown how participation in voluntary societies with a charitable, cultural or educational remit brought cohesion and a shared sense of purpose to an otherwise disparate and varied section of the urban middle class.[7] Differences in social status,

---

[1] *Hunt and Co's Directory and Topography for the Cities of Gloucester and Bristol and the Towns of Carmarthen, Kidwelly, Laugharne, Llanelly and St Clears* (London, 1849), pp. 144–7.

[2] J. Lewis, *The Swansea Guide, 1851* (Swansea, 1851), p. 5.

[3] *Slater's Royal National and Commercial Directory and Topography of the Counties of Gloucestershire, Monmouthshire, and North and South Wales* (London, 1858–9), pp. 121–2.

[4] R. Trainor, *Black Country Elites. The Exercise of Authority in an Industrial Area, 1830–1900* (Oxford, 1993), p. 18.

[5] J. Smith, 'Urban elites and urban history', *Urban History*, 27, no. 2 (2000), 255–75.

[6] See, for example, W. D. Rubinstein, *Elites and the Wealthy in Modern British History. Essays in Social and Economic History* (Brighton, 1987); N. Morgan and R. H. Trainor, 'The dominant classes', in W. H. Fraser and R. J. Morris (eds), *People and Society in Scotland*, Volume 2: *1830–1914* (Edinburgh, 1990), pp. 103–37.

[7] R. J. Morris, 'Voluntary societies and British urban elites, 1780–1850: an analysis', *Historical Journal*, 26, no. 1 (1983), 95–118.

religious denomination and occupational or business interests could be overcome through active participation in literary societies, gardening clubs, library committees or musical societies. Moreover, Simon Gunn's recent study of Manchester, Leeds and Birmingham, has shown that these elite activities amounted to a thriving 'public culture' which had a significant effect on shaping the cities themselves. He sees 'the growth of an urban bourgeois culture' as a 'central component' of the development of a town.[8]

In south Wales, more than in other parts of Britain, research on urban culture has been scarce. Intense interest in labour relations, industrial organization and the working-class experience has tended to dominate research on Welsh urban society, leaving little scope for acknowledging the existence of culture in the towns.[9] Where cultural life has been examined, for example in the work of Gareth Williams and Andy Croll on music in Welsh industrial society, the focus has been the activities of the working classes.[10] The idea of elite culture in Welsh towns remains largely obscure, marking a significant lacuna in our knowledge of Welsh urban history. But Swansea's reputation as an 'intelligent town' was closely linked to the character and behaviour of its social elites. An understanding of the town's urban identity in the middle decades of the nineteenth century therefore requires an examination of their activities. This facet of urban life was all the more important in Swansea in view of its background as a fashionable resort town, where the provision of polite entertainment for elite visitors had been a priority for town leaders since the latter decades of the eighteenth century.

The aim of this chapter is not to attempt a general survey of elite 'public culture' in Swansea, but rather to focus on the role of one particular and vital institution, the Swansea Scientific Society, in shaping the identity of the town in the mid-nineteenth century. The establishment of learned institutions, universities and societies of

---

[8] S. Gunn, *The Public Culture of the Victorian Middle Class. Ritual and Authority in the English Industrial City, 1840–1914* (Manchester, 2000), p. 187.

[9] See, for example, C. Evans, *'The Labyrinth of Flames'. Work and Social Conflict in Early Industrial Merthyr Tydfil* (Cardiff, 1933); G. A. Williams, *The Merthyr Rising* (London, 1978); D. Smith (ed.), *A People and a Proletariat. Essays in the History of Wales, 1780–1980* (London, 1980); T. Herbert and G. Elwyn Jones (eds), *People and Protest. Wales, 1815–1880* (Cardiff, 1988).

[10] G. Williams, *Valleys of Song. Music and Society in Wales, 1840–1914* (Cardiff, 1998); A. Croll, 'From bar stool to choir stall: music and morality in late Victorian Merthyr', *Llafur*, 6, no. 1 (1992), 17–27.

intellectuals in towns and cities, in which ideas could be debated and shared, could play an important role in the creation of a 'public sphere' in urban life.[11] Scientific societies, which were a commonplace in British provincial towns from the late eighteenth and early nineteenth centuries, can be viewed as part of this evolving public culture. One historian has gone so far as to suggest that the proliferation of such institutions amounted to a second scientific revolution in Britain.[12] By 1841, there were sixteen London-based societies for various scientific disciplines, such as geology, astronomy and botany, and literally dozens of provincial societies, either general in their scientific scope or devoted to a particular branch of learning.[13] In one sense, the Swansea society, established in 1835, was just another example of the growth of urban science culture in Britain in this period; but in the context of the town itself, it took on much greater significance. Apart from being the main focus for the cultural activities of the town's elite, it became Swansea's most prominent urban institution by the mid-point of the nineteenth century, and the main vehicle by which the town's status and identity were advanced on the regional and national stage.

Swansea's first attempt to found an institution of this kind was in 1821, with the establishment of the Cambrian Society for the pursuit of geology, zoology and natural history. The surgeon John Charles Collins was a leading light in the movement and Humphrey Davy and Michael Faraday were invited to become honorary members.[14] Similar initiatives in other towns dated from the same period. York, Hull and Sheffield, for example, had 'literary and philosophical' societies by 1822, and in Liverpool and Leeds their foundation had come even earlier.[15] The Cambrian Society, however, had only a short lifespan and ceased to exist by the mid-1820s, probably because of lack of support. Another body, the Swansea and Neath Horticultural Society, founded in 1832,

---

[11] D. Outram, *The Enlightenment* (Cambridge, 1995), p. 15; T. Bender (ed.), *The University and the City from Medieval Origins to the Present* (New York; Oxford, 1998); C. Calhoun, 'Introduction: Habermas and the public sphere', in idem (ed.), *Habermas and the Public Sphere* (Cambridge, Mass.; London, 1992), pp. 1–48.

[12] A. Thackray, 'Natural knowledge in cultural context: the Manchester model', *American Historical Review*, 79, no. 3 (1974), 674.

[13] Ibid.

[14] D. Tomos (ed.), *Michael Faraday in Wales, including Faraday's Journal of his tour through Wales in 1819* (Denbigh, 1972), pp. 157, 164.

[15] C. A. Russell, *Science and Social Change, 1700–1900* (London, 1983), p. 176.

attracted a following among the local botanical enthusiasts, including Lewis Weston Dillwyn, his son, John Dillwyn Llewelyn, John Henry Vivian, the banker Robert Eaton, and the surgeon George Bird,[16] but this was not a mainstream scientific society of the kind that existed in other towns. By the mid-1830s, then, Swansea had been without a functioning association to reflect the broad range of scientific interests of its inhabitants for a decade. Few other Welsh towns were any better served, although the small neighbouring town of Neath was supporting its own scientific society by this date. Science enthusiasts within Wales more commonly looked across the border to England to satisfy their intellectual interests. Ironmaster Josiah John Guest, Dowlais trustee G. T. Clark, and Poor Law reformer J. H. Moggridge, were among the Welsh-based members of the Bristol Institution for the Advancement of Science, founded in 1823.[17] When a new scientific society was finally established in Swansea in 1835, its founders acknowledged the example set by the pre-existing institutions at Bristol and Neath and admitted that:

> Previous to the formation of this society it had long been a matter of surprise and regret that a large, intelligent and populous town like Swansea, possessing in itself and in numerous connexions with foreign parts so many advantages for the encouragement and propagation of scientific research, should be without some institution of this kind.[18]

The prospects for the new Swansea Institution were good. Where the Cambrian Society had failed, the new society succeeded spectacularly. It was to be no ordinary institution peopled by enthusiastic local amateurs, but rather the focus of activities for an extraordinary wealth of scientific talent in the town in the 1830s and 1840s. The presence of three fellows of the Royal Society and the president of the Royal Geological Society among its founder members was an early signal of the prestigious and prominent position it would come to occupy in the life of the town in the middle decades of the nineteenth century. Its impressive longevity – outlasting many of the

---

[16] WGAS, RISW, GGF, F14, Societies and Institutions. Swansea and Neath Horticultural Society.

[17] M. Neve, 'Science in a commercial city: Bristol, 1820–1860', in I. Inkster and J. Morrell (eds), *Metropolis and Province. Science in British Culture, 1780–1850* (London, 1983), p. 187.

[18] *Swansea Literary and Philosophical Institution. First Annual Report, 1836* (Swansea, 1836), pp. 8–9.

urban literary and philosophical societies established in other towns in the same period – testified to the strength of its position in the town. In fact, it is not far-fetched to claim that it was the scientific society more than any other institution in Swansea, public or private, charitable or municipal, that did most to shape the town's urban identity in this period. It placed intellectual and cultural life at the centre of this identity, making this probably the clearest feature distinguishing Swansea from other Welsh towns in the eyes of both its own inhabitants and outside observers.

Signs of the scientific society's central role in town life are reflected in its membership. With 167 members by 1839, each subscribing one guinea annually,[19] it brought together the commercial, industrial and professional elites of the town as well as many of the landed proprietors of the neighbourhood (see Table 6.1). Local professionals formed the largest occupational group, accounting for more than one-fifth of the 167 subscribers. Representatives from the commercial and financial sectors accounted for a little under one-fifth, and industrialists constituted the third largest occupational group at just under 8 per cent of the total. Along with a handful from the retail and craft sectors, these made up the principal occupational classes within the membership. What was more significant, however, was the involvement of many of the leading figures from the town and neighbourhood. Two-thirds of Swansea's 1836 town council members were amongst the subscribers, and gentry members included Christopher Talbot of Margam and Penrice, H. J. Grant of Gnoll Castle, Neath, John Nicholl of Merthyr Mawr, MP for Cardiff, and Viscount Adare of Dunraven Castle. It was unusual to find such a strong representation from among the social elite in scientific societies elsewhere in Britain in this period.[20] A similar institution in Sunderland, for example, has been described by one historian as the work of a group of 'lesser known local men'.[21]

In Swansea the involvement in the scientific society of gentry, professionals, commercial, retail and trading people along with industrialists reveals the depth of interest in scientific knowledge

---

[19] *Annual Report of the Council of the RISW, 1838–39* (Swansea, 1839), pp. 10–11, 13.
[20] I. Inkster, 'The development of a scientific community in Sheffield, 1790–1850: a network of people and interests', in idem, *Scientific Culture and Urbanisation in Industrial Britain* (Aldershot, 1997), p. 109.
[21] C. A. Russell, *Science and Social Change, 1700–1900* (London, 1983), p. 177.

Table 6.1 Occupational status of RISW subscribers, 1839

Occupational group	No.	%
Commercial	31	18.5
Industrial	13	7.8
Professional	38	22.7
Independent income	26	15.5
Public Administration	6	3.6
Distribution/Processing	11	6.6
Craft	10	6
Unknown	32	19.1
Total	167	

Source: *Annual Report of the Council of the Royal Institution of South Wales, 1838–39* (Swansea, 1839); *Matthews's Swansea Directory* (Swansea, 1830); W. W. Price, *Biographical Index of W. W. Price, Aberdare*, WGAS D/D WCR, 113–35.

and discovery amongst the town's middle classes and the social elite of the wider neighbourhood. The involvement of local industrialists in scientific work in the town is relatively well known, and indeed the link between industry and scientific knowledge has been frequently noted by historians of the provincial science movement.[22] Some, like John Henry Vivian, collaborated closely with the leading scientists of the day on the issue of industrial pollution. Michael Faraday made a visit to Vivian's Hafod works in the summer of 1822 to work on the problem, resided with the Vivian family at their house, Marino, and thereafter maintained a correspondence with John Henry Vivian regarding his continuing experiments with copper.[23] Starling Benson also employed the latest scientific advances in his efforts to reduce sulphurous emissions from his Forest copper works. A keen geologist,[24] his works also became the focus for some of the most advanced geological survey work in Britain. This was due, in no small part to the expertise of William Edmond Logan, who took up a managerial post at the works in 1831 and commenced an ambitious project to produce accurate geological maps of the local

---

[22] See I. Inkster, 'Aspects of the history of science and science culture in Britain, 1780–1850 and beyond', in I. Inkster and J. Morrell (eds), *Metropolis and Province. Science in British Culture, 1780–1850* (London, 1983), pp. 1–54.

[23] Tomos, *Faraday in Wales*, pp. 149–65.

[24] D. M. Bayliffe and J. N. Harding, *Starling Benson of Swansea* (Bridgend, 1996), pp. 24, 52.

coal seams. The results of his work drew national acclaim in 1837 when they were presented at a meeting of the British Association for the Advancement of Science. Among those most impressed was Henry de la Beche, director of the Geological Survey of Great Britain who, after seeing Logan's pioneering work which he considered 'greatly superior to that usual with geologists',[25] transferred the field mapping activities of the Geological Survey to south Wales, and adopted Swansea as a base for the work.

Swansea's location in the south Wales coalfield, and the influence of local industrialists undoubtedly played an important part in its emergence as a nationally renowned centre for geological expertise, but the industrial location was never the dominant influence on the activities of the scientific institution in the way that the Yorkshire coalfield was in the case of the Geological Society of the West Riding of Yorkshire.[26] In Swansea there were also some high-profile scientific minds to be found in other quarters, not least in the ranks of the legal profession. It was William Robert Grove, a lawyer by occupation, who was perhaps the town's most distinguished and widely renowned scientist. Educated first at Swansea Grammar School and later at Bath and then Brasenose College, Oxford, his scientific achievements included pioneering the use of electric currents in the carbonation of hydrogen and oxygen and, most significantly, the development of a powerful new gas battery, now acknowledged as 'the forerunner of modern-day fuel cells'.[27] Grove's scientific publications included *The Correlation of Physical Forces*, and his achievements were recognized by his scientific peers when he was elected a fellow of the Royal Society at the age of just twenty-nine; in 1841 he was appointed professor of experimental philosophy at the London Institution. He went on to hold the presidency of the British Association on the occasion of its visit to Nottingham in 1866.[28] Similarly, John Gwyn Jeffreys, a local solicitor, distinguished himself as a conchologist, helped to found the Marine Biological Association of Great Britain, and became a

[25] M. la Terieur (ed.), *Dictionary of Canadian Biography*, Volume X: *1871–1880* (Toronto, 1872), pp. 444–5.
[26] J. B. Morrell, 'The early Yorkshire Geological and Polytechnic Society: a reconsideration', *Annals of Science*, XLV (1988), 153–67.
[27] M. L. Cooper and V. D. M. Hall, 'William Robert Grove and the London Institution, 1841–1845', *Annals of Science*, 39 (1982), 232.
[28] W. W. Price, *Biographical Index of W. W. Price, Aberdare*, Volume 10 (Aberystwyth, 1981), 183.

fellow of the Royal Society in 1840. A contemporary of Grove at Swansea Grammar School, his interests were nurtured by Lewis Weston Dillwyn, with whom he made excursions to Gower caves to collect specimens and examine fossilized remains.[29] Both Grove and Jeffreys were Swansea-born and members of established local families; their scientific interests were cultivated from a young age in their native town.

Members of the local medical profession were also active in the work of the new scientific society. Studies of the role of medical men in scientific societies elsewhere in Britain have suggested that they tended to be men of marginal social standing who involved themselves primarily for reasons of status enhancement.[30] In Swansea, however, the picture seems to have been rather different. Some of the town's leading medical practitioners were keen members of the scientific community. J. W. G. Gutch, a surgeon who was employed for a time at Swansea Infirmary, was also a keen meteorologist who recorded detailed statistics on the local climate for publication in the institution's annual reports. Along with his friend, local magistrate and 'inventor', William Edmond of Morriston, he was involved in the development of an experimental new anemometer, which they tested together in high winds in May 1839.[31] He also distinguished himself in more than just local circles, becoming editor of the quarterly *Meteorological Journal* in 1841.[32] Another stalwart of the institution was George Gwyn Bird, a product of St Bartholomew's Hospital medical school in London who was 'regarded by many as being the leading Glamorgan doctor of his day'.[33] Scientific talent was also to be found in other sections of the town's middle class. John Jenkins, watchmaker and jeweller, for example, was a keen astronomer. With an observatory in the garden of his business premises in Wind Street, he was able to collect astronomical data and gave lectures on the subject at the institution. Wider recognition of his talents came in 1842 when he was elected a fellow of the Royal Astronomical Society.[34]

[29] WGAS, D/D WCR 122, Biographical information on J. G. Jeffreys.
[30] I. Inkster, 'Marginal men: aspects of the social role of the medical community in Sheffield, 1790–1850', in idem (ed.), *Scientific Culture and Urbanisation*, pp. 129–43.
[31] *Annual Report of the Council of the RISW, 1838–1839*, p. 84.
[32] WGAS, RISW, E2, Letter from J. W. G. Gutch to Grant Francis, 7 December 1841.
[33] T. G. Davies, 'Lewis Weston Dillwyn and his doctors', *Morgannwg*, XXXII (1988), 78.
[34] R. J. Hart, 'John Jenkins of Rotherslade. A forgotten pillar of the Royal Institution of South Wales', *Minerva*, 5 (1997), 9–14.

'THERE IS A SPIRIT OF INTELLIGENCE ABROAD'   167

A further corpus of scientific enthusiasts in the Swansea area was to be found among the gentry and landowning elite of the neighbourhood. Interest in natural history, in particular, was common among the leisured classes in nineteenth-century Britain. Its appeal was particularly strong among higher status groups in society for whom the collection and display of specimens became a popular leisure pursuit.[35] In Swansea the nearby Gower coast, with its abundance of rock and plant life, provided the training ground for a number of talented botanists and geologists from local gentry families. Lewis Weston Dillwyn, owner of the Cambrian Pottery, was well acquainted with Dr Buckland, professor of geology at Oxford, meeting him regularly on visits to London and Oxford. The two men collaborated in scientific projects, including a cave excavation in Gower in January 1823.[36] Likewise, the Talbot family, with its estate at Penrice in Gower, was well placed to develop similar scientific interests. During summers at Penrice, frequent excursions were made to the beach at Oxwich to collect shells and other specimens. In 1812 Mary Talbot commented that so many 'curiosities' had been collected by various members of the family that a museum would be needed to house them all.[37]

As well as the natural history enthusiasts, there were a number of key Swansea figures involved in early photographic work. Henry Fox Talbot, renowned as one of the founding fathers of modern photography, was a cousin of the Talbots of Margam and Penrice and a close collaborator and correspondent of two Swansea photographic pioneers. Calvert Richard Jones, whose father had gifted land to the town for the site of Swansea Market, accompanied Fox Talbot on a photographic tour of the country in the early 1840s. He was an accomplished practitioner in his own right, taking some of the earliest photographic images of Swansea in the mid-1840s.[38] He also worked to advance photographic techniques, drawing on his artistic aptitudes as a skilled watercolourist to produce colour-enhanced prints. Among his photographic inventions, presented in a paper to the Royal Photographic Society in 1854, was a 'binocular

[35] G. Kitteringham, 'Science in provincial society: the case of Liverpool in the early nineteenth century', *Annals of Science*, 39, 4 (1982), 338.
[36] NLW, Lewis Weston Dillwyn 1, November 1819, October 1821, January 1823.
[37] Quoted in J. Martin, *Henry and the Fairy Palace. Fox Talbot and Glamorgan* (Aberystwyth, 1993), p. 20.
[38] D. Painting, *Swansea's Place in the History of Photography* (Swansea, 1982), pp. 6–9.

camera', designed to take broader, panoramic views.[39] John Dillwyn Llewelyn, a Swansea contemporary of Jones and the son of Lewis Weston Dillwyn, inherited his father's talents for botany and natural history, and also applied his scientific talents to photographic work. Along with Calvert Richard Jones, he served as one of the first committee members of the Royal Photographic Society of London, founded in 1853 and, like Jones, he pioneered new techniques in photography. His *Wave Breaking at Three Cliffs Bay*, taken in 1854, was awarded the silver medal of honour at the Photographic Exhibition in London that year for the precision with which it captured the movement of the sea water.[40]

In many cases, the scientific interests of these men were shared by their wives and daughters. It was the policy of the Swansea Scientific Society to allow each subscriber 'to introduce all the females and minors of his own family',[41] enabling them to make use of the library facilities and attend lectures. In addition, a small number of women became subscribers in their own right, including the wife of industrialist, Starling Benson, and the daughter of the Reverend John Collins. Women also played a prominent part in the social networks which served to unite Swansea's scientific elite. The Dillwyn family was closely linked with the Talbots, John Dillwyn Llewelyn having married Emma Talbot who ably assisted him in his photographic work.[42] Dillwyn's second son, Lewis Llewellyn, married Bessie, daughter of Sir Henry de la Beche, of the British Geological Survey. John Gwyn Jeffreys, the distinguished conchologist, married Anne Nevill, daughter of the Llanelli copper smelter and fellow Swansea Scientific Society member, Richard Janion Nevill.[43] The Penllergaer and Singleton Park estates of Dillwyn and Vivian respectively were the social focal points of this scientific world, providing hospitality to local enthusiasts and visiting dignitaries and a place to meet and exchange news of experiments, discoveries and collected specimens. Lewis Weston Dillwyn's diary entry of 15 November 1841 is illustrative of the calibre of scientific minds that gathered socially in Swansea in the Dillwyn household.

[39] R. Buckman, 'Calvert Richard Jones of Swansea', in M. Weaver (ed.), *British Photography in the Nineteenth Century* (Cambridge, 1989), pp. 55–64.
[40] C. Titterington, 'John Dillwyn Llewelyn: instantaneity and transience', in Weaver, *British Photography*, pp. 68–9.
[41] *Annual Report of the Council of the RISW, 1838–39*, p. 14.
[42] Ibid., pp. 15–16.
[43] W. W. Price, *Biographical Index*, Volume 13, 97.

That evening his dinner guests included Dr Buckland, Starling Benson, William Edmond Logan and John Gwyn Jeffreys.[44] The Dillwyn family thus stood at the centre of a close-knit social circle, drawn together by its members' common enthusiasm for scientific discovery, and cemented through marital ties and social interaction.

Although not all of its members were as closely linked in such circles, the society did have the effect of drawing together people from the town and neighbourhood who otherwise had little in common. Landowners and industrialists, men of old and new wealth, Nonconformists and Anglicans, were all represented in the membership of the Swansea Scientific Society, indicating that a common interest in the attainment of scientific knowledge was sufficient to overcome potential divisions among the elite. Just as in Bristol, where membership of both the Bristol Institution and the town's Literary and Philosophical Society can be seen to have 'transcended denominational differences',[45] so in Swansea, science brought together people from opposite ends of the religious spectrum. Although Anglicanism was probably the dominant faith among the members, reflecting the prominence of gentry and upper middle class men, there was also room in its ranks for people from a number of Nonconformist denominations. Prominent Anglicans such as Starling Benson, Christopher Talbot and George Grant Francis were to be found alongside members of some of the town's best-known Quaker families, including Robert Eaton and Henry Bath. Others from Nonconformist denominations included John Jenkins, the clockmaker and astronomer, Michael John Michael, a corn and flour merchant of Jewish descent who had joined the Unitarian faith, and Llansamlet-born Elias Jenkins, a musical-instrument maker by trade and a member of the town's Independent congregation.[46] Ministers from these different religious camps also found common ground in the scientific society. Its clerical contingent included the Reverend George Martin Maber, rector of Merthyr Tydfil, who had lived in Swansea since 1812 for health reasons after obtaining a licence to become non-resident,[47]

---

[44] NLW, Lewis Weston Dillwyn 3, 15 November 1841.
[45] M. Neve, 'Science in a commercial city: Bristol, 1820–60', in I. Inkster and J. Morrell (eds), *Metropolis and Province: Science in British Culture, 1780–1850* (London, 1983), p. 190.
[46] See WGAS, RISW, Swansea Statistical Survey 2, Statistical return for Swansea. Description of properties, details of occupant, 1839, for information on the religious affiliations of members.
[47] R. L. Brown, 'George Martin Maber, rector of Merthyr Tydfil', *Merthyr Historian*, 10 (1999), pp. 63–7.

and also Father Charles Kavanagh, Swansea's resident Roman Catholic priest, who won widespread respect in the town for his work with cholera victims during the epidemic of 1849.

As well as bridging religious divides, the institution also had a broad geographical base. By 1839 two-thirds of the members were Swansea-based; the rest were drawn from a wide geographical area extending far beyond the immediate neighbourhood, west to Carmarthenshire and east through Glamorgan, Monmouthshire and the south-west of England (see Table 6.2). This broad geographical remit testified to Swansea's growing influence as a centre for cultural and scientific learning. Even many of the Swansea-based members were incomers to the town from distant parts of Britain, such as the Northumbrian-born shipowner John Richardson, and Channel Islander Phillip Francis Poingdestre, who had only taken up residence in Swansea in 1834.[48] For these and other newcomers to the local business community, the scientific society provided a good introduction to local elite circles. Visitors to Swansea who, for the purpose of the society's rules, were defined as anyone who had been resident in the town or its neighbourhood for less than three months, were also encouraged to avail themselves of the facilities of the institution by means of introduction by a member.[49] It was hardly surprising that in a resort town, which had for decades sought to attract fashionable visitors for sea bathing during the summer months, the scientific society should be promoted as an additional visitor attraction. In short, the Swansea Scientific Society was, from its inception, an outward-looking institution with a broad membership base which testified to its non-parochial outlook and its ambition to serve the scientific interests of more than just the town and its immediate neighbourhood.

With visitors to Swansea, recently settled residents of the town and individuals from the south-west of England among its members, it is not surprising that from the outset, English was the principal language of the institution. All of its reports were published in English and, likewise, in lectures, meetings and correspondence English was the language used. Many of the leading members were either incomers to the area, like de la Beche and Logan, or, like John Henry Vivian and George Grant Francis,

[48] W. W. Price, *Biographical Index*, Volume 24, 115; WGAS, WCR 128, biographical note on Poingdestre.
[49] *Annual Report of the Council of the RISW, 1838–39*, p. 14.

Table 6.2 Residential distribution of RISW subscribers, 1839

Residential Area	Number of Subscribers
Swansea	114 (68%)
Hafod/Morriston	3
Mumbles/West Cross	3
Gower	7
Tawe valley	7
Neath/Neath valley	4
Taibach/Baglan/Margam	3
Carmarthenshire	6
Glamorgan (other)	6
Monmouthshire	2
South-west England	4
England (other)	4
Unknown	4
Total	167

Source: *Annual Report of the Council of the RISW, 1838–39* (Swansea, 1839), pp. 10–11.

members of families which had been resident in Wales for no more than a generation and were thus unlikely to use Welsh as their main medium of communication. Interest in the Welsh language and the culture and history of Wales, however, was widespread among the elite of the town and evident in the work of the scientific society. Lewis Weston Dillwyn displayed a willingness to defend the right of local Welsh speakers to express themselves in their native language, presenting a Welsh-language address at court in 1821 from his constituents in Llangyfelach and Llandeilo Tal-y-bont, successfully claiming 'a right for all his majesty's subjects to address him in their native language'.[50] Others interested themselves in the history and antiquities of Wales. A Society for the Publication of Ancient Welsh Manuscripts was supported by some high-profile local figures, including the duke of Beaufort and the earl of Dunraven, both of whom were vice-presidents, and George Grant Francis who was a corresponding member.[51]

---

[50] L. W. Dillwyn, *Contributions towards a History of Swansea* (Swansea, 1840), pp. 52–3.
[51] WGAS, RISW, GGF, F14, Societies and Institutions, 1763–1937, Society for the Publication of Ancient Welsh Manuscripts.

As far as the Swansea Scientific Society was concerned, it was in the area of library provision that the considerable resources of the institution to cater for particularly Welsh tastes and interests were evident. When Grant Francis became the institution's librarian, he developed a rich collection of texts and pamphlets which reflected his interest in local history and Welsh antiquities. He made it his policy to 'collect as many works relating to the Principality as possible'.[52] In 1839 he sent out a circular to members requesting donations of works on Wales.[53] As a result of his efforts, histories of Wales featured prominently in the library stock as did a range of Welsh poetry in both the Welsh and English languages. Reference works, including English–Welsh dictionaries and grammatical works, also featured, as did versions of the New Testament in Welsh and historical studies of the Welsh language.[54] With this sort of material at its disposal, the society was clearly not gearing itself solely towards the interests of a commercially motivated, English elite. Members whose academic tastes were quite obviously Welsh-orientated were also able to satisfy their interests. Howel Gwyn of Neath, whose main area of interest was the history of Neath Abbey, and Richard Rees of Gelligron, who collected a mass of historical material relating to Glamorgan, were subscribers in the 1830s.[55]

The library collection, as well as catering for specifically Welsh interests, contained a diverse array of reading matter. Items of interest to antiquarians and local historians were stocked, including pamphlets, Acts of Parliament and other documents relating to the town of Swansea. Many other works were donated by members, reflecting their own varied interests. An account of the Bristol riots of 1831 was donated by a native Bristolian, J. W. G. Gutch, and a coal proprietor, Charles H. Smith of Gwernllwynwyth, donated copies of the *Mining Journal*. The museum collection was even more diverse. Exhibits included numerous coins and medals and works of art as well as specimens of botany, conchology, mineralogy, geology and zoology. Compared with many other scientific societies established in British towns in the 1820s and 1830s, this was an impressive range. Some towns and cities fostered several separate

---

[52] *Annual Report of the Council of the RISW, 1838–39*, p. 56.
[53] WGAS, RISW, GGF, E1, Letter from J. E. Bicheno to Grant Francis, 12 June 1839; Letter from J. W. G. Gutch to Grant Francis, 4 August 1839.
[54] *Annual Report of the Council of the RISW, 1838–39*, pp. 56–64.
[55] For biographical information on Gwyn and Rees, see W. W. Price, *Biographical Index*, Volume 10, 236; Volume 23, 234.

societies devoted to different branches of scientific study. Dublin, for example, was home to the Geological Society of Dublin, the Royal Irish Academy and the Royal Dublin Society.[56] Sheffield had a Physical Society, a Botanical Society and a Phrenological Society.[57] A number of towns established statistical societies separate from their main scientific institutions, including Manchester in 1833 and Glasgow, which had two statistical societies, both founded in 1836.[58] By contrast, the Swansea institution was more of an umbrella society, appealing to all manner of scientific tastes. Statistical enquiry was carried out by a designated statistical subcommittee. The results of its first extensive survey, into the size, occupational description and religious affiliations of the population of Swansea, were published in the annual report of 1838–9. The range of other scientific pursuits covered by the institution can be gauged from the series of lectures offered to members. These covered subjects as diverse as entomology, phrenology, chemistry, optics, botany and geology.[59]

This very extensive menu of scientific knowledge testified to the sheer depth and breadth of interest in science among the local elite, and was also indicative of the ambition of the institution's founders. Not content with allowing it to become a run-of-the-mill provincial scientific society, within a year of its establishment it applied for royal patronage as part of a bid to become an institution of wider significance within Wales. The parallels with the establishment of *The Cambrian* newspaper, whose founders had also expressed a mission to serve the whole of Wales, were striking. John Henry Vivian, Lewis Weston Dillwyn and William Edmond Logan were among the petitioners on behalf of the scientific society who argued that their institution had already 'elicited talent, stimulated investigation and accumulated results of no inconsiderable order and value', but that 'under the powerful influence of Her Majesty's sanction, the Institution would find supporters in every part of the Principality'.[60] Their pleas were heard, and in July 1838 Lord John Russell conveyed the good news that the society had been granted

[56] J. Morrell and A. Thackray, *Gentlemen of Science. The Early Years of the British Association for the Advancement of Science* (Oxford, 1981), p. 175.
[57] Inkster, 'The development of a scientific community in Sheffield', pp. 106–8.
[58] M. J. Cullen, *The Statistical Movement in Early Victorian Britain* (Sussex, 1975), pp. 77–120.
[59] *Annual Report of the Council of the RISW, 1838–39*, p. 18.
[60] Ibid., p. 20.

the right to call itself the Royal Institution of South Wales (RISW). This was the first tangible sign that science culture in Swansea was to play more than a minor role in urban development. The founders, as well as sharing an enthusiasm for scientific knowledge, had a vision of Swansea as a national centre for learning and culture.

This early quest for increased status and wider recognition was a sign of things to come. In 1841 a new, purpose-built museum building opened its doors. The first of its kind anywhere in Wales, the premises were designed to house the growing array of scientific treasures in the possession of the RISW as well as to provide a venue for its lecture series, meetings and other events. Constructed on a prime site in the town, on land partly donated by the town council, the new building, with its elegant portico supported by four classical columns, was typical of the kind of civic architecture that was shaping the built environment in urban Britain in this period. Neoclassicism was the chosen architectural style of the provincial town halls and other public buildings constructed in industrial towns and cities throughout Britain in the middle decades of the nineteenth century.[61] Its choice for the new museum signified the scientific community's eagerness to demonstrate its own spirit of municipal pride in a similar way. Moreover, it placed science at the heart of the town's evolving urban landscape. Few contemporaries could have been left in any doubt as to the significance of scientific knowledge to Swansea's emerging identity. Key members of the RISW had a hand in reinforcing this image. Lewis Weston Dillwyn's *Contributions towards a History of Swansea*, published in 1840, gave as much space to the cataloguing of archaeological finds in the district, and the detailing of flora and fauna found in the neighbourhood, as it did to the various charters granted to the town since the medieval period.[62] The columns of the *Cambrian* regularly carried details of attendance at lectures, recent additions to the museum and library collections, and reports of meetings of subscribers to the institution.[63]

As more than simply a focal point for those with common intellectual interests, the RISW became a defining feature of the town's life, and one that was recognizable outside the town as well as within it. In March 1839 Emilius Nicholson, co-author of the *Cambrian*

[61] R. Dixon and S. Muthesius, *Victorian Architecture* (London, 1978), pp. 144–55.
[62] Dillwyn, *Contributions Towards a History of Swansea*.
[63] See, for example, *The Cambrian*, 7 May 1836.

Traveller's Guide series, was in the process of preparing a third edition of the guide and wrote to Grant Francis for details 'as would do justice to the rising importance' of Swansea. In particular, he requested information 'on the recent improvements which have taken place in Swansea which has assumed so considerable a literary importance as to render it an article of leading interest in the Principality'.[64] Perceptions of the town were undoubtedly affected by the presence of such an active institution of learning and culture. Plans to host an art exhibition at the RISW in 1841 caused one contemporary to comment that, in Swansea, 'I have no doubt there is wealth and taste enough to afford the most liberal patronage'.[65]

Swansea's reputation as an 'intelligent town' was especially secured in this period by the success with which RISW members forged links with the wider scientific community in urban Britain. As we have seen, such links already existed at an individual level, as a result of the close communication between Vivian and Faraday, Dillwyn and Buckland, and Calvert Jones and Fox Talbot. But more importantly, the development of an institutional framework for the provincial science movement in this period and, in particular, the formation of an umbrella organization in the shape of the British Association for the Advancement of Science (BAAS) gave the Swansea scientists a national stage on which to promote their town and its flourishing science culture. The BAAS was established in York in 1831 with the aim of bringing some direction and unity to the disparate work of the various provincial science institutions up and down the country.[66] Its main instrument for achieving this was its annual meeting, which saw the nation's scientific elite decamp to a different venue each year for the purpose of discussion, debate and reflection on news of recent advances in science in all its various branches. By the mid-1830s, competition between towns and cities to play host to a British Association meeting was fierce. It was 'no small matter' to be selected as a venue for a BAAS meeting and host towns stood to gain considerable advantage in enhanced status and recognition on the national stage.[67]

[64] WGAS, RISW, GGF, E1, Letter from E. Nicholson to Grant Francis, 8 March 1839.
[65] WGAS, RISW, GGF, E2, Letter from T. Brigstocke to Grant Francis, 19 December 1841.
[66] H. Mumford Jones and I. Bernard Cohen (eds), *Science before Darwin. A Nineteenth Century Anthology* (London, 1963), p. 291.
[67] Morrell and Thackray, *Gentlemen of Science*, pp. 165–75.

It was for this reason that the leading lights of the RISW decided to press Swansea's case to host the annual meeting in 1848. It was a shrewd move. The BAAS at that time was beginning to consider how best to extend its activities beyond its habitual territory of Oxford, Cambridge and York, and to hold meetings in other parts of the country.[68] Moreover, a visit to Swansea would provide a platform from which the scientific gospel could be carried to Wales. The principality was previously untried territory for the BAAS. The closest they had come was their visit to Bristol in 1836 which could, with some justice, be seen as a base from which to serve Wales as well as the south-west. Prior to the establishment of the RISW, a number of men with south Wales connections, including G. T. Clark and J. J. Guest, had been members of the Bristol institution.[69] By the 1840s, though, Bristol's scientific society was past its peak – partly perhaps because of the creation of the new institution in Swansea – and south Wales was operating in its own scientific orbit. This gave the Swansea case additional weight with the British Association. Just as, in 1835, Dublin had appeared to the BAAS to be an ideal base from which to bring science to Ireland as a whole,[70] so the wider Welsh dimension figured in the Swansea case.

The success of Swansea's bid to host the 1848 BAAS meeting was down to more than just good timing. Equally crucial was the strength of the case put forward by the town. Some of the leading figures in its scientific fraternity emerged as very effective advocates of Swansea's case. William Robert Grove, in particular, argued persuasively in favour of the town's suitability as a venue.[71] He took his case, firstly, to the town council where he impressed members with the benefits which a British Association visit might bring to the town. The councillors listened as Grove, 'in the most lucid manner painted out the benefits and advantages to be derived' from such a visit and, as a result:

> It was resolved unanimously that a visit to Swansea of the BAAS will be greatly conducive to the manufacturing, commercial and general interests of the town and neighbourhood and tend to diffuse a taste for science and to improve its practical application throughout the principality of Wales.[72]

[68] Ibid., p. 359.
[69] Neve, 'Science in a commercial city', p. 187.
[70] Morrell and Thackray, *Gentlemen of Science*, p. 177.
[71] WGAS, RISW, British Association for the Advancement of Science (BAAS) Box File 1, 83/5, President's Address.
[72] WGAS, B/S Corp, B11, 10 July 1846.

With the town council so enthusiastic, the task of persuading the British Association of the merits of Swansea as a venue was made easier. As the experience of previous years had shown, civic endorsement of this kind was essential to the success of an aspirant host town's bid.[73] When Grove took his case direct to the BAAS at its annual meeting in Southampton in 1846, he was backed by a declaration signed by the mayor, aldermen and leading inhabitants of Swansea, outlining their support for the visit.[74] Swansea's credentials as a scientific centre, with its Royal Institution, and with one of its own Royal Society fellows making its case, must have seemed enticing to the BAAS members gathered in the south-coast town, where the local Literary and Philosophical Society had already folded because of lack of support after a lifespan of just fifteen years.[75] The promise of a more vigorous scientific climate in Swansea, and the strong endorsement of municipal authorities in the town, proved impossible for the British Association to ignore.

The conviction with which the town council threw its weight behind the bid illustrated the important position which the science institution had come to occupy in Swansea by the mid-1840s. The Swansea organizers recognized that the British Association visit was a major coup for the town and they wasted no time in milking maximum capital from it. A public address was issued proclaiming it to be 'the most important [event] in the recent history of the Principality',[76] and there can be little doubt that it helped to raise the profile of the town on a regional and national stage. The sight of the country's leading scientists flocking to Swansea, and the total attendance of 847 at the meeting, forced even rival urban centres in south Wales to admit that the event was 'a triumph, and one of which Swansea may justly be proud'.[77]

The significance of the BAAS visit for the shaping of Swansea's urban identity in the mid-nineteenth century soon became evident in contemporary publications. Town and regional directories published in mid-century were quick to reflect upon the impact which science culture in general, and the British Association visit in

---

[73] Morrell and Thackray, *Gentlemen of Science*, p. 202.
[74] WGAS, B/S Corp, B11, 10 July 1846.
[75] A. Temple Patterson, *A History of Southampton, 1700–1914*, Volume 2: *The Beginnings of Modern Southampton, 1836–1867* (Southampton, 1971), p. 132.
[76] WGAS, RISW, BAAS Box File 1, 83/3, Address to the Inhabitants of the Town and Neighbourhood of Swansea and Neath, 1848.
[77] *Cardiff and Merthyr Guardian*, 26 August 1848.

particular, had had on Swansea's status as an urban centre. Those published in the late 1840s and early 1850s placed science at the centre of Swansea's recent development as an urban centre and made a direct link between the work of the RISW and the advancing status of the town. Hunt's 1849 directory noted that 'Swansea is celebrated for its scientific acquirements, and for having anteceded all the towns in Wales in building a noble institution for a museum ... its position in this particular may be estimated by its being selected for the meeting of the BAAS in 1848.'[78] Pearse's 1856 Swansea directory noted that 'Swansea justly claims to be the first and most important town in the Principality' and that 'its status is proved by its having been selected for the meetings of the British Association for the Advancement of Science in 1848'.[79] Directory authors invariably listed the Royal Institution among the key public buildings and most noteworthy visitor attractions in the town. Indeed, John Lewis's 1851 town guide devoted two pages to a detailed description of its origins and achievements.[80]

The influence of the RISW was not confined to the middle decades of the century. It continued to mark Swansea out as a cultural centre for the next fifty years, proving itself to be much more durable than many of the more narrowly focused contemporary scientific societies. Whilst elsewhere, separate institutions had to merge in order to survive, the RISW was flexible enough to adapt to changing intellectual tastes and new directions in scientific research. In particular, it was not as adversely affected as many others by the gradual professionalization of science from the mid-nineteenth century onwards. The field sciences and natural history, areas in which the Swansea institution was traditionally strong, remained relatively accessible to the talented amateur, whereas chemistry and physics shifted more decisively away from the learned society and into the laboratory.[81] Yet its ability to stand the test of time while other, comparable societies fell by the wayside as the 'Lit and Phil' movement passed its peak also owed much to its urban as well as its scientific functions. The institution united many different facets of Swansea's evolving urban identity. It was a body with which all of the influential groups in the town could identify. For

[78] *Hunt and Co's Directory and Topography*, p. 146.
[79] *Pearse's Swansea Directory* (E. Pearse, 1856), p. 5.
[80] Lewis, *Swansea Guide 1851*, pp. 25–7.
[81] Russell, *Science and Social Change*, p. 181.

industrialists seeking solutions to the environmental problems of smelting metal, for medical men keen on keeping up with advances in their profession, for the leisured classes with time to study the natural environment, for visitors seeking a place to while away the hours in respectable company, and for the resident middle classes with a thirst for collecting, cataloguing or inventing – the RISW had something to offer. In this sense, it provided a public forum which could reflect Swansea's character in all of its diversity. The resort town with industry was almost the perfect setting for the cultivation of scientific knowledge of all kinds.

Nevertheless, the institution had its limitations. Not all classes of the Swansea populace felt the effects of scientific knowledge emanating from the RISW. It was, first and foremost, an elite institution. Its annual subscription rate of one guinea ensured that membership was solidly from the middle class, and although like many similar contemporary institutions it harboured ideas of disseminating scientific knowledge, the extent to which this happened in practice was probably limited. Amongst its founders' objectives were 'the cultivation and advancement of the various branches of natural history, as well as the local history of the town and neighbourhood and the extension and encouragement of literature and the fine arts and the general diffusion of knowledge'.[82] In reality, however, 'its museum, library and laboratory were overwhelmingly for the shareholders, the subscribers, their families and guests'.[83] There were some openings by which interested members of the wider community could access this thriving scientific world. Attendance at the programmes of lectures organized annually was open to all classes, and provided one means by which the institution could claim to be fulfilling its objective of knowledge diffusion. In addition, the public were admitted free of charge to the institution and its facilities on designated days every year, usually around Whitsun. On such occasions, the library and museum were almost overwhelmed with visitors. The RISW's tenth annual report recorded that:

> Free admission of the public to the institution of the 12th and 13th ultimo, on which occasion upwards of 11,000 of the inhabitants, chiefly of the humbler

---

[82] Quoted in W. A. Beanland, *The History of the Royal Institution of South Wales, Swansea* (Swansea, 1935), p. 14.
[83] G. Gabb, 'What manner of men? The founders of the Royal Institution', *Minerva*, 3 (1995), 24.

classes, were admitted to the museum and other apartments, and were entertained each day in the theatre, by lectures and exhibitions of electrical and chemical experiments and of the phantasmagoria. It is very satisfactory to the Council and highly creditable to this vast multitude to report that they demeaned themselves with strict propriety and seemed gratified and interested by the objects of their inspection.[84]

There was a sense, then, in which the epithet 'intelligent town' truly reflected a universal interest in scientific knowledge in Swansea, although for the most part the scientific education of the working classes was confined to the mechanics' institute and other similar societies.

It was the social elite, through the RISW as its flagship institution, which was mainly responsible for Swansea's emergence in the 1830s and 1840s as Wales's 'intelligent town'. By a number of status-enhancing initiatives, this influential urban intelligentsia manoeuvred its scientific society into a position of such prominence in the town that it became Swansea's best-known and most distinctive institution. The role of intellectual elites in constructing public culture in this way has been explored in an American urban context where, as in Swansea, the nature of place was important in shaping cultural characteristics.[85] In developing a scientific institution in this period, Swansea was not simply following a lead set by other towns. The RISW was slightly different in membership and intellectual range from many similar contemporary bodies. Leading members like Grant Francis ensured that a specifically Welsh dimension was present in the institution, and made much of the Wales-wide remit set out in its royal charter. The varied industrial interests and coastal attractions of the region provided a basis for scientific study that was broad, varied and appealing to the bulk of the middle and upper ranks of the social spectrum, from the middle-class businessman to the gentry landowner. Moreover, the core of impressive scientific talent amongst the membership made it much more than simply a privileged social club for status-conscious townsfolk.

The 1830s and 1840s were years in which the Welsh urban landscape was becoming more visibly defined. A number of growing towns were developing distinctive roles for themselves. Merthyr, as the capital of the mineral districts, was the industrial centre. Cardiff,

[84] *Tenth Annual Report of the Council of the RISW, 1844–45* (Swansea, 1845), p. 9.
[85] B. M. Stave, 'A conversation with Thomas Bender: urban history as intellectual and cultural history', *Journal of Urban History*, 14, no. 4 (1988), 455–91.

the smaller, older administrative centre, was just beginning to emerge as a principal shipping outlet for the inland iron and coal belt. Newport was an expanding port-town serving the mineral districts of the Monmouthshire valleys. Swansea, with its harbour and its copper works, had industrial and commercial functions like these other towns, but it was its claim to be a centre of learning and culture that gave it a special identity in Wales. Good library and reading-room provision since the late eighteenth century had given it a head start in these urban stakes. The establishment of the scientific institution, with its purpose-built museum and library building capable of hosting a national scientific meeting, took these functions to a new level of importance. It has been noted that 'opportunities for ... acquiring scientific and technical knowledge were not widespread in Wales until the passing of the Welsh Intermediate Act of 1889',[86] and thus Swansea's achievements in the 1830s and 1840s stand out all the more starkly. Other Welsh towns followed in Swansea's footsteps by developing successful scientific institutions of their own. The Monmouthshire iron town of Ebbw Vale, for example, established a literary and scientific institute in 1849.[87] Merthyr was the original home of the South Wales Institute of Engineers, founded in 1857, though the headquarters later moved to Cardiff.[88] But there can be little doubt that by becoming the first Welsh town to make a name for itself in the world of urban science culture, Swansea's status in Wales and beyond was significantly enhanced.

---

[86] G. W. Roderick, 'South Wales industrialists and the theory of gentrification: 1770–1914', *Transactions of the Honourable Society of Cymmrodorion* (1987), 70.
[87] *The Ebbw Vale Literary and Scientific Institute. History of a Hundred Years, 1849–1949* (Pontypool, 1950).
[88] *Centenary Brochure, 1857–1957. South Wales Institute of Engineers* (Cardiff, 1957).

CONCLUSION

Within the space of a few months in 1855, two notable deaths occurred in Swansea. The first, on 10 February, was that of John Henry Vivian. *The Cambrian* carried the news of his decease in a special issue complete with black borders on every page and containing a lengthy memoir of his life. A week of mourning commenced, not only in Swansea but throughout the surrounding boroughs of Neath, Aberafan and Loughor, the area comprising the parliamentary seat left vacant by his death. Initial plans for a private family funeral were soon overtaken as public meetings held in the town resulted in a request that the inhabitants be permitted to follow the remains of their esteemed MP to his final resting place. On the day of the funeral, 'a sabbath-like stillness pervaded the whole place'. Business was suspended in the town centre and in Morriston. Public buildings, ships and manufactories displayed flags at half-mast. The funeral procession, which wound its way from the Guildhall towards Singleton Abbey, was nearly two miles in length and made up of some twelve official carriages carrying the dignitaries of Swansea and Neath and a further sixty private carriages of mourners. Several hundred of the workmen of Vivian and Sons from Hafod and Taibach were in attendance. They wore silk hatbands provided for them by the firm, and a few were selected to act as bearers. All along the route thousands of spectators gathered to see the cortège pass.[1]

Then, on 31 August, came news of the death of Lewis Weston Dillwyn. Compared with the coverage afforded to his recently deceased friend, *The Cambrian*'s reporting on this occasion was low key. After all, Dillwyn had been retired from public life for fourteen years and had long since relinquished active management of the Cambrian Pottery. Even his regular diary entries had ceased in 1852.[2] One black-bordered page was deemed sufficient to record his death, along with an affectionate memoir of the 'man of

---

[1] *The Cambrian*, 16 February 1855.
[2] H. J. Randall and W. Rees (eds), 'Diary of Lewis Weston Dillwyn', *South Wales and Monmouth Record Society*, 5 (Newport, 1963), p. 98.

CONCLUSION

science'. His friendship with the leading scientific figures of the day, including Conybeare, Buckland and de la Beche, was fondly recalled, as were some of his most important publications.[3] In life Vivian and Dillwyn had much in common. Both fellows of the Royal Society, their interest and expertise in scientific research were nationally acclaimed. Both deeply involved in public life at the local and national levels, they enjoyed many of the same honours. They were elected MPs in the same year and granted the freedom of the borough of Swansea simultaneously in recognition of their services to the town. They presided over important manufacturing establishments and were key members of Swansea's municipal, charitable and cultural institutions. It was somehow appropriate that the timing of their deaths should have coincided so closely and it provides an appropriate point from which to review the preceding half-century of urban development in Swansea.

The town they entered as unknowns in the opening years of the nineteenth century would have looked much the same as it did when, at around the same time, Francis Barrett attempted his manned balloon ascent. Had Barrett succeeded in gaining sufficient height that day in 1802, to look down on Swansea from his airborne basket, he would have been able to observe a town of modest extent – the borough boundaries covering around 230 acres – with a wide, sweeping bay. The harbour would have presented a bustling scene, receiving as it did some 2,590 vessels annually in 1800. He may have been able to make out the shapes of bathing machines dotted along the shoreline and the fine lodging houses on the Burrows described by Benjamin Malkin.[4] The distinctive shape of the kilns of the Cambrian Pottery, which Lewis Weston Dillwyn's father had purchased that year as a business for his son to manage, may also have been visible. Had he turned to look upriver, he would have been able to count seven copper-smelting works sited along the banks of the Tawe, soon to be joined by the Hafod works, founded by John Henry Vivian's father in 1809.[5] The main transport arteries of the period would also have come into view, including the line of

---

[3] *The Cambrian*, 7 September 1855.

[4] B. H. Malkin, *The Scenery, Antiquities and Biography of South Wales* (London, 1807), p. 588.

[5] A 'chronological account' of the works is contained in R. O. Roberts, 'The smelting of non-ferrous metals', in G. Williams and A. H. John (eds), *GCH*, Volume V: *Industrial Glamorgan* (Cardiff, 1980), pp. 86–91.

the Swansea valley canal, extending some fifteen miles north of the town, and the main east-to-west mail-coach route from the river Severn to Milford which crossed the Tawe upriver at Wychtree Bridge. His view of the small colliery settlements further inland, however, may well have been obscured by the plumes of sulphurous smoke issuing from the works which, more often than not, were carried away from the town by the prevailing sea breezes.

The features characterizing the Swansea which Vivian and Dillwyn first encountered in the early years of the nineteenth century were by no means unrecognizable fifty years later, yet the town they left in 1855 would have looked and felt like a very different place. Changes had taken place in its size, function, appearance, administration and reputation. In population terms it had grown from a little over 6,000 at the time of their arrival, to almost 35,000 at the time of their deaths.[6] Over the same period boundary extensions had seen the size of the borough increase geographically from 230 to 5,400 acres.[7] All of its principal economic activities had also undergone a transformation in scale. The vessels entering the port increased in size and number from 2,590 (154,264 tons) in 1800 to 5,325 (537,068 tons) by 1857.[8] The copper-smelting trade had also expanded, not so much in terms of the number of works in operation – there were ten in the vicinity of Swansea by 1850 – but rather in terms of output. The quantity of copper being produced grew from around 7,000 tons to 22,000 in the fifty-year period. Meanwhile, the number of collieries in operation in the district in 1854 stood at seventy-six.[9] There were also signs of growing diversity in the industrial economy. The production of tin plate, which was becoming increasingly concentrated in the Swansea region, rose from 4,000 tons per annum in 1805 to 37,000 by 1850.[10]

As well as its commercial, demographic and industrial growth, Swansea had grown in stature as a town during the lifetimes of Vivian and Dillwyn. By the time they died it had all the trappings of

---

[6] The latter figure from *Pearse's Swansea Directory* (E. Pearse, 1856), p. 7.

[7] I. G. Jones, 'The city and its villages', in R. A. Griffiths (ed.), *The City of Swansea. Challenges and Change* (Stroud, 1990), 80–1.

[8] Figures from W. H. Jones, *History of the Port of Swansea* (Carmarthen, 1922), p. 363.

[9] D. T. Williams, 'The economic development of Swansea and of the Swansea district to 1921', *Social and Economic Survey of Swansea and District*, 4 (Cardiff, 1940), p. 53.

[10] P. Jenkins, *"Twenty by Fourteen". A History of the South Wales Tinplate Industry, 1700–1961* (Llandysul, 1995), p. 36.

an important administrative, commercial and cultural centre, including a lavish new guildhall complete with council chamber, court rooms, judges' and jury accommodation, a nationally renowned and respected institution of scientific learning with its own purpose-built museum and library, and a weekly English-language newspaper which enjoyed extensive circulation throughout Wales and the West of England. Within a few short years it had gone from being perceived as a remote provincial outpost to becoming a relatively accessible urban centre. The main influence here was the arrival in 1850 of the South Wales Railway which connected the town to the wider rail network. Journey times from the major English population centres were significantly reduced as a result, and travellers were no longer reliant on the unpredictable sea-passage from Bristol.[11] A council resolution in November 1851, 'that the public clocks under control of the corporation be for the future kept at Greenwich time',[12] confirmed the sense that Swansea was becoming more closely linked to the rhythms of metropolitan and national urban life.

Between them, Vivian and Dillwyn had presided over all of the major urban developments of the previous fifty years which had helped Swansea to become an acknowledged industrial, legal, financial and intellectual centre in its own right. Each had been instrumental in bringing the Bank of England branch to Swansea in 1826, forming part of the powerful delegation that lobbied the bank's directors to name Swansea as one of the first three sites in the country for a branch bank. Similarly, they were to the fore in campaigning for more than a decade for the Great Sessions to be held alternately at Cardiff and Swansea, rather than exclusively at Cardiff. Each played a central role in the establishment and success of the RISW and the visit of the British Association to the town in 1848. Vivian and Dillwyn were both signatories to the letter which successfully petitioned the queen to become patron of the institution.[13] The first two Swansea men to represent their town and county in Parliament, they were also returned near the top of the poll to the first reformed town council in 1836. Through these public positions they made a direct contribution to the

[11] D. S. M. Barrie, *A Regional History of the Railways of Great Britain*, Volume XII: *South Wales* (Newton Abbot, 1980), pp. 201–2.
[12] WGAS, B/S Corp, B11, 10 November 1851.
[13] *Annual Report of the Council of the RISW, 1838–39*, p. 20.

decision-making and legislation on every issue, from the building or improvement of roads, bridges and harbours to the administration of justice and the welfare of the poor. In fact, it is difficult to think of any aspect of the town's development in this period in which they were not, to some degree, directly involved. They seem to have epitomized the optimistic spirit which underpinned Swansea's 'coming of age' in these years.

Given the scale of their joint contribution to Swansea's urban development over the previous half-century, the deaths of these two men, within six months of one another, were a significant loss. After Vivian's death, *The Cambrian*'s editors predicted that 'we shall not see his like again'.[14] As well as mourning the men, they might also have lamented the passing of an era. It is possible to conceive of the 1850s as marking a watershed in Swansea's urban history. In some senses, this had nothing to do with the deaths of two prominent townsmen. In Swansea, much as elsewhere, the decade can be seen as one of transition towards greater municipalization in urban administration. The establishment of the local board of health in 1850 and the transfer of the water supply into public hands in 1852 were two of the earliest signs of this process in Swansea; further moves in this direction were soon to follow as public bodies gradually superseded private companies and individual initiatives in the provision of public services. In this, the Swansea experience may be likened to that of other British towns which were also beginning the shift from what one historian has described as the 'lighting and watching period' to the 'public health period of local government'.[15]

In other respects, the 1850s may be viewed as the decade in which some of Swansea's earlier developments began to falter. The opening of the new North Dock on the Burrows purportedly brought an end to its days as a seaside resort by sacrificing the recreational functions of the shoreline to the needs of trade and industry.[16] The days of the fashionable sea-bathing resort were arguably over in any case. Swansea was not the only British town where leisure facilities gave way to dock construction at about this

[14] *The Cambrian*, 16 February 1855.
[15] J. Prest, *Liberty and Locality. Parliament, Permissive Legislation and Ratepayers' Democracies in the Nineteenth Century* (Oxford, 1990), p. 18.
[16] D. Boorman, *The Brighton of Wales. Swansea as a Fashionable Seaside Resort, c.1780–1830* (Swansea, 1986), p. 95.

CONCLUSION

time,[17] and Britain's social elites resumed their recreational activities overseas with grand tours of the Continent and more distant destinations. There were signs of change in other spheres too. In January 1859 Swansea's Bank of England branch, which Dillwyn and Vivian had fought so hard to attract, was closed. Doubts about its future had been expressed by bank staff since the early 1840s, when dock developments at Cardiff seemed to promise greater rewards.[18] In the event, the business of the Swansea branch was transferred to Bristol,[19] bringing to an end Swansea's thirty-year reign as the principal banking centre in south Wales. A number of significant developments in the copper trade also dated from the 1850s. Output of copper ore from the Cornish mines peaked in 1856 and its subsequent decline in the face of competition from imported ores from Latin America, Europe, Australia and the United States inevitably affected Swansea's advantages as a smelting location.[20] Rival copper-smelting enterprises began to be established overseas and newcomers from foreign ore-fields made their appearance in Swansea, notably the Chilean smelter, Charles Lambert, who arrived in 1852.[21]

There is little evidence to suggest that any of these developments caused great concern in Swansea at the time. In fact, the optimism of previous decades continued well into the 1850s and beyond. There were signs, for instance, that the town's bathing-resort functions were adapting to the changing circumstances. The hub of seaside life on the Burrows, though disrupted by dock construction, simply relocated further west along the shoreline at the 'slip'.[22] Here facilities developed to cater for the needs of the new breed of working-class sea bather, which was increasingly dominant among visitors to Britain's coastal resorts from mid-century

---

[17] E. M. Sandell, 'Georgian Southampton: a watering place and spa', in J. B. Morgan and P. Peberdy (eds), *Collected Essays on Southampton* (Southampton, 1958), pp. 86–7.

[18] R. O. Roberts, 'Banking and financial organisation, 1170–1914', in Williams and John (eds), *GCH*, Volume V, p. 378.

[19] BoEA, C148/9, Swansea 4. Letter book from London, 1854–9, 20 January 1859.

[20] E. Newell, 'The British copper ore market in the nineteenth century with particular reference to Cornwall and Swansea' (unpublished D.Phil. thesis, University of Oxford, 1988), p. 53.

[21] L. Valenzuela, 'Challenges to the British copper smelting industry in the world market, 1840–1860', *Journal of European Economic History*, 19 (1990), 663–74; Pyrites, *The Copper Trade in Swansea, 1860–1914* (Edinburgh, n.d.), p. 7.

[22] W. W. Moore, *The Advantages of Swansea as a Summer Resort* (Swansea, 1905), pp. 14–32.

onwards.[23] In addition, the loss of the Burrows was the catalyst for a number of initiatives in the second half of the nineteenth century to provide public recreational space elsewhere in the town in the shape of parks and gardens.[24] The improvement of rail links made the town more accessible to the day-tripper and the holidaymaker, and one mid-century town guidebook noted that, 'since the advent of the South Wales Railway, the resort of sea-bathing people has been very considerable'.[25]

The economic changes of the 1850s evoked a similarly untroubled response. The loss of the Bank of England branch aroused barely a flicker of concern in *The Cambrian*, which merely reported the date of the closure and the fact that customers would be eligible to transfer their accounts to the Bristol branch.[26] Likewise, the changes afoot in the world market for copper did not appear immediately threatening to Swansea's pre-eminence as a smelting centre. Not until the late 1860s was it apparent that a 'great change' had taken place in this regard, prompting contemporaries to look to steel, zinc, tin plate and other products as the future basis of the town's economy.[27] Many of the town's leading copper industrialists achieved considerable success in diversifying into other non-ferrous products and, in addition, the introduction of open-hearth steel production at Landore in 1867 gave an extra dimension to the town's already strong repertoire of metal industries. Tin-plate production, in particular, was given a boost by the availability of Siemen's steel, which quickly became the favoured base metal. The three decades after 1870 witnessed 'remarkable developments' in steel and tin-plate production.[28] The town's peak years of industrial prosperity were arguably still some way off in the 1880s, so perhaps the air of complacency that greeted the subtle economic shifts of the 1850s was in some senses justified.

Swansea's role as a cultural and congressional centre also seemed set to continue. No doubt buoyed by the success of the BAAS visit,

---

[23] J. K. Walton, 'The demand for working-class seaside holidays in Victorian England', *Economic History Review*, 34 (1981), 249–65.

[24] J. A. Owen, *Swansea's Earliest Open Spaces. A Study of Swansea's Parks and their Promoters in the Nineteenth Century* (Swansea, 1995), pp. 17–20.

[25] J. Lewis, *The Swansea Guide, 1851* (Swansea, 1851), p. 12.

[26] *The Cambrian*, 28 January 1859.

[27] G. G. Francis, *The Smelting of Copper in the Swansea District of South Wales* (2nd edn, London, 1881), p.148.

[28] Williams, 'Economic development of Swansea', p. 117.

CONCLUSION

the town council, in 1851, resolved to invite the Royal Agricultural Society of England to hold its annual meeting in Swansea the following year.[29] Founded in 1838 at a time when there was no comparable Welsh body in existence, its annual shows were the agricultural world's equivalent of the BAAS meetings, and were usually held in or close to large urban centres where the prospect of high visitor numbers was good.[30] A more ambitious, although ultimately unsuccessful, council initiative dating from the same period was the resolution to pursue an offer from Sir Thomas Phillipps, the antiquarian and prolific collector of books and manuscripts, to deposit his library in 'some eligible, central town in Wales', and to press Swansea's claim to be the most suitable recipient town.[31] Given the size and importance of Phillipps's collection, the manuscript portion of which alone ran to over 60,000 items, this would have been an extraordinary coup for the town.

To a large extent it was the emergence of a new generation of individuals, with similar values and ambitions for Swansea as those of Dillwyn and Vivian, which ensured this continuity. By the 1850s such people were already making their mark as the cultural and civic leaders of the next generation. George Grant Francis, for example, librarian of the RISW, was another Swansea man whose career embraced both public life and the pursuit of learning.[32] Mayor of the town in 1853, he was also a founder member of the Cambrian Archaeological Association and a great preserver of Swansea's written and physical heritage.[33] Along with the next generation of the Vivian and Dillwyn families, he ensured that there was continuity in Swansea's cultural and political life. John Dillwyn Llewelyn inherited many of his father's interests in botany and natural history and also pursued new scientific techniques in photography. Lewis Llewelyn Dillwyn, meanwhile, assumed the political mantle, gaining election to the parliamentary seat vacated by Vivian's death in 1855 and retaining it for thirty years. Henry

---

[29] It is referred to as the 'British Agricultural Society' in the minutes. See WGAS, B/S Corp, B11, 13 June 1851.
[30] N. Goddard, 'Agricultural institutions: societies, associations and the press', in R. J. T. Collins (ed.), *The Agrarian History of England and Wales*, Volume VII: *1850–1914*, part 1 (Cambridge, 2000), pp. 652–6.
[31] WGAS, B/S Corp, B11, 28 October 1850.
[32] S. Thomas, *George Grant Francis of Swansea, 1814–1882. Antiquary, Philanthropist and Civic Dignitary* (Swansea, 1993).
[33] *Dictionary of Welsh Biography down to 1940* (London, 1959), p. 270.

Hussey Vivian followed in John Henry's footsteps as a Member of Parliament, first for Glamorgan and later for Swansea, and as the head of the Hafod copper works where he used his considerable scientific expertise and initiative to develop new products and processes. With such figures in place, there was every reason to expect that Swansea would continue to occupy the prominent role in Welsh urban life which had been attained over the previous half-century.

Yet the element of continuity in Swansea was offset by change elsewhere in urban Wales. Significant developments in the economy and transport infrastructures of the principality were profoundly affecting patterns of urban development. In economic terms, developments in the coal industry were crucial in shifting the momentum of urban growth eastwards. Ironically, science – and a Swansea scientist – played a part in this. Trials in the mid-1840s, funded by the Admiralty and carried out in part by Henry de la Beche, a stalwart of the RISW, revealed that the steam-raising properties of Merthyr Tydfil and Aberdare coals were superior to those of the western district of the coalfield around Swansea, Llanelli and Neath.[34] Something resembling a classic 'take-off' in output levels followed, first in Aberdare where production rose from 177,000 tons in 1844 to over two million tons twenty years later, and then in the Rhondda valleys where output topped two million tons per annum by 1874.[35] The coastal towns of south-east Wales were the chief beneficiaries of these developments. Cardiff already had the dock and rail links in place to serve the newly expanding coal industry of the eastern Glamorgan valleys. At Newport, too, investment in dock construction and conversion of miles of tramroads into railways linked the town more efficiently with the industrial districts of the Monmouthshire valleys.[36] As a result, both towns had overtaken Swansea as coal-shipping ports by 1851 and the ensuing demographic growth brought their population totals close to the 20,000 mark by the same date.

Swansea, of course, was not the only town in the country whose status was affected in these years by industrial and commercial growth elsewhere. Bristol lost its 'second city' tag during the first half of the nineteenth century in the face of expansion in the textile

---

[34] J. Williams, 'The coal industry, 1750–1914', in Williams and John (eds), *GCH*, Volume V, p. 178.
[35] M. J. Daunton, *Coal Metropolis. Cardiff, 1870–1914* (Leicester, 1977), pp. 5–6.
[36] Barrie, *Railways of Great Britain: South Wales*, pp. 48–53, 84–91.

CONCLUSION 191

industry in the north-west of England which saw Liverpool and Manchester grow rapidly as centres of industry, commerce and manufacture.[37] In Scotland in the same period, similar shifts were taking place. Glasgow overtook Edinburgh in terms of population size as the cotton industry, new town expansion and port developments made their effects felt. On the east coast, Dundee had pulled ahead of Aberdeen by 1851 and embarked on a new phase of growth as the centre of the British jute industry.[38]

Reflecting on the urban growth of the previous decade, the general report published after the 1861 census identified some seventy-two large towns in England and Wales with populations of over 20,000.[39] By this measure, a top flight of Welsh towns had clearly emerged, consisting of the 'big four' of Cardiff, Merthyr Tydfil, Newport and Swansea. What was less clear, however, was the status of these four relative to one another. Merthyr Tydfil was still Wales's largest town in terms of population size, but its growth had slowed compared with that of Cardiff and Newport. In the face of these developments, Swansea's claim to be the principal Welsh town was less secure in the 1850s than it had been in the 1830s and 1840s when it had only Merthyr for company in the 20,000-plus population category and enjoyed primacy as a coal port, smelting location and intellectual centre. After carrying all before it in the early decades of the nineteenth century, it was now being caught by the rising tide of urban development elsewhere.

Swansea by no means abandoned its claims to the status of 'Welsh metropolis' in response to these developments. It entered fully into the contest over the location of the new university college of Wales in the 1880s.[40] Guidebooks for that period continued to use the phrase 'metropolis of South Wales',[41] and even into the twentieth century, when Cardiff gained city status, ambitious

[37] B. W. E. Alford, 'The economic development of Bristol in the nineteenth century: an enigma?' in P. McGrath and J. Cannon (eds), *Essays in Bristol and Gloucestershire History* (Bristol, 1976), pp. 252–83; P. Ollerenshaw and P. Wardley, 'Economic growth and the business community in Bristol since 1840', in Dresser and Ollerenshaw (eds), *The Making of Modern Bristol*, pp. 124–55.
[38] For population figures of Scottish towns, see S. G. E. Lythe and J. Butt, *An Economic History of Scotland, 1100–1939* (Glasgow, 1975), p. 245.
[39] *Census of England and Wales, 1861, volume III: General Report* (London, 1863), pp. 11–12, 102–3.
[40] N. Evans, 'The Welsh Victorian city: the middle class and civic and national consciousness in Cardiff, 1850–1914', *WHR*, 12, no. 3 (1985), 371.
[41] S. C. Gamwell, *The Official Guide and Handbook to Swansea and its District* (Swansea, 1880), p. 17.

municipal improvement schemes were afoot for a 'greater Swansea', suggesting that 'perhaps the leadership of Wales and the status of capital had not been lost to its larger rival after all'.[42] The reputation gained from its emergence as a centre of scientific learning in the 1830s and 1840s also endured. The longevity of the Royal Institution of South Wales and the return of the British Association for the Advancement of Science in 1880 distinguished it from other Welsh urban centres and ensured that there was mileage still to be made from the 'intelligent town' image, cultivated so profitably in earlier decades. Yet in this respect, too, there was progress elsewhere. The Newport Mechanics' Institute was reborn as Newport Athenaeum in 1847 in recognition of the potential middle-class interest in its art exhibitions, library and reading-room facilities.[43]

The importance of Swansea's urban development in the 1780–1855 era lies less in the position the town had attained by the end of this period – this was still uncertain – than in the processes through which it had passed in the preceding decades. Patterns of urbanization in Wales are intriguing precisely because the position of 'principal town' was much less clear-cut than in other parts of Britain in the first half of the nineteenth century. Whatever advantages Swansea may have gained over rival Welsh towns in this period, it was no Edinburgh, Dublin or London. It had not achieved a permanent and unassailable lead over its rivals and had no official status as a centre of Welsh urban life. Nevertheless, its rise to prominence in the early nineteenth century, helped by a passing fashion for sea bathing among the social elites, a flourishing provincial science movement and a strong industrial base, was unique in Wales. What this combination of factors produced in Swansea was an urban world that differed markedly from the kinds of communities and societies associated with Merthyr iron or Rhondda coal. The aim of this book has been to construct a picture of this urban world as it evolved in the early decades of the nineteenth century. In some respects, the result is a history that is more at home with recent traditions of British urban historical writing, embracing culture, elites and institutional life, than with some modern Welsh historical

---

[42] N. Evans, '"A Nation in a Nutshell": the Swansea disestablishment demonstration of 1912 and the political culture of Edwardian Wales', in G. H. Jenkins and R. R. Davies (eds), *From Medieval to Modern Wales*, p. 219.

[43] J. Wilson, *Art and Society in Newport: James Flewitt Mullock and the Victorian Achievement* (Newport, 1993), pp. 36–7.

research in which industry, workplace relations and the politics of labour have predominated. Yet it is a history without which the development of urban life in early nineteenth-century Wales and Britain cannot be fully understood.

BIOGRAPHICAL APPENDIX[1]

BENSON, STARLING

He was born in 1808 into a wealthy London merchant family whose connection with Swansea began in 1827 when his father's business partnership purchased the Forest copper works, originally built by Robert Morris. After his schooling at Eton, Starling arrived in Swansea in 1830 to enter the business. He quickly became active in public life, gaining election to the new town council in 1836, serving as a member of the harbour trust and becoming mayor of Swansea in 1843. He was also one of the original subscribers to the new Scientific Society, formed in 1835, and was honorary curator of the geological section at the British Association meeting in Swansea in 1848.

CAMERON, COLONEL NATHANIEL

Born in March 1787, he came into possession of Gellihir estate, Gower, on the death of his mother-in-law. He rented several properties in Swansea, including Ffynone house and Danygraig house. Cameron was one of the original subscribers to the Swansea Scientific Society and a prominent figure in town government. The first mayor of Swansea after the 1835 Municipal Reform Act, he was proposed by John Henry Vivian and supported by Lewis Weston Dillwyn and John Morris. He had extensive coal interests in the Loughor area and, in 1845, formed the Cameron Coalbrook Steam Coal Company and the Loughor Railway Company, with a view to working coal and transporting it by rail to Swansea. The railway, however, was never constructed. He died in April 1860.

---

[1] The main biographical sources are *Oxford Dictionary of National Biography* (online edition, Oxford, 2004); *Dictionary of Welsh Biography down to 1940* (London, 1959); W. W. Price, *Biographical Index of W. W. Price, Aberdare* (Aberystwyth, 1981); WGAS, W. C. Rogers Collection.

COLLINS, CHARLES

Surgeon of Swansea, he played a prominent part in the public life of the town, becoming a burgess in 1765, a common attorney in 1771, alderman in 1801 and portreeve in 1802 and again in 1812. Described as 'an indefatigable champion of progress', he was a leading supporter of harbour improvement – the issue over which he came to blows with Gabriel Powell and his son during a corporation meeting in November 1787. He died in January 1817 aged seventy-four. Other members of his family were also involved in public life: his brother, Reverend John Collins, was a burgess, alderman and harbour trustee; his son, John Charles Collins, entered the medical profession like his father, was appointed surgeon to Swansea Infirmary in 1811, and became portreeve in 1821.

DILLWYN, LEWIS WESTON

His father, William Dillwyn, a Quaker and prominent anti-slavery campaigner, purchased the Cambrian Pottery in 1802 as a business for his son to run. He did so successfully, in conjunction with George Haynes, who looked after the day-to-day management of the business. After five years in Swansea, Lewis married the heiress to a local estate, Penllergaer, which he subsequently inherited. This distanced him somewhat from work at the pottery, but not from the affairs of the town in which he was immersed, as a paving commissioner, magistrate and town council member from 1836. He also became high sheriff of Glamorgan in 1818 and MP for the county in 1832. He was well known in scientific circles, both in Swansea and beyond, as a distinguished botanist. A fellow of the Royal Society since 1804, he published a number of important works on natural history, including *British Confervae*, completed in 1809. He was a leading light in the Royal Institution of South Wales from its creation in 1835 and was vice-president at the British Association meeting in Swansea in 1848. His sons, John Dillwyn Llewelyn and Lewis Llewelyn Dillwyn, inherited his scientific and political interests, the former as a pioneer photographer and natural scientist, the latter as a Welsh Liberal MP.

Francis, John

A coach-maker, born in Somerset, who relocated to Swansea in 1811 and opened business premises in the town's High Street. Francis became active in public life, serving as a member of the Swansea Paving Commission and the Association for the Prosecution of Felons. He was also chair of the Swansea Commercial Society in 1827. An ardent supporter of political reform, he marked the passage of the 1832 legislation through Parliament by decorating the front of his works with a portrait of the king and the slogan, 'the bill, the whole bill and nothing but the bill'. He organized the celebratory procession to mark the election of John Henry Vivian as MP in 1832. He was also an active member of the Royal Institution of South Wales. He died in February 1841.

Francis, George Grant

The son of John Francis, George Grant Francis was born in Swansea in 1814. Educated at Swansea Grammar School, he developed a taste for antiquarianism and became a keen collector and preserver of historical documents. He was active in the cultural life of the town. A founder member of the Royal Institution of South Wales, he became its first librarian. He was also an original member of the Cambrian Archaeological Association in 1846. In 1840 he married Sarah Richardson, daughter of John Richardson, a prominent Swansea shipowner of Northumbrian origin. Grant Francis was also active in local government, becoming mayor of Swansea in 1853. He died in 1882.

Grenfell, Pascoe

Born in Cornwall in 1761, he became a copper ore merchant before entering into partnership with the Anglesey 'copper king', Thomas Williams, who had two copper-smelting works in operation in Swansea by the 1790s, at Upper and Middle Bank. By 1825, Grenfell had taken over the Williams family's interest in these works, and placed them in the charge of his own firm, Pascoe Grenfell and Sons. Grenfell did not reside in Swansea and had extensive interests to attend to elsewhere, including his political duties as MP, first for Great Marlow in Buckinghamshire and later for Penryn in Cornwall. He died in London in 1838.

GRENFELL, PASCOE ST LEGER

Third son of Pascoe Grenfell, Pascoe St Leger shouldered the main responsibility for continuing his father's copper-smelting interests in Swansea. Educated at Eton, and a staunch Anglican, he contributed to educational and religious provision in the town, maintaining his own works' schools and supporting religious instruction in Sunday school classes. He took up residence at Maesteg House, in close proximity to the works, and took an active part in public life in Swansea and district in his capacity as a justice of the peace, deputy lieutenant of Glamorgan and a member of Swansea corporation and harbour trust. He died in 1879.

GROVE, WILLIAM ROBERT

Born in Swansea in 1811 into a local merchant family, Grove was educated at Brasenose College, Oxford, and pursued a legal career. It was for his scientific interests, nurtured at the Royal Institution of South Wales, however, that he was to become best known. Among his inventions was the nitric acid battery, an achievement which led to his election as a fellow of the Royal Society in 1840. A year later he was appointed professor of experimental philosophy at the London Institution. He was instrumental in securing the visit of the British Association for the Advancement of Science to Swansea in 1848 and later held the presidency of the BAAS. Despite his preoccupation with scientific research, he continued to pursue his legal career, becoming a QC in 1853 and being appointed to Queen's Bench in 1880. He died in London in 1896.

HAYNES, GEORGE

Although facts about his early life are sketchy, George Haynes is known to have been born in 1745 into a Warwickshire Quaker family. As a young man he spent some time in Philadelphia, before returning to England. By 1789 he was resident in Swansea, where he went into business with John Coles at the Cambrian Pottery. It was management skills rather than technical expertise which Haynes brought to the partnership. He was credited with organizing production at the Cambrian along the lines of the Wedgwood factory. In addition to the pottery, Haynes involved himself in numerous other ventures in the town, including the establishment of *The Cambrian* newspaper and the Glamorgan Library. He also had banking and brewing interests and, in 1814, after falling out with the owner of the Cambrian Pottery, Lewis Weston Dillwyn, he established his own rival business in Swansea, the Glamorgan Pottery.

JERNEGAN, WILLIAM

Swansea's most influential early nineteenth-century architect was possibly a native of the Channel Isles. Little is known of his early training, although he may have been a pupil of the English architect John Johnson, who designed Clasemont for John Morris. Jernegan's work in Swansea consisted of a range of buildings, from the remodelling of Marino house for the Vivian family, to the Regency-style terraces of Prospect and Cambrian Place. The public buildings he designed included the Countess of Huntingdon's chapel and the Assembly Rooms. He also took on commissions for work outside Swansea, including Cardiff gaol in 1795. He never married, and died in 1836 aged eighty-five.

JONES, CALVERT RICHARD

Born in Swansea in 1802, he was the son of Calvert Jones who presented the town with land on which to build a new market in the 1820s. Calvert Richard studied at Oriel College, Oxford, where he befriended C. R. M. Talbot and his cousin, the pioneer photographer Henry Fox Talbot. His own artistic and scientific interests prompted him to undertake a number of photographic tours with Fox Talbot, and he developed considerable expertise himself. He photographed housing and maritime scenes in Swansea in the 1840s, and also travelled abroad capturing images which he would later enhance using watercolour tints. He left Swansea in the early 1850s and eventually died in Bath in 1877.

MORRIS, JOHN (FIRST BARONET)

Born in 1745, he inherited industrial interests on the outskirts of Swansea from his father, Robert, who had built the Forest copper works there *c.*1748. Like his father, who had constructed housing for his workers in the form of a large tenement known as 'Morris Castle', completed *c.*1750, John Morris also sought to provide suitable worker accommodation in the area. He engaged the bridge-builder, William Edwards, to plan and construct a worker settlement, named Morriston. Another architect, John Johnson, was commissioned to build Morris's own new residence, Clasemont, in 1775. A member of the Swansea corporation and harbour trust, Morris participated fully in public life in Swansea. He was also an advocate of agricultural improvement and was awarded the medal of the Glamorgan Society for the Cultivation of Agriculture in 1774 for successfully introducing the cultivation of cabbages into the county. He was created a baronet in 1806 and died in 1819. His son, also named John, inherited his title, lands and industrial assets at Morriston.

PADLEY, WILLIAM

Although he started out as an ironmonger, William Padley became a prominent boat-yard owner, merchant and trader in late eighteenth-century Swansea. A member of the Society of Friends, he was closely connected with other members of the town's Quaker community, including Henry Bath, senior, to whom his sister was married. Admitted a burgess in 1765, he became closely involved in the work of the corporation, as a common attorney and a member of the harbour trust. Along with Charles Collins and Robert Morris, he opposed Gabriel Powell's attempt to block harbour improvement plans in 1787, although his religious sensibilities prevented him from joining them in a legal action against the Reverend Thomas Powell in the aftermath of the turbulent corporation meeting of November of that year. His son, Silvanus, increasingly looked after his business interests from the 1790s onwards and later played a similarly active role in local administration.

PHILLIPS, RICHARD

Phillips came from a Cornish, Quaker family whose connection with Swansea was established when his father, John Phillips, became agent at the White Rock Copper Works in the town. Richard was educated for a legal career and in 1774, after his father's death, he established himself as a lawyer in London. It was there that he first became involved in work with charitable institutions, helping to found a hospital for contagious diseases. He became increasingly aware of the need for similar charitable initiatives in Swansea during return visits to his sister's house in the town. It was largely thanks to his fund-raising efforts that a dispensary was established there in 1808 and a boy's school in 1810. In London, Phillips also became well known as an anti-slavery campaigner and was a close associate of the leading abolitionist, Thomas Clarkson.

PRICE, HENRY HABBERLEY

The Prices were another Quaker industrialist family active in the Swansea and Neath area in the late eighteenth and early nineteenth centuries. Peter Price was a partner in Neath Abbey Ironworks and his sons, Henry Habberley and Joseph Tregelles, took over his industrial interests in the region. Henry was born in 1749 and gained considerable expertise as an engineer. While his brother, Joseph, was the more involved of the two in management at Neath Abbey, Henry gravitated towards Swansea where he set himself up as a civil engineer and lived at the Rhyddings. From the 1820s onwards, he seems to have become increasingly interested in the development of transport infrastructures. He was employed by Thomas Telford to build new piers on the Severn estuary, worked on harbour schemes in Ireland, Scotland and south Wales, and took a particular interest in the planning of the new dock at Swansea. He died in 1839, long before Swansea's new North Dock opened.

SMITH, CHARLES AND CHARLES HENRY

Charles Smith was the son of John Smith and Elizabeth, daughter of Chauncey Townsend, whose lands and coal interests at Gwernllwynchwyth he inherited. Charles became a member of the Swansea Harbour Trust in 1797 but his involvement in the affairs of the town did not extend any further. Instead he pursued a career as a barrister at Lincoln's Inn. He died in 1813. His son, Charles Henry Smith, was born in Swansea in 1804. He opened new coal levels at Llansamlet and developed the railway and canal network serving the industrial sites in the area. He also maintained a school for the children of his workmen in Llansamlet. He became high sheriff of Glamorgan in 1839 and mayor of Swansea in 1845, but was defeated in the council election of 1848. His career in local politics revived when he moved to Tenby in later life and became mayor of the town, where he died in 1878.

SMITH, WILLIAM HENRY

He was a man of multiple interests and business concerns in Swansea. Listed in *Pearse's Swansea Directory* of 1856 as a barrister, brick- and tile-maker, resident at Burrows Gardens, it was for his association with the first private scheme to introduce a piped water supply to Swansea in 1836 that he became better known. He became manager of the new water company and earned himself the nickname 'Waterworks Bill'. He was a fierce critic of the harbour trust and its handling of Swansea's harbour improvement plans and felt that representatives from the outlying industrial areas enjoyed a disproportionate influence in the local government of the town. Although his criticisms made him unpopular in some quarters, his experience as a paving commissioner was called upon in 1844 when he was asked by the council to draw up a new improvement bill for the better paving and lighting of the town. He was also responsible for the founding of Swansea's second English-language weekly newspaper, the *Swansea Journal*, in 1843.

SOCKETT, HENRY

A barrister in Swansea's High Street, Henry Sockett was a well-known and respected townsman who was closely associated with many of the improvements to Swansea's urban infrastructure and facilities in the early nineteenth century. His contribution to town life was recognized in 1830 when he was awarded the freedom of the borough. Despite this, little is known about his background. As a paving commissioner, he played a leading role in the initiative, from 1819 onwards, to improve the condition of Swansea's streets. His activities in the 1830s suggest that he was no great champion of municipal reform. He resigned his post as a paving commissioner in 1833, before the responsibilities of the commission were transferred to the town council, and in 1836, when the first town council was elected in Swansea, Sockett made a speech calling on the newly elected councillors to continue the good work of the old corporation in improving the town.

TENNANT, GEORGE

Born in 1765, probably in Lancashire, Tennant studied law and established a legal practice in London. One of his clients was the earl of Jersey and it was possibly his knowledge of Jersey's estate in south Wales that led him to develop his own interests there. In 1814 he purchased the Rhyddings estate, near Neath. Recognizing the limitations of Neath harbour as an outlet for shipping coal, he began to work on improving transport communication with Swansea. The first phase of his work involved the construction of a canal and he also set about building a dock at its point of termination in Swansea. At a time when Swansea harbour trustees were making little headway with their own improvement plans, Port Tennant showed what could be achieved through individual initiative.

VIVIAN, JOHN

John Vivian was born in Devon in 1750 but developed many of his diverse business interests in Cornwall, where he was an investor or 'adventurer' in a number of copper mines, a partner in the Miners' Bank at Truro and a founder member of the Cornish Metal Company. His interest in copper smelting began when he worked as Cornish agent for the Cheadle Brass and Wire Company. By 1800 he had entered into partnership in their works in Penclawdd, and installed his son, John Henry Vivian, as manager there in 1806. The experience gained at Penclawdd must have given Vivian cause for optimism about the business potential of copper smelting as, by 1809, he had set up his own firm, Vivian and Sons, at Hafod on the northern fringes of Swansea. Again it was John Henry Vivian who looked after the day-to-day management of Hafod. His father maintained close links with Cornwall where he was a justice of the peace and a keen huntsman. He died there in 1826 after a hunting accident.

VIVIAN, JOHN HENRY

Although it was his father who first developed the Vivian family's links with Swansea, John Henry Vivian's interests were far more firmly rooted in the town. He took over as head of the business on his father's death, and developed it into one of the largest copper-smelting firms in existence. He built workers' housing and schools at Hafod, applied his scientific interests to the question of reducing copper smoke, and expanded the business to nearby Margam, where the property of the English Copper Company was acquired in 1838. John Henry also became one of the most influential townsmen of his time in Swansea, first as a harbour trustee and later as a member of the town council. He was also elected the first member for Swansea Boroughs, the new parliamentary seat created in 1832. He played an active role in securing royal patronage for Swansea's scientific society in the 1830s and was also instrumental in the relocation of a session of the assizes to the town in 1833. His death, in 1855, prompted widespread public mourning in the town and district.

Voss, John

Like many of Swansea's most successful merchants in the late eighteenth and early nineteenth centuries, Voss's business interests were diverse. Mainly engaged in the drapery, printing and banking businesses, he also dealt in corn, an activity which made him unpopular during times of dearth, such as in 1766 when attacks on his property were threatened. He married the daughter of the dissenting minister, Solomon Harris, but it is not known whether Voss himself attended Harris's services. Voss was not a member of Swansea corporation, but he did participate with other local businessmen in founding the Association for the Prosecution of Felons in 1792. His son, also named John, took over his banking interests after his death in 1818, and became the first treasurer of Swansea town council in 1836.

BIBLIOGRAPHY

1. MANUSCRIPTS
2. OFFICIAL PUBLICATIONS
3. NEWSPAPERS
4. WORKS OF REFERENCE
5. CONTEMPORARY WORKS
6. SECONDARY WORKS
7. UNPUBLISHED THESES

1. MANUSCRIPTS

(a) Bank of England
Branch Committee Minute Book A, 12 January – 3 June 1826
Branch Committee Minute Book B, 4 June – 31 August 1827
Swansea Private Letter Book, 1826–9
Swansea (2) Private Letters from London, 1829–34
Swansea (3) Letter Book from London, 1834–54
Swansea (4) Letter Book from London, 1854–9

(b) Glamorgan Record Office
Dowlais Company Letter Books

(c) National Library of Wales
Lewis Weston Dillwyn Diary (catalogue summary)
Nevill Collection
Penrice and Margam Muniments
Vivian Collection

(d) National Archives, Kew
Board of Health Records (MH32)
Home Office Records (HO44, HO45)
Railway and Canal Companies (RAIL 877)

(e) Royal Institution of South Wales (held at West Glamorgan Archives Service)
British Association for the Advancement of Science
Collins Collection
Grant Francis Collection
Swansea Statistical Survey

(f) Swansea Central Library
Introductory Discourse on Swansea's Mechanics' Institute (SW2126)
Papers, Reports and Prospectuses (SW714)
Reports on Swansea Harbour (S87.1)
Swansea Improvement Act, 1844 (X387/7)

(g) University of Wales Swansea Archives
Archive of St David's Priory, Swansea
Grenfell Collection
D. T. Eaton Papers
Miscellaneous (papers on banking in Swansea)
Morris Collection
Yorkshire Imperial Metals (Vivian papers)

(h) West Glamorgan Archives Service
A Carol for Christmas 1839 (S/L WM3 36)
Acts of Parliament relating to Swansea, 1791–1822
Council Minute Books, 1835–52
Hall Day Minute Books, 1783–5
Minutes of Swansea Infirmary, 1817–18
Paving Commissioners' Minute Books, 1809–50
Reports and Correspondence relating to Swansea Harbour, 1794–1847
Swansea Theatre Tontine
W. C. Rogers Collection

2. Official Publications

A Collection of Acts of Parliament Relating to Swansea Harbour (Swansea, 1902)
Census of England and Wales, Reports: 1841, 1851, 1861, 1901.
PP 1835 XXIII, Report of the Commissioners on Municipal Corporations in England and Wales, appendix 1, part 1.
PP 1837 XXVIII, Report of the Commissioners Appointed to Report and Advise on the Boundaries and Wards of Certain Boroughs and Corporate Towns.
PP 1847 XXVII pt. 1, Royal Commission on the State of Education in Wales.

3. Newspapers

The Cambrian
Cardiff and Merthyr Guardian
Swansea Journal
The Times

BIBLIOGRAPHY

4. WORKS OF REFERENCE

A List of the Names and Residences of the High Sheriffs of Glamorgan from 1841–1966 (Cardiff, 1966).
Alban, J. R., *Calendar of Swansea's Freemen's Records from 1760* (Swansea, 1982).
Oxford Dictionary of National Biography (online edition, Oxford, 2004).
Dictionary of Welsh Biography down to 1940 (London, 1959).
James, B. Ll., *Parliamentary Papers, 1801–1914, as Sources of the History of Wales: A Guide and Bibliography* (Library Association, 1973).
Jones, D., *Statistical Evidence relating to the Welsh Language, 1801–1911* (Cardiff, 1998).
La Terieur, M. (ed.), *Dictionary of Canadian Biography*, Volume X: *1871–1880* (Toronto, 1872).
Price, W. W., *Biographical Index of W. W. Price, Aberdare* (Aberystwyth, 1981).
Wales: Historical, Biographical and Pictorial (London, 1908).
Williams, J., *Digest of Welsh Historical Statistics* (2 vols., Cardiff, 1985).

5. CONTEMPORARY WORKS

Annual Report of the Council of the Royal Institution of South Wales, 1838–9 (Swansea, 1839).
Cambrian Tourist (London, 1821).
Clark, G. T., *Report to the General Board of Health on the Sanitary Condition of the Town and Borough of Swansea* (London, 1849).
Contemporary Portraits. Men and Women of South Wales and Monmouthshire (Cardiff, 1897).
Cooke, G. A., *Topographical and Statistical Description of the Principality of Wales*, Part 2: *South Wales* (London, n.d.).
De la Beche, H. T., *Report on the Sanitary Condition of Swansea* (London, 1845).
Dillwyn, L. W., *Contributions Towards a History of Swansea* (Swansea, 1840).
Feltham, J., *Guide to the Watering and Sea-bathing Places* (London, 1806).
Francis, G. G., *The Smelting of Copper in the Swansea District of South Wales* (2nd edn, London, 1881).
Gabb, G. (ed.), *Mr Dillwyn's Diary* (Swansea, 1998).
Gamwell, S. C., *The Official Guide and Handbook to Swansea and its District* (Swansea, 1880).
Ginswick, J. (ed.), *Labour and the Poor in England and Wales, 1849–1851*, Volume 3: *South Wales – North Wales* (London, 1983).
Gwent, D., *The Swansea Stage. A Biographical and Anecdotal Sketch of its History. Articles from the South Wales Daily News* (Swansea, n.d.).
Hunt and Co.'s Directory and Topography for the Cities of Gloucester and Bristol and the Towns of Carmarthen, Kidwelly, Laugharne, Llanelly and St Clears (London, 1849).
Lewis, J., *The Swansea Guide, 1851* (Swansea, 1851).
Malkin, B. H., *The Scenery, Antiquities and Biography of South Wales* (London, 1807).
Mathews's Swansea Directory (Bristol, 1816).

Mathews's Swansea Directory for the year 1830 (Swansea, 1830).
Moore, W. W., *The Advantages of Swansea as a Summer Resort* (Swansea, 1905).
Morris, M. G. R. (ed.), *Romilly's visits to Wales, 1827–54* (Llandysul, 1998).
New Swansea Guide (Swansea, 1823).
Nicholas, T., *Annals and Antiquities of the County Families of Wales* (London, 1872).
Nicholson, G., *The Cambrian Traveller's Guide* (Stourport, 1808).
Nicholson, G., *Nicholson's Cambrian Traveller's Guide* (3rd edn, London, 1840).
Pearse's Swansea Directory (E. Pearse, 1856).
Phillips, M., *Memoir of the Life of Richard Phillips* (London, 1841).
Pigot's London Provincial Directory (London, 1822–3).
Pyrites, *The Copper Trade. Swansea, 1860–1914* (Edinburgh, n.d.).
Randall, H. J., and Rees, W. (eds), 'Diary of Lewis Weston Dillwyn', *South Wales and Monmouth Record Society*, 5 (Newport, 1963).
Richards, J. W., *Reminiscences of the Early Days of the Parish Church of St Joseph's Greenhill, Swansea* (Swansea, 1919).
Slater's Royal, National and Commercial Directory and Topography of the Counties of Gloucestershire, Monmouthshire, and North and South Wales (London, 1858–9).
Smyth, W. H., *Nautical Observations on the Port and Maritime Vicinity of Cardiff* (Cardiff, 1840).
Swansea Guide: containing such information as was deemed useful to the traveller through the counties of Glamorgan and Monmouthshire (Swansea, 1802).
Swansea Philosophical and Literary Institution. First Annual Report (Swansea, 1836).
Thomas, H. M. (ed.), *The Diaries of John Bird of Cardiff. Clerk to the First Marquess of Bute, 1790–1803* (Cardiff, 1987).
Tomos, D. (ed.), *Michael Faraday in Wales, including Faraday's Journal of his Tour through Wales in 1819* (Denbigh, 1972).

6. Secondary works

(a) Books

Alban, J. R., *Portreeves and Mayors of Swansea* (Swansea, 1982).
Aldis, A. S., *Cardiff Royal Infirmary, 1883–1983* (Cardiff, 1984).
Allen, G. C., *The Industrial Development of Birmingham and the Black Country, 1860–1927* (London, 1966).
Atkinson, M. and Baber, C., *The Growth and Decline of the South Wales Iron Industry, 1760–1880: An Industrial History* (Cardiff, 1987).
Ayris, I., *A City of Palaces. Richard Grainger and the Making of Newcastle upon Tyne* (Newcastle, 1997).
Baber, C. and Williams, L. J. (eds), *Modern South Wales. Essays in Economic History* (Cardiff, 1986).
Baker Jones, T., *History of the Royal Gwent Hospital, 1839–1948* (Newport, 1948).
Barker, H., *Newspapers, Politics and English Society, 1695–1885* (Harlow, 2000).
Barrie, D. S. M., *A Regional History of the Railways of Great Britain*, Volume XII: *South Wales* (Newton Abbot, 1980).

BIBLIOGRAPHY

Bayliffe, D. M. and Harding, J. N., *Starling Benson of Swansea* (Bridgend, 1996).
Beanland, W. A., *The History of the Royal Institution of South Wales, Swansea* (Swansea, 1935).
Bender, T. (ed.), *The University and the City from Medieval Origins to the Present* (New York and Oxford, 1998).
Berg, M., *The Age of Manufactures. Industry, Innovation and Work in Britain, 1700–1820* (Oxford, 1985).
Boorman, D., *The Brighton of Wales. Swansea as a Fashionable Seaside Resort, c.1780–1830* (Swansea, 1986).
Briggs, A., *The Age of Improvement, 1783–1867* (Harlow, 1979).
Bush, G., *Bristol and its Municipal Government, 1820–1851* (Bristol, 1976).
Cadogan, P., *Early Radical Newcastle* (Consett, 1975).
Calhoun, C. (ed.), *Habermas and the Public Sphere* (Cambridge and London, 1992).
Carter, H., *The Towns of Wales. A Study in Urban Geography* (Cardiff, 1965).
Carter, H. and Wheatley, S., *Merthyr in 1851. A Study of the Spatial Structure of a Welsh Industrial Town* (Cardiff, 1982).
Clapham, J., *The Bank of England. A History*, Volume II: *1797–1914* (Cambridge, 1944).
Clark, P., *The English Alehouse. A Social History* (London, 1983).
Idem (ed.), *The Cambridge Urban History of Britain*, Volume 2: *1540–1840* (Cambridge, 2000).
Cotter, P., *Calvert in Camera* (Cardiff, 1990).
Cragoe, M., *Culture, Politics and National Identity in Wales, 1832–1886* (Oxford, 2004).
Croll, A., *Civilizing the Urban. Popular Culture and Public Space in Merthyr, 1870–1914* (Cardiff, 2000).
Crouzet, F., *The First Industrialists. The Problem of Origins* (Cambridge, 1985).
Cullen, M. J., *The Statistical Movement in Early Victorian Britain* (Sussex, 1975).
Daunton, M. J. (ed.), *The Cambridge Urban History of Britain*, Volume 3: *1840–1950* (Cambridge, 2001).
Daunton, M. J., *Coal Metropolis. Cardiff, 1870–1914* (Leicester, 1977).
Davies, J., *Cardiff and the Marquesses of Bute* (Cardiff, 1981).
Idem, *A History of Wales* (London, 1993).
Davies, J., *Cardiff. A Pocket Guide* (Cardiff, 2002).
Davies, J. H., *History of Pontypridd and District from Earliest to Modern Times* (Llandybïe, 1967).
Davies, T. G., *Deeds Not Words. A History of the Swansea General and Eye Hospital, 1817–1948* (Cardiff, 1988).
Idem, *Howel Gwyn of Dyffryn and Neath* (Neath, 1992).
Devine, T. M. and Jackson, G. (eds), *Glasgow*, Volume 1: *Beginnings to 1830* (Manchester, 1995).
Dixon, R. and Muthesius, S., *Victorian Architecture* (London, 1978).
Dodd, A. H. (ed.), *A History of Wrexham, Denbighshire* (Wrexham, 1957).
Dresser, M. and Ollerenshaw, P. (eds), *The Making of Modern Bristol* (Tiverton, 1996).
Eaton, G., *From Castle to Civic Centre. A History of Local Government in Neath, c.1100–1972* (Neath, 1975).

The Ebbw Vale Literary and Scientific Institute. History of a Hundred Years, 1849–1949, (Pontypool, 1950).

Egan, D., *Coal Society. A History of the South Wales Mining Valleys, 1840–1980* (Llandysul, 1987).

Evans, A. L., *The Story of Taibach and District* (2nd edn, Port Talbot, 1982).

Evans, C., *'The Labyrinth of Flames'. Work and Social Conflict in Early Industrial Merthyr Tydfil* (Cardiff, 1993).

Evans, E. and Spurgeon, C. J., *Swansea Castle and the Medieval Town* (Swansea, 1983).

Evans, L. W., *Education in Industrial Wales, 1700–1900* (Cardiff, 1971).

Firth, G., *A History of Bradford* (Chichester, 1997).

Fraser, D., *Urban Politics in Victorian England* (Leicester, 1976).

Idem (ed.), *Municipal Reform in the Industrial City* (Leicester, 1982).

Fraser, H. and Maver, I. (eds), *Glasgow*, Volume 2: *1830–1912* (Manchester, 1996).

Freeman, E. C., and Gill, E., *The Story of Lord Nelson and Sir William and Lady Hamilton's Tour in Wales and Monmouthshire, Sunday 25 July – Friday 20 August 1802* (Newport, 1962).

Gauldie, E., *One Artful and Ambitious Individual: Alexander Riddoch (1745–1822) (Provost of Dundee, 1787–1819)* (Dundee, 1989).

Gauldie, E., Lenman, B. and Lythe, C., *Dundee and its Textile Industry, 1850–1914* (Dundee, 1969).

Grant, R., *The Parliamentary History of Glamorgan, 1542–1976* (Swansea, 1978).

Greenlaw, J., *Swansea Clocks. Watch and Clockmakers of Swansea and District (Llanelli, Llandeilo, Neath)* (Swansea, 1997).

Grenfell Hill, J. (ed.), *Growing up in Wales, 1895–1939* (Llandysul, 1996).

Griffiths, R. A. (ed.), *The City of Swansea. Challenges and Change* (Stroud, 1990).

Gunn, S., *The Public Culture of the Victorian Middle Class. Ritual and Authority in the English Industrial City, 1840–1914* (Manchester, 2000).

Hadfield, C., *The Canals of South Wales and the Border* (Cardiff, 1967).

Haley, B., *The Healthy Body and Victorian Culture* (London, 1978).

Hallesy, H. L., *The Glamorgan Pottery, Swansea, 1814–38* (Llandysul, 1995).

Harris, J. R., *The Copper King. A Biography of Thomas Williams of Llanidan* (Liverpool, 1964).

Hartwell, R. M., *The Industrial Revolution and Economic Growth* (London, 1971).

Hassan, J. A., *A History of Water in Modern England and Wales* (Manchester, 1998).

Hennock, E. P., *Fit and Proper Persons. Ideal and Reality in Nineteenth Century Urban Government* (London, 1973).

Herbert, T. and Jones, G. E. (eds), *People and Protest. Wales, 1815–1880* (Cardiff, 1988).

Hewitt, M., *The Emergence of Stability in the Industrial City. Manchester, 1832–1867* (Aldershot, 1996).

Hibbert, C., *Nelson: A Personal History* (2nd edn, London, 1985).

Hignell, A., *A 'Favorit' Game. Cricket in South Wales before 1914* (Cardiff, 1992).

Hobsbawm, E. J., *Industry and Empire. An Economic History of Britain since 1750* (London, 1968).

Hughes, S. R., *Copperopolis. Landscapes of the Early Modern Industrial Period in Swansea* (Aberystwyth, 2000).
Hughes, S. R. and Reynolds, P., *A Guide to the Industrial Archaeology of the Swansea Region* (Swansea, 1988).
Hunt, W. W., *'To Guard my People'. An Account of the Origin and History of the Swansea Police* (Swansea, 1957).
Ince, L., *Neath Abbey and the Industrial Revolution* (Stroud, 2001).
Idem, *The Neath Abbey Iron Company* (Eindhoven, 1984).
Inkster, I., *Scientific Culture and Urbanisation in Industrial Britain* (Aldershot, 1997).
Inkster, I. and Morrell, J. (eds), *Metropolis and Province. Science in British Culture, 1780–1850* (London, 1983).
Jenkins, E., *Neath and District. A Symposium* (Neath, 1974).
Jenkins, G. H. and Davies, R. R. (eds), *From Medieval to Modern Wales. Historical Essays in Honour of Kenneth O. Morgan and Ralph A. Griffiths* (Cardiff, 2004).
Jenkins, Paul, *'Twenty by Fourteen'. A History of the South Wales Tinplate Industry, 1700–1961* (Llandysul, 1995).
Jenkins, Philip, *The Making of a Ruling Class: The Glamorgan Gentry, 1640–1790* (Cambridge, 1983).
Idem, *A History of Modern Wales, 1536–1990* (London, 1992).
Jones, A. G., *Press, Politics and Society. A History of Journalism in Wales* (Cardiff, 1993).
Jones, B. P., *From Elizabeth to Victoria. The Government of Newport (Monmouthshire), 1550–1850* (Newport, 1957).
Jones, D., *The Quakers of Swansea and Neath* (Swansea, 1936).
Jones, D. J. V., *The Last Rising: the Newport Chartist Insurrection of 1839* (Cardiff, 1999).
Idem, *Before Rebecca. Popular Protests in Wales, 1793–1835* (London, 1973).
Jones, G. E. and Roderick, G. W., *A History of Education in Wales* (Cardiff, 2003).
Jones, H. M., *Llanelli Lives* (Swansea, 2000).
Jones, I. G., *Mid-Victorian Wales. The Observers and the Observed* (Cardiff, 1992).
Jones, O. V., *The Progress of Medicine; A History of the Caernarfon and Anglesey Infirmary, 1809–1948* (Llandysul, 1984).
Jones, P. H. and Rees, E. (eds), *A Nation and its Books. A History of the Book in Wales* (Aberystwyth, 1998).
Jones, W. H., *History of Swansea and of the Lordship of Gower*, Volume 1: *From the Earliest times to the Fourteenth Century* (Carmarthen, 1920).
Idem, *History of the Port of Swansea* (Carmarthen, 1922).
Jones, W. Tudor, *The Rise and Progress of Religious Free Thought in Swansea* (Swansea, 1900).
Joyce, P., *Work, Society and Politics. The Culture of the Factory in Victorian England* (New Brunswick, 1980).
Koditschek, T., *Class Formation and Urban Industrial Society. Bradford, 1750–1850* (Cambridge, 1990).
Lenman, B., *From Esk to Tweed. Harbours, Ships and Men of the East Coast of Scotland* (Glasgow, 1975).
Lewis, E. D., *The Rhondda Valleys. A Study in Industrial Development, 1800 to the Present Day* (London, 1959).

Lieven, M., *Senghennydd. The Universal Pit Village, 1890–1930* (Llandysul, 1994).
Lowe, J. B., *Welsh Industrial Workers' Housing, 1775–1875* (Cardiff, 1977).
Lucas, R., *Reynoldston* (Swansea, 1998).
Lythe, S. G. E. and Butt, J., *An Economic History of Scotland, 1100–1939* (Glasgow, 1975).
Malet, H., *The Canal Duke* (London, 1961).
Marcus, S., *Engels, Manchester and the Working Class* (2nd edn, London, 1985).
Martin, J., *Henry and the Fairy Palace. Fox Talbot and Glamorgan* (Aberystwyth, 1993).
Minchinton, W. E. (ed.), *Industrial South Wales, 1750–1914. Essays in Welsh Economic History* (London, 1969)
Miskell, L., Whatley, C. A. and Harris, B. (eds), *Victorian Dundee. Image and Realities* (East Linton, 2000).
Morgan, R., *A History of Taibach to 1872* (trans. A. L. Evans) (Port Talbot, 1987).
Morgan, J. B. and Peberdy, P. (eds), *Collected Essays on Southampton* (Southampton, 1958).
Morrell, J. and Thackray, A., *Gentlemen of Science. The Early Years of the British Association for the Advancement of Science* (Oxford, 1981).
Morris, B., *The Houses of Singleton. A Swansea Landscape and its History* (Swansea, 1995).
Idem (ed.), *Gabriel Powell's Survey of the Lordship of Gower and Kilvey in 1764* (Swansea, 2000).
Morris, R., *Penllergare: A Victorian Paradise: A short history of the Penllergare estate and its creator, John Dillwyn Llewellyn (1810–82)* (Llandeilo, 1999).
Morris, R. J., *Class, Sect and Party. The Making of the British Middle Class: Leeds, 1820–1850* (Manchester, 1990).
Morton Nance, E., *The Pottery and Porcelain of Swansea and Nantgarw* (London, 1942).
Mumford Jones, H. and Bernard Cohen, I. (eds), *Science Before Darwin. A Nineteenth Century Anthology* (London, 1963).
O'Leary, P., *Immigration and Integration. The Irish in Wales, 1798–1922* (Cardiff, 2000).
Idem (ed.), *Irish Migrants in Modern Wales* (Liverpool, 2004).
Outram, D., *The Enlightenment* (Cambridge, 1995).
Owen, J. A., *Swansea's Earliest Open Spaces. A Study of Swansea's Parks and their Promoters in the Nineteenth Century* (Swansea, 1995).
Painting, D., *Swansea's Place in the History of Photography* (Swansea, 1982).
Penny, J., 'Up, up and away. An account of ballooning in and around Bristol and Bath, 1784–1999', *Historical Association Local History Pamphlet* (Bristol, 1999).
Phillips, D. R., *The History of the Vale of Neath* (Swansea, 1925).
Phillips, M., *The Copper Industry in the Port Talbot District* (Neath, 1935).
Prest, J., *Liberty and Locality. Parliament, Permissive Legislation and Ratepayers' Democracies in the Nineteenth Century* (Oxford, 1990).
Rees, R., *King Copper. South Wales and the Copper Trade, 1584–1895* (Cardiff, 2000).
Rees, W., *Cardiff: A History of the City* (Cardiff, 1962).
Robins, N. A., *The Enclosure of Townhill. An Illustrated Guide* (Swansea, 1990).
Rogers, W. C., *The Genealogy and some Historical Notices of the Families of Collins of Swansea, Powell of Cantreff and Swansea, Thomas of Glanmor* (Swansea, 1946).

Rolt, L. T. C., *The Aeronauts. A History of Ballooning, 1783–1903* (Gloucester, 1985).
Rubinstein, W. D., *Elites and the Wealthy in Modern British History. Essays in Social and Economic History* (Brighton, 1987).
Russell, C. A., *Science and Social Change, 1700–1900* (London, 1983).
Salmon, D., *Swansea Hospital: History, 1817–1917* (Swansea, 1917).
Salmon, H. M., 'The Cardiff Naturalists' Society: a condensed history' (1974), www.cardiffnaturalists.org.uk.
Saunders, N. H., *Swansea Hebrew Congregation, 1730–1980* (Swansea, 1980).
Smith, C. (ed.), *Bishop Gore's Grammar School. Founded 14 September 1682. A History Published to Celebrate the Tercentenary of Foundation* (Swansea, 1982).
Smith, D. (ed.), *A People and a Proletariat. Essays in the History of Wales, 1780–1980* (London, 1980).
The South Wales Institute of Engineers. Founded 1857, Incorporated by Royal Charter, 1881. Centenary Brochure, 1857–1957 (Cardiff, 1957).
Spencer, F. H., *Municipal Origins. An Account of Private Bill Legislation Relating to Local Government, 1740–1835* (London, 1911).
Spencer, G., *Catholic Life in Swansea. The Centenary of St David's Church Swansea, 1847–1947* (Swansea, 1947).
Symons, M. V., *Coal Mining in the Llanelli Area*, Volume 1: *Sixteenth Century to 1829* (Llanelli, 1979).
Temple Patterson, A., *A History of Southampton, 1700–1914*, Volume 1: *An Oligarchy in Decline, 1700–1835* (Southampton, 1966).
Idem, *A History of Southampton, 1700–1914*, Volume 2: *The Beginnings of Modern Southampton, 1836–1867* (Southampton, 1971).
Thomas, N. L., *The Story of Swansea's Districts and Villages*, Volume 1, parts 1–3 (Swansea, 1964).
Idem, *The Story of Swansea's Markets* (Swansea, 1965).
Idem, *The Story of Swansea's Districts and Villages*, Volume 2, parts 4–8 (Swansea, 1969).
Thomas, S., *George Grant Francis of Swansea, 1814–1882. Antiquary, Philanthropist and Civic Dignitary* (Swansea, 1993).
Thomas, W. S. K., *The History of Swansea: From Rover Settlement to the Restoration* (Llandysul, 1990).
Toomey, R. R., *Vivian and Sons, 1809–1924. A Study of the Firm in the Copper and Related Industries* (London, 1985).
Trainor, R., *Black Country Elites. The Exercise of Authority in an Industrial Area, 1830–1900* (Oxford, 1993).
Tucker, K., *A Scratch in Glamorganshire* (Cilfrew, 1998).
Wallace, R., *Organise! Organise! Organise! A Study of Reform Agitations in Wales, 1840–1886* (Cardiff, 1991).
Weaver, M. (ed.), *British Photography in the Nineteenth Century* (Cambridge, 1989).
Webb, S. and B., *English Local Government from the Revolution to the Municipal Corporations Act*, part 2 (London, 1924).
Wilkes, L. and Dodds, G., *Tyneside Classical. The Newcastle of Grainger, Dobson and Clayton* (London, 1964).

Wilkins, C., *The South Wales Coal Trade and its Allied Industries from the Earliest Days to the Present Time* (Cardiff, 1888).
Idem, *History of the Iron, Steel, Tinplate and other Trades of Wales* (Merthyr Tydfil, 1903).
Williams, C., *Democratic Rhondda. Politics and Society, 1885–1951* (Cardiff, 1996).
Idem, *Capitalism, Community and Conflict. The South Wales Coalfield, 1898–1947* (Cardiff, 1998).
Williams, D., *John Frost. A Study in Chartism* (Cardiff, 1939).
Idem, *The Rebecca Riots. A Study in Agrarian Discontent* (Cardiff, 1955).
Williams, Gareth, *Valleys of Song. Music and Society in Wales, 1840–1914* (Cardiff, 1998).
Williams, G. (ed.), *Swansea. An Illustrated History* (Swansea, 1990).
Williams, G. and John, A. H. (eds), *Glamorgan County History*, Volume V: *Industrial Glamorgan* (Cardiff, 1980).
Williams, G. A., *The Merthyr Rising* (London, 1978).
Idem, *When Was Wales?* (London, 1985).
Williams, L. J., *Was Wales Industrialised? Essays in Modern Welsh History* (Llandysul, 1995).
Wilson, J., *Art and Society in Newport: James Flewitt Mullock and the Victorian Achievement* (Newport, 1993).
Youngson, A. J., *The Making of Classical Edinburgh, 1750–1840* (Edinburgh, 1966).

(b) Articles and Essays

Alford, B. W. E., 'The economic development of Bristol in the nineteenth century: an enigma?', in P. McGrath and J. Cannon (eds), *Essays in Bristol and Gloucestershire History* (Bristol, 1976), pp. 124–55.
Bowen, E. G., 'Carmarthen: an urban study', *Archaeologia Cambrensis*, 17 (1968), 1–17.
Brown, R. L., 'George Martin Maber, Rector of Merthyr Tydfil', *Merthyr Historian*, 10 (1999), 63–7.
Campbell, T. M., 'C. R. M. Talbot (1803–1890): a Welsh landowner in politics and industry', *Morgannwg*, 44 (2000), 66–104.
Cardy, B., 'Nathaniel Cameron: the first Reform Mayor of Swansea', *Minerva*, 3 (1995), 12–16.
Chadwick, R., 'Trading in ores, 1600–1900', *Tamar*, 5 (1983).
Collins, M., 'The Bank of England at Liverpool, 1827–44', *Business History*, 14, no. 2 (1972), 144–65.
Cook, L. A., 'The Vivians of Cornwall', *Minerva*, 4 (1996), 22–6.
Cooper, M. L., and Hall, V. M. D., 'William Robert Grove and the London Institution, 1841–1845', *Annals of Science*, 39 (1982), 229–54.
Coopey, R. and Roberts, O., 'Public utility or private enterprise? Water and health in the nineteenth and twentieth centuries', in A. Borsay (ed.), *Medicine in Wales, c.1800–2000. Public Service or Private Commodity?* (Cardiff, 2003), pp. 21–39.
Croll, A., 'From bar stool to choir stall: music and morality in late Victorian Merthyr', *Llafur*, 6, no. 1 (1992), 17–27.

Davies, J., 'Aristocratic town-makers and the coal metropolis: the marquesses of Bute and the growth of Cardiff, 1776–1947', in D. Cannadine (ed.), *Patricians, Power and Politics in Nineteenth Century Towns* (Leicester, 1982), pp. 17–67.
Davies, J. M., 'The Morris family and Swansea', *Gower*, 5 (1952), 26–30.
Davies, T. G., 'Lewis Weston Dillwyn and his doctors', *Morgannwg*, 32 (1988), 70–89.
Emery, V., 'Contact between north Devon and south Wales in the 1840s', *Devon and Cornwall Notes and Queries*, 27, no. 8 (1957), 198–206.
Evans, C., 'Global commerce and industrial organisation in an eighteenth century Welsh enterprise: the Melingriffith Company', *Welsh History Review*, 20, no. 3 (2001), 413–34.
Evans, D. O., 'The non-ferrous metallurgical industries of south Wales and Welshmen's share in their development', *Transactions of the Honourable Society of Cymmrodorion* (1929–30), 1–37.
Evans, N., '"The first charity in Wales": Cardiff Infirmary and south Wales society, 1837–1914', *Welsh History Review*, 9, no. 2 (1979), 319–46.
Idem, 'Urbanisation, elite attitudes and philanthropy: Cardiff, 1850–1914', *International Review of Social History*, 27 (1982), 290–323.
Idem, 'The Welsh Victorian city. The middle class and civic and national consciousness in Cardiff, 1850–1914', *Welsh History Review*, 12, no. 3 (1985), 350–87.
Evans, N., 'Immigrants and minorities in Wales, 1840–1990: a comparative perspective', *Llafur*, 5, no. 4 (1991), 5–26.
Idem, 'Patterns of protest and regional labour implantation in South Wales and the north-east of England', *Tijdschrift voor Sociale Geschiedenis* (1992), 212–29.
Idem, 'Writing the social history of modern Wales: approaches, achievements and problems', *Social History*, 17, no. 3 (1992), 479–92.
Gabb, G., 'Some cracks in the fabric of Victorian Swansea', *Gower*, XLIV (1993), 50–6.
Idem, 'What manner of men? The founders of the Royal Institution', *Minerva*, 3 (1995), 19–25.
Gill, C., 'Birmingham under the street commissioners, 1769–1851', *University of Birmingham Historical Journal*, 1, no. 2 (1948), 255–87.
Goddard, N., 'Agricultural institutions: societies, associations and the press', in E. J. T. Collins (ed.), *The Agrarian History of England and Wales*, Volume VII: *1850–1914*, part 1 (Cambridge, 2000), pp. 650–90.
Griffiths, R. A., 'Wales and the Marches', in D. M. Palliser (ed.), *The Cambridge Urban History of Britain*, Volume 1: *600–1540* (Cambridge, 2000), pp. 681–714.
Gwyn, D., 'The industrial town in Gwynedd', *Landscape History*, 23 (2001), 71–89.
Hargest, L., 'Cardiff's "spasm of rebellion" in 1818', *Morgannwg*, 21 (1977), 69–88.
Hart, R. J., 'John Jenkins of Rotherslade: a forgotten pillar of the Royal Institution of South Wales', *Minerva*, 5 (1997), 9–17.
Hassan, J. A., 'The growth and impact of the British water industry in the nineteenth century', *Economic History Review*, 38, no. 4 (1985), 531–47.

Howell, D. W., 'Pembrokeshire gentry in the eighteenth century', in T. Barnes and N. Yates (eds), *Carmarthenshire Studies. Essays Presented to Major Francis Jones* (Carmarthen, 1974), pp. 158–85.

Idem, 'Society, 1660–1793', in B. Howells (ed.), *Pembrokeshire County History*, Volume III: *Early Modern Pembrokeshire* (Haverfordwest, 1987), pp. 32–59.

James, D. C., 'The genesis of sanitary reform in Cardiff, 1774–1850', *Welsh History Review*, 11, no. 1 (1982), 50–66.

Jenkins, P., 'Jacobites and Freemasons in eighteenth-century Wales, *Welsh History Review*, 9, no. 3 (1979), 391–406.

Idem, 'Tory industrialism and town politics. Swansea in the eighteenth century', *Historical Journal*, 28, no. 1 (1985), 103–23.

Jones, I. G., 'Denominationalism in Swansea and district: a study of the ecclesiastical census of 1851', *Morgannwg*, 12 (1968), 67–96.

Jones, O. V., 'Bangor – the growth of a city during the first half of the nineteenth century', *Caernarvonshire Historical Society Transactions*, 46 (1985), 23–43.

Jones, W., 'Robert Morris, the Swansea friend of John Wilkes', in R. Denning (ed.), *Glamorgan Historian*, Volume 11 (Barry, 1975), 126–36.

Jordan, H., 'The 1842 general strike in south Wales', *Our History*, 75 (1983), 1–23.

Keith, T., 'Municipal elections in the royal burghs of Scotland, II: from the union to the passing of the Scottish burgh reform bill in 1833', *Scottish Historical Review*, Volume 13, no. 51 (1916), 266–81.

Kitteringham, G., 'Science in provincial society: the case of Liverpool in the early nineteenth century', *Annals of Science*, 39, no. 4 (1982), 329–48.

Lambert, W. R., 'Some impressions of Swansea and its copper works in 1850', in S. Williams (ed.), *Glamorgan Historian*, Volume 5 (Cowbridge, 1968), pp. 206–12.

Lloyd, T., 'The architects of Regency Swansea', *Gower*, 41 (1990), 56–67.

Marwick, J. D., 'The municipal institutions of Scotland', *Scottish Historical Review*, 1, no. 2 (1904), 274–90.

Minchinton, W., 'Bristol – metropolis of the west in the eighteenth century', *Transactions of the Royal Historical Society*, 5th series, 4 (1954), 69–89.

Miskell, L., 'From conflict to co-operation: urban improvement and the case of Dundee, 1790–1850', *Urban History*, 29, no. 3 (2002), 350–71.

Idem, '"Separate spheres"? Rethinking the history of the metalliferous industries in south Wales', *Welsh History Review*, 21, no. 2 (2002), 249–70.

Idem, 'The making of a new "Welsh metropolis": science, leisure and industry in early nineteenth-century Swansea', *History*, 88, no. 1 (2003), 32–52.

Miskell, L. and Whatley, C. A., '"Juteopolis" in the making: linen and the industrial transformation of Dundee, c.1820–1850', *Textile History*, 30, no. 2 (1999), 176–98.

Miskell, L. and Kenefick, W., '"A flourishing seaport": Dundee harbour and the making of the industrial town, c.1815–1850', *Scottish Economic and Social History*, 20, no. 2 (2000), 176–98.

Morgan, K. O., 'Consensus and conflict in modern Welsh history', in D. W. Howell and K. O. Morgan (eds), *Crime, Protest and Police in Modern British Society: Essays in Memory of David J. V. Jones* (Cardiff, 1999), pp. 16–41.

Morgan, N. and Trainor, R., 'The dominant classes', in W. H. Fraser and R. J. Morris (eds), *People and Society in Scotland*, Volume 2: *1830–1914* (Edinburgh, 1990), pp. 103–37.
Morrell, J., 'The early Yorkshire Geological and Polytechnic Society: a reconsideration', *Annals of Science*, 45, no. 2 (1988), 153–67.
Morris, B., 'Swansea houses: working-class houses, 1800–1850', *Gower*, 26 (1975), 53–61.
Morris, R. J., 'Voluntary societies and British urban elites, 1780–1850: an analysis', *Historical Journal*, 26, no. 1 (1983), 95–118.
Newell, E., '"Copperopolis": the rise and fall of the copper industry in the Swansea district, 1826–1921', *Business History*, XXXII (1990), 75–97.
O'Gorman, F., 'Campaign rituals and ceremonies: the social meaning of elections in England, 1780–1860', *Past and Present*, 135 (1992), 79–115.
Parry, G., '"Queen of the Welsh resorts": tourism and the Welsh language in Llandudno', *Welsh History Review*, 21, no. 1 (2002), 118–48.
Penrhyn Jones, G., 'Cholera in Wales', *National Library of Wales Journal*, X (1957–8), 281–300.
Phelps, M., 'Maritime, medical and municipal matters: the Richardson family and Swansea in the nineteenth century', *Annual Report of the County Archivist* (Swansea, 1997–8), pp. 16–18.
Phillips, M., 'The copper industry in the Port Talbot district', *Transactions of the Aberafan and Margam District Historical Society*, VI (1933), 91–113.
Pritchard, J. W., '"Fit and proper persons": councillors of Denbigh, their status and position, 1835–94', *Welsh History Review*, 17, no. 2 (1994), 186–204.
Idem, 'Water supply in Welsh towns, 1840–1900: control, conflict and development', *Welsh History Review*, 21, no. 1 (2002), 24–47.
Quinault, R., 'The French invasion of Pembrokeshire: a bicentennial assessment', *Welsh History Review*, 19, no. 4 (1999), 618–42.
Rees, E. and Walters, G., 'Swansea libraries in the nineteenth century', *Journal of the Welsh Bibliographical Society*, X (1966–71), 43–57.
Rees, R., 'The great copper trials', *History Today*, 43, no. 12 (1993), 38–44.
Ridd, T., 'The health of a town: Swansea in the 1840s', in S. Williams (ed.), *Glamorgan Historian*, Volume 1 (Cowbridge, 1963), pp. 171–9.
Idem, 'Gabriel Powell: the uncrowned king of Swansea', in S. Williams (ed.), *Glamorgan Historian*, Volume 5 (Cowbridge, 1968), pp. 152–60.
Roberts, G., 'The municipal development of the borough of Swansea to 1900', *Social and Economic Survey of Swansea and District*, 1 (Swansea, 1940), pp. 3–55.
Roberts, G. B., 'Swansea and Wedgwood', in J. Gray (ed.), *Welsh Ceramics in Context*. Part 1 (Swansea, 2003), pp. 75–98.
Roberts, R. O., 'Dr John Lane and the foundation of the non-ferrous metal industries in the Swansea valley', *Gower*, 4 (1951), 18–24.
Idem, 'A comment: John Hughes, manager of the Upper Bank copper works, Swansea, *c.*1800', *Gower*, 7 (1954), 32–4.
Idem, 'Bank of England branch discounting, 1826–59, *Economica*, n.s., XXV (1958), 230–45.

Idem, 'The White Rock copper and brass works near Swansea, 1736–1806', in R. Denning (ed.), *Glamorgan Historian*, Volume 12 (Cowbridge, 1971), pp. 136–51.

Idem, 'Enterprise and capital for non-ferrous metal smelting in Glamorgan, 1694–1924', *Morgannwg*, 23 (1979), 48–81.

Roderick, G., 'South Wales industrialists and the theory of gentrification: 1770–1914', *Transactions of the Honourable Society of Cymmrodorion* (1987), 68–83.

Idem, 'Educating the worker: the mechanics' institute movement in south Wales', *Transactions of the Honourable Society of Cymmrodorion* (1991), 161–74.

Rowlands, J., 'Essay on the history of Cwmavon', in *Aeron Afan: sef y cyfansoddiadau buddugol yn Eisteddfod Ifforaidd Aberfan, Mehefin 23 1853: dan nandd y bwrdd Ifforaidd* (Caerfyrddin, 1855), pp. 10–76.

Shapin, S. and Barnes, B., 'Science, nature and control: interpreting mechanics' institutes', *Social Studies of Science*, 7, no. 1 (1977), 31–74.

Smith, C., 'Urban improvement in the Northamptonshire market town, 1770–1840', *Midland History*, XXV (2000), 98–114.

Smith, J., 'Urban elites, c.1830–1930, and urban history', *Urban History*, 27, no. 2 (2000), 255–75.

Stave, B. M., 'A conversation with Thomas Bender: urban history as intellectual and cultural history', *Journal of Urban History*, 14, no. 4 (1988), 455–91.

Sullivan, K., '"The biggest room in Merthyr": working-class housing in Dowlais, 1850–1914', *Welsh History Review*, 17, no. 2 (1994), 155–85.

Sweet, R., 'Stability and continuity: Swansea politics and reform, 1780–1820', *Welsh History Review*, 18, no. 1 (1996), 14–39.

Thackray, A., 'Natural knowledge in cultural context: the Manchester model', *American Historical Review*, 79, no. 3 (1974), 627–709.

Thomas, B., 'The growth of industrial towns', in A. J. Roderick (ed.), *Wales Through the Ages*, Volume 2 (Llandybïe, 1960), pp. 185–92.

Thomas, H., 'The industrialisation of a Glamorganshire parish', *National Library of Wales Journal*, 19 (1975–6), 227–42.

Thomas, P. S., 'Industrial relations: a short study of the relations between employers and employed in Swansea and neighbourhood from about 1800 to recent times', *Social and Economic Survey of Swansea and District*, 3 (Swansea, 1940), pp. 7–125.

Thomas, S., 'J. Francis, coach-maker', *Minerva*, 2 (1994), 29–33.

Thomas, W. G., 'The coal mining industry in West Glamorgan', in S. Williams (ed.), *Glamorgan Historian*, Volume 6 (Cowbridge, 1969), pp. 201–27.

Thomas, W. S. K., 'Municipal government in Swansea, 1485–1640', in S. Williams (ed.), *Glamorgan Historian*, Volume 1 (Cowbridge, 1963), pp. 27–36.

Trott, A. L., 'The British School movement in Wales, 1806–1846', in J. L. Williams and G. R. Hughes (eds), *The History of Education in Wales*, Volume 1 (Swansea, 1978), pp. 83–104.

Valenzuela, L., 'Challenges to the British copper smelting industry in the world market, 1840–1860', *Journal of European Economic History*, 19 (1990), 657–86.

Von Tunzelmann, N., 'Technology in the early nineteenth century', in R. Floud and D. McCloskey (eds), *The Economic History of Britain since 1700*, Volume 1: *1700–1860* (Cambridge, 1994), pp. 271–99.

Walton, J. K., 'The demand for working-class seaside holidays in Victorian England', *Economic History Review*, 34 (1981), 249–65.

Williams, C., '"The great hero of the Newport Rising": Thomas Phillips, Reform and Chartism', *Welsh History Review*, 21, no. 3 (2003), 481–511.

Williams, D. T., 'The economic development of Swansea and of the Swansea district to 1921', *Social and Economic Survey of Swansea and District*, 4 (Cardiff, 1940), pp. 7–189.

Williams, G. A., 'The Merthyr election of 1835', *Welsh History Review*, Volume 10, no. 3 (1981), 359–97.

7. Unpublished Theses

Anthony, C. R., 'Seaport, society and smoke: Swansea as a place of resort and industry, c.1700–1840' (Ph.D. thesis, University of Leicester, 2002).

Bevan, C. J., 'The rise and fall of Back Street: a study of workers' dwellings in Swansea, 1803–1879' (Swansea Local History dissertation, University of Wales Swansea, 1991).

Callison, J. E., 'Politics, class and water supply in Dundee, 1831–1845' (M. Phil. thesis, University of Dundee, 1985).

Cook, L. A., 'An examination of the social impact of the Vivians on Swansea, 1809–1894' (Ph.D. thesis, University of the West of England, 1997).

Evans, D. G., 'The growth and development of organised religion in the Swansea valley, 1820–1890' (Ph.D. thesis, University of Wales Swansea, 1977).

Evans, T., 'Elementary schools in Swansea in the nineteenth century' (MA thesis, University of Wales Swansea, 2003).

Fielder, G. D., 'Public health and hospital administration in Swansea and West Glamorgan since the end of the eighteenth century to 1914' (MA thesis, University of Wales Swansea, 1962).

Light, J., '"Of inestimable value to the town and district"? A study of the middle classes in south Wales with particular reference to Pontypool, Bridgend and Penarth, 1850–1890' (Ph.D. thesis, University of Wales Swansea, 2003).

Matthews, M. D., 'In pursuit of profit? Local enterprise in south-west Wales in the eighteenth century' (Ph.D. thesis, University of Wales Swansea, 1998).

Newell, E., 'The British copper ore market in the nineteenth century with particular reference to Cornwall and Swansea' (D. Phil. thesis, University of Oxford, 1988).

Peres Le Roy, M., 'Decline of the Welsh language in the Swansea region' (MA thesis, University of Wales Swansea, 1989).

Rees, J. C. M., 'Evolving patterns of residence in a nineteenth-century city: Swansea, 1851–1871' (Ph.D. thesis, University of Wales Swansea, 1983).

Ridd, T., 'The development of municipal government in Swansea in the nineteenth century' (MA thesis, University of Wales Swansea, 1955).

Roberts, O. G., 'Sanitary reform, civic politics and ideas of health in Wales, 1870–1900' (Ph.D. thesis, University of Wales Aberystwyth, 2003).

Thomas, J. E., 'Poor law administration in West Glamorgan from 1834–1930' (MA thesis, University of Wales Swansea, 1950).

Williams, E. C., 'The Nonconformist movement in industrial Swansea, 1780–1914' (M.Phil. thesis, University of Wales Swansea, 1993).

INDEX

Aber-craf 89
Aberafan 88, 90, 91, 120, 182
Aberdare 190
Aberdeen 191
Aberdulais 78
  see also Neath and Neath valley
Abergavenny 39, 94
Adare, Viscount, of Dunraven Castle
  see Dunraven, earl of
Adelaide Place 48
Afan valley 100
agriculture 83, 106, 199
aldermen 19, 24, 36, 135, 137, 138–9
Anglesey, and copper manufacture
  76–7, 78
Anglicanism 120–1, 169
Anglicization 13
architecture 48–9
assembly rooms 42, 45–7, 48, 198
assizes 43, 64–5, 185, 203
Association for the Prosecution of
  Felons 38, 196, 204
Aubrey, Richard (merchant) 138
Aubrey, Richard (Unitarian minister)
  53
Ayton, Richard 70

balloon flight attempt (1802) 1–5
Bangor 7
  health care 56, 57
Bank of England
  branch 13, 14, 43, 66–8, 122–3,
    157, 185, 187, 188
  control of Cwmafan copper works
    117, 121
banking 61–2, 128
  see also Bank of England
Baptists 52–3
Barrett, Francis 1, 2–5, 183
Bassett, Miles 21, 59

Bassett, Sarah 21
Bath
  balloon flights 3, 5n
  health tourism 58
Bath, Henry 58, 169
Bath, Henry (senior) 199
bathing resort(s) 4, 8, 14, 18, 130, 156,
  160, 192
  end of Swansea as 186–8
  and industrialization 6, 70–1, 95–6
  urban improvement 42–3, 45, 51,
    55, 58–9, 69, 98
Beaufort, duke of 19, 21, 22, 24, 25,
  26, 28, 47, 59, 67, 134, 135, 171
Benson, Starling 117, 138, 139, 140,
  164, 168, 169, 194
Berrington, J. D. 147
Bevan, William 107–8
Biddulph, John 121
Bigg, Thomas 58, 59
Bird, George Gwyn 110, 162, 166
Bird, John 43, 46
Birmingham 89
  and Swansea copper manufacture
    31, 76, 79, 94
Birmingham Mining and Copper
  Company 58, 76
Black Country 89
Blackpill 85
Blaenafon 119
Blanchard, Jean-Pierre-François 1, 5
book trade see printing and publishing
Bordell, Samuel 58
Boulton, Matthew 5, 79, 94
boundaries see Swansea
Bradford 11, 50, 105
Brecon 18, 39
Briggs, Asa 41
Brighton 58
Bristol 13, 19, 94, 97, 190

INDEX

balloon flights 3
Bank of England branch transferred to 187
investment in copper manufacture 75
local government 133, 137, 140
scientific interests 169, 176
Bristol Institution for the Advancement of Science 162, 176
British Association for the Advancement of Science (BAAS) 165, 175–8, 185, 188, 192, 194, 195, 197
British schools 59–60
Briton Ferry 122
Brock, G. B. 53
Buckland, Dr 167, 169, 175, 183
Budd, James Palmer 85
Burgess, Thomas, bishop of St David's 63
burgesses 19, 21–2, 24, 27, 29, 30, 36, 44, 135–6, 151
Burrows, the 23, 24, 47–8, 58, 83, 183, 186, 187–8
Bute family 8, 20, 65, 66, 134, 149–50

Caernarfon 7, 18
Cambrian 53–4, 115, 116–17, 118, 137, 139, 150, 151, 152, 153, 154, 173, 174, 182, 186, 188, 198
Cambrian Archaeological Association 189, 196
Cambrian Place 48, 198
Cambrian Pottery 33–5, 61, 139, 182, 183, 195, 198
Cambrian Society 161, 162
Cambrian Tourist, The (1821) 52, 69
Cambrian Traveller's Guide, The (1808) 14, 46, 70
Cambrian Traveller's Guide (1840) 175
Cameron, Nathaniel 138, 139, 140, 142, 194
Cameron Coalbrook Steam Coal Company 194
canals 31–2, 35, 74, 88, 98, 102, 147, 184, 202
Cape copper works 122

Cardiff
banking 67, 187
coal industry 90, 126, 190
education for the poor 60
harbour and port 90, 126, 149–50, 157, 180–1
health 57, 105
historiography 8, 12
industrial development 31, 96
local government 20, 134
population 9, 102–3, 190, 191
rivalry with Swansea 64–9, 157, 191–2
social and industrial relations 112, 123, 126
urban improvement 39
Carmarthen 7, 18, 39, 56
Carter, Harold 5
Castle Square 143
Census: (1841) 98n, 123–4; (1851) 93; (1861) 191; (1901) 9–10
chapels 53
Chartism 100, 114–15
Cheadle Brass and Wire Company 203
Chester 13
Child, Henry 62
Chile 95, 187
cholera 105, 121, 127, 170
circulating libraries 51–2
Clark, George T. 104, 130, 155–6, 162, 176
Clark, R 54
Clarkson, Thomas 200
Clasemont 98, 199
Clifton 58
Clive, George 87
Clydach 89, 120
Clyne 85
coach-building 61
coal industry 5, 18, 19, 71–4, 78, 88, 89, 90, 93, 184, 190, 194
philanthropy 58
poverty 15
and proposals for harbour improvements 147–8
social and industrial relations 98, 113, 119, 122

INDEX

Coles, John 33, 198
Coles, William 34
Collins, Charles 23, 26, 27, 38, 49, 138, 195, 199
Collins, John 26, 168, 195
Collins, John Charles 55, 57, 161, 195
commercial sector 13, 14, 16, 85–7, 91–3, 95, 96, 156–7
 and culture 163–4
 and local government 20, 21, 29, 30–3, 37, 39, 138–40, 143
 and urban improvement 58, 60–9
conflict thesis 101
Conybeare, William Daniel 183
Cooke's *Topographical and Statistical Description of the Principality of Wales* 55
copper manufacture 4, 5, 8, 71, 73–83, 88–97, 156, 184, 187, 188
 environmental pollution 6, 82–3, 99, 164
 and local government 18, 19, 24–5, 30–1, 37
 overseas contacts 77, 94–5, 97, 106, 187
 pay and social status 107, 112–13, 115–16
 philanthropy 58
 and proposed harbour improvements 146–9
 social and industrial relations 98–9, 100–1, 106–31
Copper Trade Association 78
Cornish Metal Company 76, 78, 79, 203
Cornwall
 and copper manufacture 75–6, 77, 78, 93, 97, 187
 in-migration 93, 125, 126
corporation 13, 19–40, 135–8
 ceremonial functions 23–4
 development of cooperation 39–40
 and education 62–3
 and environmental pollution 82
 law and order 37–8, 43–4
 period of factionalism in 1780s 20, 26–30, 132

 property management 22–3, 33–4, 48
 urban improvement 20, 25, 27–9, 32–40, 41, 45, 47, 48, 50, 62–3, 68–9, 84, 98, 124, 130, 195, 199
Coster, Thomas 75
Countess of Huntingdon's chapel 48, 198
Coventry 28, 135
crafts 86, 98, 123, 137
 and culture 163–4
 industrial relations 113–14
cricket 23, 117
Croll, Andy 8, 160
Crown Copper and Spelter Company 76, 80
Cuba 95
cultural history 17, 159–60
culture 6, 10–12, 13, 16, 51–2, 156, 157, 158–81, 188–9
 and social relations 99, 119–21
 for workers 128–9
Cwmafan 121
Cwmafan copper works 89, 116, 117, 122
Cwmbwrla 125

Danygraig house 194
Daunton, Martin 8, 12
Davies, John 138, 140n
Davies, Walter 108
Davies, William 52
Davy, Humphrey 161
de la Beche, Bessie 168
de la Beche, Henry 99, 109–10, 126, 155, 165, 168, 170, 183, 190
Delamotte, George Orleans 14
Denbigh 12
Devon, connection with 92–3, 125
Dillwyn, Lewis Llewelyn 116, 168, 189, 195
Dillwyn, Lewis Weston 14, 15, 52, 53, 59, 61, 66, 67, 68, 84, 94, 114–15, 127, 136, 138, 139, 140, 194, 195
 death and legacy 182–9
 scientific interests 162, 166, 167, 168–9, 171, 173, 174, 175

INDEX

Dillwyn, William 195
Dillwyn family 168–9, 189
Dillwyn-Llewelyn *see* Llewelyn, John Dillwyn
Dowlais 110, 111, 112
drainage 41–2, 130
Dublin, scientific societies 172–3, 176
Dundee 36, 110–11, 133, 191
Dunraven, earl of 163, 171
Dyer, George 122

Eaton, Robert 56, 59, 62, 66, 68, 162, 169
Eaton family 26
Ebbw Vale 181
Edinburgh 49, 191
Edmond, John 87
Edmond, William 166
education 68, 131
  for middle class 62–3
  for the poor 59–60
  for working class 111–12, 119–20, 122, 128–9, 180, 197
Edwards, D. 138
Edwards, William 108, 199
English Copper Company 81, 88, 89, 90, 117, 121, 203
entertainment facilities 22, 42–3, 45–8, 98, 130, 131, 160
Essery, T. B. 53
Evans, Chris 7, 10
Evans, Neil 12
Evans, R. J. W. 17
Evans, T. 111n

Faraday, Michael 161, 164, 175
Feltham's *Guide to the Watering and Sea-bathing Places* (1806) 55, 70–1, 99
Fendall and Co. 46
Ffynone house 194
financial sector 13, 128, 157
  and culture 163–4
  see also banking
Fleming, William 22
food riots 37, 43
Forest copper works 108, 164, 194, 199
Fox family, of Falmouth 76

France
  balloon flights 1, 2
  wars with 2, 44–5
Francis, George Grant 14, 74, 137, 152, 169, 170, 171, 172, 175, 180, 189, 196
Francis, John 61, 87, 118, 146, 196

Gabb, G. 179n
Garnerin, Monsieur 2
gentry 22, 24–6, 45–8, 138–9
  scientific interests 163, 167–9
Geological Society of the West Riding of Yorkshire 165
Geological Survey of Great Britain 165
Gerstenhöffer's furnace 82
Gibbins, Joseph 62, 66
Glamorgan Library 52, 198
Glamorgan Pottery 61, 198
Glamorganshire Canal 32, 102
Glasgow 105, 191
  historiography 11
  local government 133
  scientific societies 173
Gloucester Place 48
Goat Street 47, 125, 129
Gore, Hugh, bishop of Waterford and Lismore 62
Gorseinon 120
grammar schools 62–3, 90
Grant, H. J., of Gnoll Castle, Neath 163
Great Sessions 43, 64–5, 185, 203
Greenhill 110, 125, 126–7
Grenfell, Alys 93n, 126n
Grenfell, C. P. 95
Grenfell, G. N. 107
Grenfell, Madelina 84
Grenfell, Pascoe 73, 151, 196–7
Grenfell, Pascoe St Leger 84, 111, 119, 197
Grenfell, Riversdale William 120
Grenfell family 76, 98, 117, 120
Griffiths, David 87
Griffiths, James 107
Grove, John 56, 138, 140n, 142, 146
Grove, Thomas 138

INDEX

Grove, William 138
Grove, William Robert 165, 176–7, 197
Grove's ropeworks 113
Guest, Josiah John 107, 111, 149, 162, 176
Guest family 110
Guide to the Watering and Sea-bathing Places (1803) 51
guildhall 142
Gunn, Simon 11, 160
Gutch, J. W. G. 152, 166, 172
Gwyn, Howel 172

Hafod works 74, 79, 80, 85, 94–5, 98, 108, 111, 112–13, 125, 139, 164, 182, 183, 190, 203
Hamilton, Sir William and Lady 44
harbour 19, 88, 133, 135
 improvement 25, 27, 35–7, 142, 144–53, 158, 195, 199
Harbour Acts 36–7, 142, 144, 151
harbour trust 13, 36–7, 39, 74, 118, 140, 144, 148, 150–2, 201
Harford family 60
Harris, Joseph 52–3
Harris, Moses 27
Harris, Solomon 53, 204
Hassan, John 9
Haverfordwest 18
Haynes, George 33–4, 35, 37, 52, 53, 61, 68, 195, 197–8
Haynes and Co. 66
health and health care 9, 60, 170, 186
 for the poor 15, 55–9
 social and industrial relations 99, 105, 109–10, 121, 126, 127, 130, 131
 see also infirmary
health tourism 58–9
Hennock, E. P. 12
Hermann, G. B. 95
High Street 33, 61, 196
Hobbes, Thomas 55, 57
Homfray, Samuel, of Merthyr 46
housing 48–9, 61
 middle class 48–9, 61, 83–4, 96, 98–9

 for workers 107–11, 112, 122, 199
Houston, R. A. 54
Howell, David 11–12
Hull 161
Hunt and Co's Directory and Topography (1849) 158–9, 178
hygiene *see* health and health care; sanitation

improvement commissions *see* street maintenance and improvement; urban improvement
in-migration 31, 84, 93–4, 95, 100–2, 124–8
 scientific interests 170
Independents 169
industrial history 7–11, 17, 71–2, 99–101, 160, 192–3
industrial relations 99–101, 106–31
industrial sector 3, 5, 17, 18, 42, 69, 70–97, 184, 188, 192
 and culture 163–5; and local government before municipal reform 20, 22, 24–6, 29, 30–3, 35, 37, 39
 and local government following municipal reform 136, 139–40, 143–51, 192
 philanthropy 58
 social relations 102, 131
 see also coal industry; copper manufacture; iron manufacture; potteries
infirmary 14, 56–9, 69, 166
intelligentsia *see* urban elite
Irish 101, 121, 125, 126–8
iron manufacture 71–2, 78, 80, 85, 88, 89, 147–8
 industrial relations 100, 101, 106, 107, 110, 112, 113, 119, 122
 and Swansea's bathing facilities 130

James, Christopher 157
Jeffrey, Gabriel 22
Jeffrey family 21
Jeffreys, John Gwyn 165, 168, 169
Jeffries, John 1, 5
Jenkins, Elias 169

Jenkins, Elizabeth and Georgina 52
Jenkins, John 166, 169
Jenkins, Philip 7, 24, 28
Jenkins, Samuel 138, 140n
Jenkins, Thomas 53
Jernegan, William 49, 61, 65, 94, 198
Jews 125–6, 169
Johnson, John 48, 98, 198, 199
Jones, Calvert Richard 37, 56, 124, 167–8, 175, 198–9
Jones, Ieuan Gwynedd 15
Jones, Phillip 90, 121–2
Jones, William 29, 138
Joyce, Patrick 102

Kavanagh, Charles 127, 170
Kenfig 91
Kenrick, G. S. 119
Kilvey 98, 111, 120
Kilvey copper works 117
Knight, Henry 68
Koditschek, Theodore 11

labour history 12, 160, 193
Lambert, Charles 95, 187
Lancaster, Joseph 59
Landore 105, 119, 120, 188
Landore copper works 24–5, 30, 31, 74, 75, 77, 79, 107
Lane, John 24, 74, 75, 78, 107
Latin America, and copper manufacture 77, 95, 97, 187
law and order 37–8, 43–4, 114, 127
  see also Great Sessions
Leeds 11, 161
legal profession 165–6
  see also Phillips, Richard; Sockett, Henry
Leicester 135
Lettsom, Samuel Fothergill 89
Lewes, Sir Watkin 22, 28
Lewis, E. D. 7
Lewis's *Swansea Guide, 1851* 142, 159, 178, 188
libraries 51–2, 129, 181, 189
  Swansea Scientific Society 172, 179–80, 181
Light, Julie 12

Lindsay, Robert 90, 121
Linnean Society 4
Liverpool 13, 19, 68, 161, 191
Liverpool Chronicle 68
Llan-giwg 98
Llandeilo Tal-y-bont 171
Llanelli 73, 88, 89, 90, 106, 118, 190
Llangyfelach 15, 98, 171
Llangyfelach copper works 37, 78
Llansamlet 120, 155, 201
Llewellyn, Griffith 84
Llewelyn, John, of Penllergaer 47, 59, 120
Llewelyn, John Dillwyn 116, 162, 168, 189, 195
local government 10, 12, 13, 14;
  1780–1800 18–41, 195
  after Municipal Corporations Act (1835) 132–57, 158, 186, 194, 196
  historiography 133–4
  see also corporation; town council
Lockwood, Robert 25
Lockwood, Thomas 30, 74
Logan, William Edmond 164–5, 169, 170, 173
London 13, 94
  balloon flights 1, 2
London Institution 165
Loughor 91, 182, 194
Loughor Railway Company 194
Lucas, John 48
Luce, John 50
Lunardi, Vincent 1, 2

Maber, George Martin 169
Mackworth, Sir Herbert 28, 31, 62
Mackworth, Sir Humphrey 88
Mackworth Arms hotel 38, 45–6, 55, 77, 87
Mackworth family, of Neath 25
Maddocks, Thomas 21, 62
Maesteg House 98, 197
Malkin, Benjamin 19, 49, 183
Manchester 11, 96, 154, 173, 191
Mansfield, Thomas 62
Margam copper works 88, 121, 122
  industrial relations 109

Marine Biological Association of
    Great Britain 165
Marino house 98, 198
market 23, 33, 87, 123–4, 142
Martin, William 138
Mason, Hugh 22
Mathews's *Swansea Directory* 70, 72n
mechanics' institute 128–9, 180
medical profession 55, 56, 166
Melincryddan copper works 79, 88
Merthyr Tydfil 71, 94
    banking 62, 67
    canals 31–2
    health 105
    historiography 7, 8
    industries 71, 78, 180, 190, 191
    language 119
    population 10, 18, 102–3, 108, 191
    scientific interests 181
    social and industrial relations 99,
        100, 108, 113, 114, 123, 131
    and Swansea bathing facilities 130
    urban improvements 10, 145–6
Michael, Michael John 138, 169
Middle Bank works 77, 196
middle class 11–12, 15, 60–3, 74
    and culture 158–81
    housing 83–4, 96, 98–9
    see also urban elite
Mines Royal Company 78, 88
Mining Journal 172
Moggridge, J. H. 162
Montgolfier brothers 1
Morfa colliery 90, 109
Morning Chronicle 99, 104, 108–9,
    112–13
Morris, Sir John (junior) 114, 138,
    139, 140, 194, 199
Morris, Sir John (senior) 29, 30, 38,
    48, 56, 58, 66, 67, 73, 98, 108,
    120n, 198, 199
Morris, R. J. (Bob) 11, 159
Morris, Robert (junior) 26, 27–8, 199
Morris, Robert (senior) 24–5, 30, 74,
    75, 77, 107–8, 194, 199
Morris family 32, 73
Morriston 73, 92, 105, 140, 151, 155,
    182, 199

social and industrial relations 108,
    119, 120, 125
Mount Pleasant 83
Mowatt, Mr (manager of Cwmafan
    copper works) 122
Moyse, William 138
Mumbles 85
Municipal Corporations Act (1835)
    39, 104, 132–3, 134, 137, 141
Muntz, G. F. 81
museum 13, 172, 174, 179–80, 181
Mynydd Bychan colliery 88

Nance, E. Morton 34
national security 44–5
Neath and Neath valley 62, 90–1,
    182
    canals 31
    culture 162
    industrial relations 100, 115
    industries 78, 88, 93, 190
    local government 139
Nelson, Horatio, Viscount 44–5
Nelson Terrace 125
Nevill, Anne 168
Nevill, Charles 80, 89, 106
Nevill, Charles William 90
Nevill, Richard Janion 118, 168, 118
New Swansea Guide, 1823 41, 47, 62n,
    92
Newcastle upon Tyne 2, 49
Newport
    banking 67
    and coal industry 73, 90, 126
    culture 192
    harbour and port 73, 90, 126, 149,
        157, 181, 190
    health care 57
    historiography 7
    industrial unrest 100, 114, 131
    population 10, 102–3, 190, 191
    roads 38
    social relations 126
newspapers 13, 52–5, 69, 152
Nicholl, John, of Merthyr Mawr 163
Nicholson, Emilius 174–5
Nicholson's *Cambrian Traveller's Guide*
    (1808, 1840) 14, 46, 70, 175

Nonconformity 52–3, 169
   and social relations 120–1

Oldisworth, John 63

Padley, Paul 14
Padley, Silvanus 199–200
Padley, William 26, 27, 49, 199–200
Padley family 26–7
parks and gardens 47–8, 188
parliamentary representation 65–6, 91–2, 140, 189–90, 203
   see also Dillwyn, Lewis Weston; Vivian, John Henry
Parry, Caleb Hillier 5n
Pascoe Grenfell and Sons 196
paving maintenance and improvement 10, 13, 28, 39, 41–2, 49–51, 104–5, 140, 141, 153–6, 196, 201, 202
Pearse's Swansea Directory (1856) 178, 201
Pembrokeshire 11–12
Penclawdd copper works 31n, 203
Penllergaer estate 168, 195
philanthropy 12, 15, 55–6, 57–8, 118, 200
Phillipps, Sir Thomas 189
Phillips, John 55, 200
Phillips, R. M. 138, 140
Phillips, Richard 15, 37, 55–6, 58, 59–60, 200
photography 167–8, 189, 198–9
Pigot's London Provincial Directory (1822–3) 60, 96
Plasmarl 125
Poingdestre, Phillip Francis 170
policing 38, 104, 127, 133, 135
political history 9
Polkington, Henry 61
Pontardawe 89
Pontypool 119
Popkin, Thomas 25, 31, 74
population 3, 6, 9, 18, 19, 20, 31, 39, 42, 140, 190
   and social relations 98, 101, 102–3, 105, 125, 131
   see also Swansea, boundaries

port, Swansea as 5, 18, 25, 90, 92–3, 126, 156, 157, 184, 190
   see also harbour
Port Tennant 95
portreeve 19, 21, 24, 36, 43–4, 50, 64, 135
postal services 24, 140
potteries 5, 42, 98
   see also Cambrian Pottery; Glamorgan Pottery
poverty 15, 87
   education for the poor 59–60
   health care 55–9
Powell, Gabriel 25, 26–30, 33, 35, 39, 49, 136, 138, 154, 195, 199
Powell, Thomas 27, 199
Powell family 21
Presbyterians 53
Price, Gruffydd 25
Price, Henry Habberley 145–6, 149, 200
Price, Joseph Tregelles 200
Price, Peter 145, 200
Price family, of Penllergaer 25
printing and publishing 13, 52, 86, 112
Pritchard, John Wyn 9, 12
Pritchard, Rowland 21, 22, 138
professional sector 55–6, 86, 96, 195
   and culture 163–4, 165–6
   and local government 29, 136, 138
Prospect Place 198
public health *see* health and health care; sanitation
Public Health Act (1848) 156
public houses 129

Quakers 59, 169
   see also Bigg, Thomas; Dillwyn, Lewis Weston; Eaton, Robert; Haynes, George; Padley, William; Padley family; Phillips, John; Phillips, Richard

Raby, Alexander 89
railways 145–6, 152, 185, 188, 194
Rebecca riots 99–100, 116, 131
Rees, Richard, of Gelligron 172

INDEX

Rees, Ronald 101, 107, 112n
Rees, William, of Aberpergwm 46
Reform Act (1832) 91, 140
refuse collection 41–2, 103–5, 130
religion 16, 52–3, 197
   and science 169–70
   social and industrial relations 26–7, 99, 119, 120–1
retail sector 85–7, 137
   and culture 163–4
   social and industrial relations 98, 102, 123–4, 130–1
Rhondda valley 7, 9–10, 71, 190, 192
Rhyddings 200
Richardson, John 138, 139, 170, 196
Richardson, Sarah 196
Ridd, Tom 134, 141
roads 33, 38–9, 83, 87, 143, 184
Roberts, John 138
Roberts, Owen 9
Roderick, G. W. 181n
Roman Catholics 121, 125, 126–7, 170
Ropewalk 33
Rose Copper Smelting Company 31, 76, 80, 127
Rosser, John 22
Royal Aeronautical Society 5
Royal Agricultural Society of England 189
Royal Astronomical Society 166
Royal Geological Society 162
Royal Institution of South Wales (RISW)
   Swansea Scientific Society *see* Royal Institution of South Wales 14, 127, 158, 160–81, 185, 192, 194, 195, 196, 197
   granted right to call itself Royal Institution of South Wales 173–4, 203
   host to BAAS meeting (1848) 176–8, 185
Royal Photographic Society of London 167, 168
Royal Society 82, 162, 165, 166, 177, 183, 195, 197
Russell, Lord John 173

St John's parish 92, 111, 140
St Thomas's parish 92, 140
Sanders, David 138, 140n
sanitation 10, 41–2, 49, 103–5, 109–10, 130, 131, 153–6
   see also health and health care
science, interest in 3, 4–5
   see also Royal Institution of South Wales
Scotch Cattle 100
Scottish Historical Review 134
Seccombe, Nathaniel 29
Seren Gomer 52–3
sewerage 41–2, 103–5
Sheffield 161, 173
Sheffield, W. E. 81
shipping 86, 138, 139, 144, 146
Shrewsbury 13
Singleton Abbey 84, 111
Singleton Park estate 98, 168
Sketty 120
Sketty Hall 84
Sketty Park 98
Slater's Royal National and Commercial Directory and Topography (1858–9) 96n, 159
Smith, Charles 201
Smith, Charles Henry 142, 172, 201
Smith, John 32, 37, 151, 201
Smith, Leonard 89
Smith, William Henry 142, 150–2, 154, 155, 156, 201
social relations 98–101, 168–70
   reasons for little unrest in Swansea 60, 101–31
Society for the Publication of Ancient Welsh Manuscripts 171
Society for the Supporters of the Bill of Rights 26
Sockett, Henry 50–1, 68, 87, 137, 141, 202
Somerset Place 48, 142
South Wales Association for the Improvement of Roads 38
South Wales Institute of Engineers 181
South Wales Railway 152, 157, 185, 188

Southampton 6, 133, 177
spelter production 81
Spencer, F. H. 134
Spry, John Hume 46
steel manufacture 188
Stepney, Sir Thomas 22, 89
street cleaning 49, 153–6
 see also refuse collection
street lighting 10, 41–2, 50–1, 104, 153–6
street maintenance and improvement 10, 41–2, 49–51, 104–5, 130, 133, 153–6, 201; see also paving maintenance and improvement; sanitation
strikes 107, 114, 115–16, 117, 122, 131
Stroud, William 68
Sunderland 163
Swansea
 in 1802 1–6, 18–19, 183–4
 in 1855 182–93
 boundaries 14, 23, 91–2, 133, 140, 150, 151, 155, 156, 184
 cosmopolitanism 97, 126
 diversity as urban centre 5–7, 87–8, 98, 123–4, 143–57
 early history 19
 historiography 7–8, 19–20
 regional status 88–97
 reputation for intelligence 6, 158–9, 160, 175, 180, 192
 sources 13–15
 urban identity 43, 69, 72, 97, 131, 157, 158, 160, 161, 163, 174, 177–9, 181, 192
 urban improvement before municipal reform 18, 20, 25, 27–9, 32–70, 84, 98, 124, 130, 195, 199
 urban improvement following municipal reform 103–5, 132, 140, 141–56, 158, 186
 visual depictions 14
Swansea, Neath and Glamorganshire Bank 62
Swansea Bank 62
Swansea Commercial Society 83, 86–7, 146, 196
Swansea Guide (1802) 73n
Swansea Guide, 1851 142, 159, 178, 188
Swansea Herald 152n
Swansea Journal 152, 201
Swansea Literary Improvement Society of Working Men 129
Swansea and Llanelly Union Bank 62
Swansea Mercantile Society 26
Swansea and Neath Horticultural Society 161–2
Swansea to Oystermouth tramroad 84–5
Swansea Philosophical and Literary Institution *see* Swansea Scientific Society
Swansea Royal Volunteers 44, 100
Swansea Savings Bank 128
Swansea Scientific Society *see* Royal Institution of South Wales
Swansea Society for the Education of the Children of the Poor 59
Swansea Statistical Society 119, 125
Swansea Tontine Society 45–7
Swansea valley *see* Tawe valley
Swansea valley canal 32, 74, 98, 184
Sweet, Rosemary 20, 39

Taibach copper works 81, 88, 90, 122, 182
Talbot, Christopher (C. R. M.), of Margam and Penrice 109, 163, 169, 198
Talbot, Emma 168
Talbot, Henry Fox 167, 175, 198
Talbot, Mary 167
Talbot, Thomas Mansel 25, 38, 44, 46, 47, 52, 88
Talbot family, of Margam and Penrice 26, 167, 168
Tawe valley 32, 76, 88, 89, 92, 98, 100, 183–4
Taylor, Thomas 142
Telford, Thomas 145, 146, 200
Tennant, George 147, 202
textile industry 80, 190–1
Thackray, A. 161n
theatre 42, 45–7
Thomas, Dylan 6

INDEX 231

Thomas, Iltid 22
Thomas, P. S. 100n
Thomas, Thomas Edward 138
Times, The 115–16, 117, 122
tin-plate manufacture 89, 184, 188
Toomey, R. 73n, 82
tourism 3–4, 5, 49, 55, 68–9, 98
   effect of industries 70–1, 84–5,
      95–6, 99
   and scientific interests 170
   see also bathing resort(s)
town council 118, 132–57, 185, 194
   adoption of Greenwich mean time
      185
   financial constraints 142–3, 153–4
   scientific interests 158, 163, 176–7,
      189
   social relations 127
   and urban improvement 103–5,
      132, 140, 141–56, 158
Townhill 24
Townsend, Chauncey 32, 89
transport 31–2, 74, 84–5, 94, 140,
   145–6, 183–4, 200
   see also canals; railways; roads
Trevivian 108–9
Trinity Church 120
truck shops 102, 122–3, 124
Tunbridge 58
Turton, William 1, 4, 55

Unitarians 53, 169
University College of South Wales 65,
   191
University of Freiburg 94–5
Uplands 49, 83
Upper Bank works 30, 77, 196
urban elite 16, 83–4, 96
   and culture 4, 11–12, 158–81
   entertainment facilities for 45–8
   local government before and after
      reform 20–2, 138–40
   see also middle class
urban governance *see* local government
urban history 6, 7–17, 160, 192–3
urban improvement 10–11, 41–2,
   49–50
   in Swansea *see* Swansea

Vaughan, John, of Golden Grove 38
Vernon, Lord, of Briton Ferry 46
Vigurs, John 89
Vigurs, Louis 116–17
Vivian, Henry Hussey 82, 94, 190
Vivian, John 73, 75–6, 79, 202–3
Vivian, John Henry 51, 67, 80, 81, 82,
   84, 85, 90, 94, 111–12, 117–18,
   121, 131, 136, 139, 140, 142,
   146, 148–9, 194, 196, 203
   death and legacy 182–9
   scientific interests 162, 164, 170,
      173, 175
Vivian, Sarah 111
Vivian family 4, 73, 78, 90, 189
   social and industrial relations 98,
      108–9, 120, 121, 168
Voss, John (junior) 87, 204
Voss, John (senior) 38, 62, 204

Wallace, R. 100n
Walters, John 62
Walters, Thomas 138
water supply 9, 103–5, 130, 142,
   153–6, 186, 201
Watt, James 5
Webb, S. and B. 133–4
Weeks, J. 38
Welsh culture 12, 15–16, 171
Welsh history 171–2
Welsh identity 12
Welsh language 12, 15–16, 99, 119,
   122, 171, 172
   newspaper 52–3
Wesleyan Methodists 53, 125
Weymouth 58
White Rock copper works 37, 79, 200
Whitehouse, T. L. 157
Wilkes, John 26
Wilkins, Charles 87–8
Williams, Chris 9
Williams, Gareth 160
Williams, Glanmor 16
Williams, John 93
Williams, L. J. 17
Williams, Michael 138, 140n
Williams, Thomas, of Anglesey 30,
   76–7, 78, 196

Williams family, of Scorrier near Redruth 76
Williams and Grenfell copper works 80
Wind Street 52, 61, 83
women 16
    employment 112–13
    financial facilities for 128
    scientific interests 168
working class 160
    education and cultural interests 111–12, 119–20, 122, 128–9, 180, 197
    social relations 98–131
Wrexham 7, 18
Wyndham, Thomas, of Dunraven Castle 46, 47

Yniscedwyn iron works 147
Ynishowell copper works 58
Ynysygerwyn tin-plate works 89
York 161
Ystalyfera ironworks 85
Ystradgynlais 89, 98

zinc production 81, 106